Our Sweetest Hours

Our Sweetest Hours

*Recreation and the
Mental State of Absorption*

by

Gene Quarrick

McFarland & Company, Inc., Publishers
Jefferson, North Carolina, and London

790
Q1o

British Library Cataloguing-in-Publication data available

Library of Congress Cataloguing-in-Publication Data

Quarrick, Gene, 1930–
Our sweetest hours.

Bibliography: p. 215.
  Includes index.
  1. Recreation — Psychological aspects.
2. Attention. I. Title.
GV14.4.Q37 1989   790'.01'32   88-43571

ISBN 0-89950-404-3 (lib. bdg. : 50# alk. paper)

Manufactured in the United States of America.

McFarland   Box 611   Jefferson NC 28640

To Helen

Contents

Can we deny that all our sweetest hours
are those of self-forgetfulness? — *Ethel D. Puffer*

Psychological Diversion as Adult Play

> Man staggers through life ·yapped at by his reason, pulled and shoved
> by his appetites, whispered to by fears, beckoned by hopes. Small wonder
> that what he craves most is self-forgetting. — *Eric Hoffer*

If the behavioral and social sciences have taught us anything, it is that
we are not as free as we think. The issue is not political but psychological
freedom; it turns out that the human being is continually subjected to subtle
forms of control from both inside and outside of the body. For example, the
central nervous system is really a system of codes and programs which, unseen
and silent, determine the nature of all thought and action. Habits, mental sets,
motives, unconscious needs, and many other determinants — identified and
unidentified by psychologists — continually function to select our world and
our responses to it. Indeed, we have all been programmed, and in a sense are
prisoners of our programs. In like manner, the external world is the source
of many forms of control. In order to compete and survive, everyone has to
accept the coercions and confinements of family, job, and society. Day after
day, these bind us to the same locations, the same activities, the same people,
the same identity.

All these internal and external constraints add up to a kind of gravitational field in the psychological domain, a field of forces which undoubtedly
is responsible for the sense of pressure and drudgery that so often characterizes
everyday living. As long as we are alive, we never escape these constraints
in an absolute way — except when we fall asleep and become unconscious.
Most of the time, like the planet we live on, we stay in the orbit of our pre-
scribed patterns.

Not surprisingly, it is one of the deepest human yearnings to break out
of this gravitational field, even though we value the security and stability it
provides. It is not perversion or escapism but our very humanity that tells us
that there should be more — more new experience, more aliveness, more range
and scope than everyday life permits. Every vacation, every daydream, every
bet on the lottery is precisely this wish to break away. In a recent psychological

study, people were asked: "If you had the time and money to do *anything* you wanted, what would you do?" The reactions were almost unanimous: Most respondents said they would travel. At first glance, this does not sound like a very profound goal. Based on current mental health notions, one might have thought these people would have chosen to pursue other things like love, power, sex, material possessions, or peace of mind. Instead they simply wanted to get away; the authors of the study concluded "that people wish, above all, to be somewhere else, doing something different."[1]

Actually, we do not have to travel to get away. We can stay put, and in a psychological way accomplish something just as good or even better. It so happens that the very organism that imprisons us, also gives us a way out. Unlike electronic computers, the human organism has the capability of suspending and neutralizing its own programs. Also, it can turn off external reality and its pressures without causing any harm to itself. In other words, the organism has the capability of negating these internal and external factors—negating them almost as completely as they are during sleep—yet all the while we remain alert, and open for new experiences. This, of course, is only a temporary breaking away, but it may be the most significant respite we have. It does not beat winning the lottery but it is better than daydreaming, engaging in play activities, or perhaps even taking a trip, because this psychological diversion offers the only possible way of breaking that most insidious of bonds—the human self.

What we are talking about is the sense of escape and diversion that occurs when we get absorbed in something. Absorption is but a simple switch of attention, yet it can open us up psychologically to a degree that is not possible in the everyday frame of mind. Absorption seems to be just an intense attention, but it is much more than that. It is a qualitatively different kind of consciousness, almost a psychological reversal of how we are in everyday life.

In point of fact, absorption is nothing less than a form of hypnosis. In the hypnotic state, the control of attention is surrendered to the hypnotist. In the absorbed state, it is surrendered to some entertainment or object of fascination, like a story or show. Just as hypnosis makes it possible for people to do things they normally cannot, so absorption makes it possible for people to *experience* things they normally do not. In this way, experience is expanded beyond the everyday boundaries.

In a manner of speaking, absorption is the hypnosis of the common people. It is also the heart of adult play experience, and must be examined if we are to understand recreation as a phenomenon in its own right. In the first chapter we shall review the scientific evidence for the close relationship between absorption and hypnosis, and throughout the remainder of the book we will attempt to show how adults have used this absorbed-hypnotic capability to bring diversion into their lives.

Although this book is divided into certain content areas, the interest here is primarily in the structure of play, i.e., how a particular psychological state (absorbed involvement) is realized through the different kinds of content. Stories, shows, intoxication, sex, music, dancing, art, and meditation are the principal content areas of adult recreation. These diversions might seem as different as night and day; we have been conditioned to see some of it as desirable and some as undesirable. When all is said and done, however, all these different recreations share a basic psychological kinship. They all come alive for us in the same way — through the state of absorbed attention.

Chapter 1

Absorbed Attention

At its best mass communication allows people to become
absorbed in subjective play. — *William Stephenson*

Most of us were probably last absorbed while enjoying a story or watching
a show on television. In order to get absorbed, we implicitly make a subtle
yet important change in our attention. It is a two-step process. First, all attention is withdrawn from the many things that we monitor in everyday life. Then
the total attentional force is focused on one object, usually some curiosity or
entertainment. This switch-over into the absorbed state, of course, is made un-
consciously because the object we attend to is usually high in fascination value,
and so captivates total attention. When attention is captured, the first effect we
experience is mental relaxation, i.e., we become oblivious of self, reality and
everyday concerns. The second effect is enhanced experiencing. William James
wrote, "My experience is what I agree to attend to."[1] Therefore, if all attention
is on one particular object, it is experienced more completely.

This switch-over into the absorbed state makes us feel different, and it is
this feeling that is the basis for adult play experience. Adults play by getting
absorbed in something. Without absorbed involvement our recreations would
be processed in the everyday frame of mind. Absorption is what makes them
different. Throughout this book we shall see that absorption is the basis for the
whole range of adult diversion. It is the basis for the feeling of getting high when
intoxicated, or falling in love. When enjoying stories, absorption is what makes
possible the feeling of being in a different world and living a different life. Absorbed attention does not do much for the self-concept, but it certainly enhances
our experience. It puts a point on life and so is sweet to us.

All this may or may not be true of children; child play is not a concern
of this book. In adulthood — when the organism is matured and programmed —
play has a specific function. It acts to remove the adult from his programmed
status. It relieves the burdens of maturity by allowing the adult to step
"sideward into another reality," as Erik Erikson pointed out.[2] Thus, for
adults, play experience is primarily a matter of feeling different, and this

4

might come from taking a drink, watching television, or even reading the newspaper.

For example, adults will talk about losing themselves in their pastimes. One might have thought that "losing oneself" would be a bad experience, but people find it to be the epitome of enjoyment. The highest praise one could offer about an entertainment would be to say that "it really got me out of myself." Such expressions refer to the fact that in absorption we stop attending to ourselves, and so the sense of self fades. This is experienced as mental relaxation, as being released from a constraint, and it is liberating and enjoyable.

Scholars agree that we do indeed lose ourselves when we get absorbed; this is not just a way of speaking. It is generally accepted that the self is nonfunctional in hypnosis.[3] Likewise, as we will show in this book, absorbing entertainments are experienced as egoless, nonself states; e.g., when the literary scholar says that story enjoyment requires a "willing suspension of disbelief," he is talking about something comparable to the "suspension of the generalized reality orientation" that is essential for hypnotic induction. Both concepts refer to the suspension of judgmental self-functions. The same thing is implied when the art scholar says that "psychic distance" is necessary for aesthetic enjoyment. In other words the self must be put at a distance before the art object can be enjoyed for its own sake. In intoxication, the self is weakened when the alcohol or other recreational drug neutralizes the forebrain which mediates self-related functions. Thus, it is not only possible to suspend self-functions while awake, it is the basis of our most enjoyable experiences.

The concept of absorption has been generally overlooked by scholars. Perhaps one reason is that this state is so brief and elusive. Because self-awareness is dimmed when we are absorbed, we fail to make the necessary discrimination. However, a much more important reason for the neglect is that the concept of absorption is completely at odds with the mind-set and paradigms currently popular in psychology. The absorbed state, with its negation of self-functions, runs counter to a concept that has had a monumental role in psychology, namely, the concept of self.

For the last fifty years, self psychology and ego psychology have been dominant influences in the study of personality. These schools of thought have always emphasized the importance of strengthening self-functions, not decreasing them. The self has been the cornerstone of theorizing about personality and mental health. Self is generally viewed as all-important in coordinating conscious, voluntary activities. On it rests our sense of identity and the ability to function effectively in social roles. From our earliest years, society conditions us to be aware of ourselves, to give an account of ourselves, and to express ourselves. The educational and mental health establishments reinforce this teaching by continually urging us to "actualize" ourselves, raise our self-esteem, have self-confidence, develop a positive self-concept, and so on. A weakened self is defined as an abnormal condition. Schizophrenic regression, dissociative neurotic disorder, and frontal lobe damage are thought to be the basic kinds of ego weakness, and they of course result in extensive impairment to psychological functioning.

Implicit in these traditional views on self are the following assumptions: (1) that the self is necessary for meaningful and purposeful interaction with the environment, and so is a constant in psychological functioning; (2) that self is a fixed trait, resulting from a long-standing learning process, and the stronger and more developed it is, the better; and (3) decrease or loss of self function always represents a regressive and pathological condition.

Given such assumptions, it is difficult to accept the phenomenon of absorption which implies almost the opposite, i.e., that it is possible to suspend self-functioning without pathological consequences, and that the resulting nonself state can be enjoyable.

It is likely that in the long run psychology will have to adopt a more relativistic view which recognizes self, not as a fixed trait, but as a variable function. As some psychologists have already noted, there will have to be scientific acceptance of that other domain of human existence that lies beyond self. For example, Gardner Murphy, an ardent "self psychologist," ended his classic text on personality with a sense of dissatisfaction about his science, and in the last chapter he wrote that although culture requires a "belief in immutable selfhood . . . it has become probable from research with drugs and with hypnosis that the self is no immutable entity."

> If, moreover, we are serious about understanding all we can of personality, its integration and disintegration, we must understand the meaning of depersonalization, those experiences in which individual self-awareness is abrogated and the individual melts into an awareness which is no longer anchored upon selfhood. . . .
>
> Now this relativity of the concept of selfhood suggests that both consciousness and behavior may well take on very different forms of organization if the self can be filtered out. The norms or laws of individual existence relating to a non-self-oriented type of reality may at present be largely masked or obscured by the omnipresent role of figure which the self plays in our figure-ground situation. . . . The true role of selfhood would be better understood and therefore more effectively used if this deeper non-self context were appreciated. It is quite likely that (as in a dialectical movement) selfhood will be better understood when reference is made to the primordial non-self matrix from which it arises, and that the synthesis, the capacity of human nature to function at self and non-self levels at the same time, or to alternate when it so desires, may prove to be an enrichment of personality far greater than that which the cult of self-contained, self-directed individuality can grant.[4]

Much has been going on in the modern world to validate Murphy's observations. As we shall see shortly, our recreations have become powerful sources of nonself experience, and there have been numerous developments in society and psychology related to such conditions, e.g., the interest in altered states of consciousness, peak experience and recreational drugs. However, while there has been some study of specific nonself areas, no one has yet offered a comprehensive look at how and why the person should have this capability to lose himself in absorbed diversion.

Nonself experiences are usually discredited by social critics and by religious and mental health institutions. Presumably, such experiences have no social value, and are perceived as being escapist. In a way, all of this is true but it must be remembered that these are transient states. They are essentially diversions; they are not meant to be a way of life. Everyone recognizes that the first priority of existence is found in everyday life, where we have to conduct continual self-related business to insure comfort, social accommodation, and survival.

Absorbed diversions have a function that transcends pragmatic values. They represent a vital function of the organism because they reinforce our basic sense of aliveness. Because they provide contrast and new experience, diversions help offset the depressing and deadening effects of anxieties and monotonies which are so endemic to everyday life. Although there is much contrast in the physical and social environments, much of it is filtered out by our perceptual programs. Many scholars feel that modern society itself, because it is becoming increasingly regulated and routinized, is an ever greater source of monotony. There is, or course, an extensive line of research showing that prolonged monotony has adverse effects on the organism; it not only saps vitality but almost impairs the ability to experience and to feel.[5] Thus contrast, diversion, and variety are vital needs of the organism, perhaps more important than those that mental health specialists are so fond of emphasizing. People can survive for long periods of time without affection, self-esteem, status, and even sex. But we need a certain amount of contrast almost on a daily basis. This is provided by our recreational diversions. Diversions make us come alive, and thus provide a significant kind of psychological nourishment — no matter that they are impractical or escapist. Diversions are not an optional or frivolous aspect of life but represent an absolute requirement for a sane existence.

The ability to lose oneself should be viewed as something of an achievement rather than demeaned as mere escapism. In our absorbing diversions we come as close as possible in removing the shackles from the mind in a controlled way. Given the powerful constraints exerted by habit, conditioning, and social pressure, it is indeed a marvel that the organism has the capability to suspend its everyday orientation and replace it with an experienced reality that is often more vivid and exciting. More than we realize, we are locked into the business of living. It is not easy to break out of this gravitational field, but we can do so through absorbed diversion. This makes it a capability of the organism worthy of study and deeper understanding.

Degrees of Diversion

The opposite of play is not being serious, but reality. — *Sigmund Freud*

To most people, the terms "play" and "recreation" refer to such activities as games or get-togethers. These are the conventional recreations, derived mostly from children's play activities, but they are not especially conducive to absorption. On the other hand, there are strictly adult recreations that have more to do with diversion, rather than just performing some fun activity — diversions such as story and show entertainment, intoxication, sex, music, dancing, art, meditational experience, and intensely cultivated hobbies. As we shall see, absorbed attention is necessary for the realization of such diversions. It is also interesting to note that the most significant recreational developments of the twentieth century have been in the direction of creating diversions that are ever more absorbing.

As a first step in formulating a psychology of diversion, it is necessary to identify the different degrees of this variable. We might follow this formula contained in an old text on music:

> There are three main lines of activity which take us away from the purely practical, everyday aspect of our experiences. The simplest and most primitive is play. This fundamentally consists in giving a fictitious value to our motor behavior. The second is phantasy, in which . . . we allow our imagination full play, regardless of the realities of our environment. The third consists in the mystical experience in which we lose the normal awareness of our own individuality, and of its relation to our surroundings.[6]

Indeed, the mildest degree of diverison consists of play activities, i.e., games, outdoor sports, etc. All these activities occur under conditions that are usually described as "not serious," "for fun," or "let's pretend." In other words, they are conditions that give a "fictitious value to our motor behavior." Unlike a movie, which can plunge us into a new reality, these conventional recreations leave us in the everyday reality; they just dilute it a little. We continue to behave much as we do in everyday life, but under slightly altered, more relaxed conditions. We continue to talk and interact with people (as at parties), we compete (as in games), we strive to stand out (as in sports), and we develop our skills (as in arts and crafts). We continue to have a self but presumably it is less evaluative and less preoccupied with standards. This kind of diversion is brought about by social definition; society attempts to divert us from the business side of life by calling a time-out and redefining our social behavior as being "not serious."

The charm of conventional recreation is that it intermingles work and play, and gives us something of both worlds. When effective, it allows us to experience people in a relaxed way, taking the sting out of competition and failure, and it allows us to exercise almost without knowing it. Magically, it takes many of the unpleasant aspects of life and turns them into fun.

By the same token, however, conventional recreation is an in-between kind of play, and so creates only a weak feeling of diversion. Because there is no complete break with reality, there is a tendency to slip back into the everyday orientation. Since the stimuli of life are always present in conventional recreation, there is the danger they will activate everyday thoughts and anxieties, which would be nonrecreational. Workaday stimuli are always stronger and more insistent than the promptings to relax and be less serious. Thus, conventional recreational activities are notorious for failing to bring off the diversion they are supposed to. Everyone has had experiences of taking the game too seriously, being nervous at parties or feeling frustrated by a hobby. Furthermore, it seems that conventional recreations are not as effective in refreshing us as they once were. Thus, more and more we hear about weekends and holidays making people depressed, and family vacations turning into "bad trips." Leisure experiences are supposed to be healing, but now psychiatrists talk about Sunday neurosis. Even Christmas is considered a stress factor for adults. Indeed, it seems that many traditional forms of recreation have become irrelevant or inadequate in modern times.

When society was cohesive, tradition-oriented, and mostly rural, social rituals and time-outs were more binding. Thus, a holiday would really be experienced as a holiday, e.g., the person was almost *forced* to stop and feel different. Likewise, in a close-knit society, group consensus and peer pressure would operate to enhance the recreational effect. Conventional recreations probably did make a contrast in times when human existence was dominated by work, and the social climate was strict and religious. However, such recreations simply do not stand out in today's more permissive conditions. In modern urban society, recreation as a social time-out tends to lose its meaning when people have opportunities to socialize during work and do not share the same rituals and values.

The second level of diversion is the absorbed state. Absorption can be considered extreme diversion because there is a complete break with self and reality. The absorbed individual is in a trance, completely unmindful of his normal self and the surrounding world. This second level of diversion was described above as allowing "our imagination full play, regardless of the realities of the environment." But it is not so much allowing imagination full play as allowing *attention* full play.

A brief look at story experience shows us how completely absorption can divert us from everyday patterns. In a psychological way, a story can bring about a feeling of having a new identity and being in a new reality. If we can forget ourselves and get totally absorbed in a story, then it takes complete control of our experience and plays upon it in a most enjoyable way. The first effect is usually the feeling of being in another world. In fact, for the time that we are involved in it, absorption will make the world of the story more real than the reality that physically surrounds us. Similar alterations occur in regard to self and sense of identity. We cease being ourselves, and identify with the story characters so much so that what happens to them seems to be happening to us. We care about story characters — we feel fear when danger threatens, we cry when they cry and we want revenge when they are hurt. In this manner the story is experienced completely and wholeheartedly because all attention is focused on it, and we are not distracted by self or reality. Thus, people do not just read or watch stories, they *live* them. All this makes a strong contrast to everyday life.

There are other effects typically found in absorption. For example, there is mental relaxation, which occurs as we stop attending to the cues of everyday life and the internal, self-referent programs are suspended. Absorbed experience can be described as "relaxed arousal," meaning that the experiencing occurs when the mind is relaxed. This phenomenon is unusual and does not occur in everyday reality, where arousal always activates both body and mind. A striking example of relaxed arousal can be found in story entertainment, where we seem to have the magical ability of *enjoying* negative emotions. Fear in everyday life is very unpleasant because self is threatened. But in the relaxed conditions of the story, when self has been suspended, the fear can be enjoyed as a thing in itself. Thus relaxed arousal greatly enriches and expands our experiencing.

All these effects — suspension of everyday self, the feeling of a new identity and reality, relaxed arousal — add up to a powerful diversion effect. These effects are different from the qualities of everyday life, and when they occur in the absorbed state, they give a sense of contrast that is enlivening. The result is a strong experience of having been diverted out of the everyday patterns.

There is, finally, a third level of diversion, a profound and radically absorbing condition that is exemplified by altered states of consciousness. Most people do not experience absorption at this intensity; it is not possible to voluntarily induce level-three diversion as easily as we slip into a story spell. Nevertheless, the organism apparently has this capability, and it can be induced by psychedelic drugs or by long-term cultivation of meditational techniques. At this level, the effects of absorption are experienced in a very convincing way, so much so that individuals come to believe they have indeed entered another reality and are one with another being. As in the case of story enjoyment, however, most of the effects of altered consciousness can be explained by the dual aspect of absorption, i.e., mental relaxation and enhancement of experience. At this extreme level, thinking itself can stop, and there can be a wholesale suspension of the psychophysical codes that stabilize perception and anchor it to reality. The result is hallucinatory perception, cosmic experience and ecstasy. According to reports this is a condition more vivid and pure than anything else experienced by the human organism. Although mystical and altered states are not usually regarded as recreation, there is no doubt they have a continuity with lesser kinds of absorption. Such experiences obviously belong in the domain of play, not work. This is a radical kind of play which the counterculture movement and other groups have experimented with and striven for, apparently with some success.

Although we generally think of play as healthful and desirable, it does not follow that its radical forms are always beneficial. Just as harsh and prolonged work is harmful and too much sleep is undesirable, so the same would be true of an excess of play and diversion. Whatever level of play makes a contrast, that suffices. Human existence seems best served by fluctuations of work and play.

The three levels of diversion discussed here show how play experience is intensified. This analysis shows that play can occur only where there has been some situational engineering. A person cannot simply make himself have play experience by act of will. The experience must be induced by the situation, and the more complete the situational support, the greater the involvement. What is needed, of course, is a situation that engineers attention, diverting it from everyday channels and focusing it completely on some object. Obviously, some recreations do this well; they are very effective in capturing attention and creating intense involvement. Other recreations do it poorly, primarily because they allow everday stimuli to compete for attention and dilute the diversion. All in all, the intensity of play is dependent on the degree of diversion. The greater the diversion, the greater the play experience.

It is often assumed, however, that play is intensified in other ways. For example, a common assumption is that play is intensified by making it more physically active. Because of the tendency to think of play in terms of certain activities like games or hobbies, intense play has been equated with intense activity. However, it is doubtful that the quality of play is enhanced in this manner. This is how work is intensified; play is the opposite of work, and so it should involve less effort.

In itself, physical activity contributes nothing to recreational effect; if anything, it works against it. Physical activity, like mental activity, requires evaluative processing, decision-making and a functional self. There are exceptions, as we shall see in a later chapter; for the most part, they consist of activities that are sexual, rhythmic, or highly cultivated. Otherwise, activity recreations engage only the perceptual-motor system and do not possess us totally as some spectator entertainments can. David Riesman pointed out that much recreation "which appears to be active may be merely muscular: its lactic acid content is high, but there may be little other content, or contentment. And conversely, such supposedly passive pursuits as movie-going can obviously be the most intense experience, the most participative." Roger Caillois seconded this when he asserted that "play is not exercise."[7]

A related stereotype about play emphasizes the importance of the out-doors. The outdoors conjures up associations of exercise, fresh air, and the wholesome participation in strenuous activity. Textbooks tend to promote such an impression; for example, in one book the chapter on outdoor recrea-tion starts with a picture of three people in a canoe, fighting the rapids in rug-ged back country. But such an image is misleading if it was meant to represent the typical outdoor recreation of adults. In a time-budget study wherein a na-tional sample of some 1,200 respondents was asked to make a log of all activities for a particular day, Robinson found that only about 1 percent engaged in out-door recreational sport (hunting, fishing, playing basketball). From his data, Robinson concluded that "20 percent of the adult population accounts for 90 percent of total sports activity."[8] Another survey taken at state parks yielded similar findings and revealed that for most adults outdoor recreation is close to being a spectator sport.[9] Of the fourteen most popular outdoor recreations, half are nearly as passive as watching television. These consist of sight-seeing, driving and walking for pleasure, boating, attending sports events, and visiting zoos, fairs, or parks. Most other outdoor recreations are intermediate, neither very passive nor very active: picnicking, camping, fishing, hunting, golf, and bicycling. It was estimated that only 5 to 20 percent of the people participate in what might be called "strenuous" outdoor recreation such as ten-nis, canoeing, water-skiing, and backpacking. Thus, for adults it would seem that the goal of outdoor recreation is changing their attentional orientation — by communing with nature — rather than getting exercise or fighting the rapids.

Finally, another popular stereotype about play holds that it consists of having fun. The more fun, the more intense the play experience. Fun is the by-product of any activity that pleases us intensely, and as such it can occur in workaday life as well as during play. It is a particular kind of enjoyment, usually associated with humorous and social situations. This kind of arousal is not necessarily associated with mental relaxation. Fun is sometimes hostile and self-promoting, and can occur in tense situations. The fun in "to make fun of" would not be consistent with the spirit of play. Of course there are many legitimate adult recreations such as art, music, tragic literature, and meditation where the term "fun" simply does not do justice to our enjoyment.

Qualities like fun, activity, and the outdoors are very much in evidence in conventional recreation. But we would argue that the true nature of play is only dimly perceived in conventional recreation in which the activities so closely mimic everyday actions and values. If play is really the opposite of workaday life, then its essence resides in things that cannot be found in every-day life, such as mental relaxation, expanded experiencing, and a feeling of contrast and diversion.

Throughout history conventional recreation has been overshadowed by a strong work ethic, and so has existed as a weak form of play. This is probably why it has been so weakly conceptualized. Maybe this is why we know so little about play, and why it has such a tenuous conceptual status in the social and psychological sciences. Actually, the concept of play has no scientific standing in the mainstream of psychology; most general texts ignore the topic. Most so-called theories of play are conceptions borrowed from other areas of psychology. For example, there is a psychoanalytic theory of play, a behavioral theory, a Piagetian theory, etc. Scholarly speculation about the nature of play has been going on for several centuries, but it has been very ideological, emphasizing that play should be active, educational, upbeat, constructive. Not surprisingly, there has been no agreement on the critical element in play that makes it unique from everything else in human existence.

The Changing Relationship between Work and Play

Adults' play requires constant new excesses to be entertaining.
— *Barbara Tuchman*

Classifying diversions (from mild to radical) as we have just done would probably not have been possible a hundred years ago. Throughout history the masses have generally known only the mild, conventional kind of diversion. But in the twentieth century, there has been an influx of new diversions extremely absorbing and distanced from everyday life. Examples of these are the movies, television, recreational drugs, and meditation.

What brought on these new diversions? In a general way, it was the affluence of Western society, which is where most of this recreational development took place. Technological resources were available, and people had the time and money to indulge in these new pastimes. Just as the twentieth century made great advances in workaday life, it made similar advances in play.

Another factor which might help explain why these recreational changes took the direction they did consists of the changing relationship between work and play. If the rule is that play must make a significant contrast to workaday life, then the nature of work through the ages must be considered.

It is difficult to imagine the toil and drudgery that was the lot of most people in ages past. Work was often brutalizing for both men and women. In pre-industrial times, most of the world's work had to be done by human energy; thus, people often worked as beasts of burden. Physical conditions were primitive, and social conditions were exploitative. Under slavery and serfdom, people existed helplessly in a permanent state of work. Most of this was agricultural work and consisted of a back-breaking, never-ending struggle against the land and the elements. In the United States in 1800, just before the arrival of farm technology, 80 percent of the people worked in an agricultural setting compared to about 5 percent today.[10] Paradoxically, the industrial revolution did not at first relieve the human race of its burden of work, but brought only the drudgeries of working in mass production.[11]

In the past, work so dominated daily living there was not the time or means for diversion as we know it. Just being away from the grueling workplace must have made a contrast so that these brief intervals of nonwork constituted a primitive kind of relaxation and play. Otherwise, when recreation was permitted it was usually of a social or religious nature. Thus, given the strong work ethic and the control exerted by religious institutions, there is little doubt that play and recreation were on the mild side.

Such a work-and-play relationship has been reversed, starting with the revolutionary changes that have occurred in the workplace. The nature of work has changed so drastically that it is now a relatively mild experience for most people. The most dramatic indication of this change is the fact that work is shorter. In 1850, the average worker spent seventy hours a week on the job; in 1900, sixty hours; and by 1950, forty hours.[12] In addition, work is not so demanding and exhausting as it once was. It is no longer centered around physical labor; much of it consists of the routines of attending to machines, paperwork or service procedures. As technology has taken the physical toil out of work, so also much of the psychological pressure has been removed by the unions, enlightened management, and government regulation. Furthermore, steps have been taken to make work a more sociable and leisurely experience. Modern work conditions offer opportunities for communication, association, and friendship — in other words, all the enjoyments of sociability that in times past were obtained *after* work. "Now work itself is judged in terms of leisure values," wrote C. Wright Mills. "The sphere of leisure provides the standards by which work is judged; it lends to work such meanings as work has."[13] There are, of course, exceptions, but there is no question that the burden has been lifted to a significant degree. Today, work is generally shorter, easier, safer, and more comfortable than in the past.

Ironically, work has changed in another important way. It is no longer restricted to time on the job. Although work has become milder, it has spread to all areas of life.

As more free time has become available, people use it to take care of activities that they carry on as seriously and with as much effort as they do their jobs. Such activities consist of various kinds of personal and family business — home improvements, community responsibilities, adult education, and perhaps even a second job. Thus leisure has become a continuation of work. As one observer of the modern scene noted, "even as the time spent on the job has steadily grown shorter, and thus the so-called leisure time greater, people have become busier and busier. The old work ethic seems to have carried over into the leisure area, with the result that most of us feel compelled to use our leisure time fruitfully."[14] Thus, what we do after work is much the same as what we do at work; the actual activities and motions may be different, but the experiencing is the same. The saying that we are in a leisure age should be the cause of jubilation, but nobody gets excited about it simply because people continue to work in one way or another during their free time.

Thus the old work-and-play cycle has been flattened out, and the two domains of life now merge into each other. There is just the general business of living, and all of it is conducted with the same mental orientation of mild work. Where is the contrast in such an existence? Indeed, it would seem that we have passed into an Orwellian world of reversed values where work is play, and play is work.

Well, not exactly. In the last fifty years, as work and leisure have blurred into each other, new and extreme forms of play have emerged to provide contrast to modern existence. Unlike conventional recreation, which is made up primarily of social activities, the new kinds of play consist of solitary experiences derived from spectator entertainments and other absorbing diversions. The twentieth century has witnessed a continuing invasion of these new diversions. Movies came first, reaching prominence in the 1930s; then television in the 1950s; recreational drugs in the 1960s; and in the 1970s and 1980s we could add to the list meditation, rock music and recreational sex. All these pastimes involve us in some type of intense experiencing usually attained in an absorbed, near-hypnotic state.

Indeed, it seems that modern diversions have stripped away the extraneous functions — socializing, competition, effortful activity — which diluted conventional recreation, making it half work and half play. Instead, the new diversions provide enriched experience distanced from the distractions of everyday life. It is for this reason that Alvin Toffler referred to these new recreations simply as "experience makers."[15] Movies, television, drugs, and the various spectator entertainments provide a purer form of recreation, and maybe this is why they have become so popular. Until this century, recreation had remained simple and static. In this century, however, it has been revolutionized and has become highly specialized.

Extreme play and mild work: There is no doubt that the old dichotomy has been reversed. Today, recreational diversions wax strong while the work ethic wanes. Modern society shines on play and shades work. Never before has recreational diversion been so much in the forefront of human consciousness. All about us today we see evidence of extreme play — the ubiquitous television set, a prestigious entertainment industry, the big business of travel and tourism with all kinds of new vehicles to whisk us out of everyday life, massive new stadiums and coliseums that stand out in our metropolitan skylines, the rapid proliferation of meditation centers and programs. The modern diversions are unsurpassed in their ability to capture the ultimate human resource — attention. They are so diverting that they alarm us; witness the national concern over television and drugs. At the same time, in the scientific community there is an unprecedented interest in drugs and meditation which can be used to probe the outer reaches of human diversion. Today, recreation is not just a toning down of everyday life; it is emerging with qualities and experiences all its own. Thus in these new recreations we can more clearly discern the nature of play, and what we see, of course, is diversion and absorbed experience.

Social critics have a low regard for these new recreations; presumably they are escapist and represent an illegitimate form of play. In spite of such attitudes, however, these diversions have literally taken over the modern recreational scene. This popularity, rather than being blamed on human perversity, should be accepted as a scientific datum. In other words, if recreation is becoming more escapist, then that should tell us something about the nature of adult recreation and play. Play, it is universally agreed, cannot be forced but is to be freely chosen. Thus, when surveys consistently show that on any particular day many more people watch television than engage in other recreations, and when it is found that attendance figures for spectator sports have increased since 1950 by about 130 percent,[16] then such overwhelming choices must be respected as indicating significant recreational value. What such data indicate is that so-called escapist recreation is not the exception but the rule. It is, in fact, the very thing that needs to be explained. And it is explained when play is viewed as diversion.

It is interesting to note that the traditional play theories do not account for the phenomenal growth or the extreme nature of modern play. In fact, traditional play theories would have predicted the opposite of what has actually happened. According to these theories, play does not add a contrasting dimension to life; it simply makes up for the deficiencies of everyday existence.[17] Presumably, play provides the gratifications and solutions that elude us in everyday life and is thus a continuation of that life. But if play makes up for the frustrations of everyday life, then today — as workaday life becomes more secure and easygoing — there should be less need for recreation. In reality, of course, just the opposite is the case; there has been a veritable recreational explosion that has occurred as working conditions have moderated.

It may not seem fair that as life becomes more comfortable, people need more powerful recreations. According to the Protestant work ethic and Judeo-Christian values, play is something that is earned and deserved by virtue of hard work. It would seem that when work is decreased, play should also be decreased, much like the principle expressed in the old dictum, "Whoever does not work, shall not play." However, such notions are not consistent with the psychological reasons for play, which is to provide variety in human existence.

It seems that modern recreational developments have bypassed the traditional theories. The traditional approaches have little to say about hypnotic diversions; what they emphasize is how recreation serves reality. Such approaches may have made sense in the past when conventional recreational activities did mimic everyday life, but they seem outmoded now. Play is close to superseding work in human consciousness, in value if not in duration. Therefore, it deserves its own perspective, which should emphasize its uniqueness and emergent qualities. Social and therapeutic functions are of minor importance. By looking at recreation strictly in terms of experience and enjoyment, we can achieve an understanding of the phenomenon it represents.

Chapter 2

Breaking Out of Everyday Consciousness

> Desire to escape is not necessarily degenerate, still less a sign of defeat.
> It may be a desire for liberation. — *Holbrook Jackson*

Absorption is a particular kind of attention that is qualitatively different from the orientation maintained in everyday life. It is a nonordinary function that makes possible those nonordinary states like hypnosis and mystical experience. But the capability for absorption also makes possible the whole range of adult diversions such as story-entertainment, aesthetic feeling, intoxication, sexual passion and meditational experience. All these things would be flat and unsatisfying if experienced with everyday attention. Absorption is seen even in the play of children. In a recent text on leisure, the author prefaced his discussion of play with this observation:

> As I write this, some children are playing in the street. What strikes me first about their play is how totally *absorbed* they are with each of their games. It is as if all the rest of the world were suspended. They have entered a magic kingdom in which nothing else matters. There is a very high degree of concentration among those children, a level of attentiveness that is probably seldom if ever reached in school.[1]

Invisible and Silent Recreation

Adults, too, get absorbed when they play, and in fact this may be the only evidence of their recreation. Thus, play experience in adults is deceptive. Who, for example, would have thought that reading the newspaper is a form of play?

> Newspaper reading, subjectively regarded, has all the earmarks of play. One reads one thing at one moment, and another at the next moment, with no relation between them. Reading a newspaper is voluntary, that is, it is not a task or duty. It is not related to the person's everyday life; it is a temporary interlude, satisfying in itself and ending there. The commuter trains in New York City are full of men who sit, two by two, each absorbed in his own

18

newspaper, all deadly silent. The reader is in a sense disinterested in what he is reading; he might look at stock exchange prices to see how his recent purchase of shares is faring, but normally what he reads about is entirely out-side the immediate satisfactions of his needs or specific interests. Yet the reading creates a certain order, as in a child's playing, a brief grasp of the reader's own world. It casts a light spell upon the person — not of rapture, but of deep absorption.[2]

This quote is from media psychologist William Stephenson, who con-sidered reading the paper a significant form of adult play experience by virtue of the absorption and diversion provided. It is important to distinguish this kind of absorbed play from its attentional opposite, which occurs when we con-centrate on something. The terms *concentration* and *absorption* are often used interchangeably to denote intense attentional involvement; however, two different psychological states are involved. Concentration is everyday con-sciousness; absorption is not. Concentration is work; absorption is play and diversion. Concentration involves intense mental activity — cognitive process-ing, problem-solving, analyzing. Absorption is the suspension of all of this internally initiated activity. Concentration is interactive, ego-involving, and effortful; it is aimed at getting practical results. Absorption is reactive, sug-gestible, relaxed — losing oneself and being harmoniously carried along by some fascination. Concentration gives evidence of dual control of attention as organism interacts with environment; there is a strong self-object dichotomy, a sense of "me" *vs.* what is out there. Absorption is unitary control of attention resulting in a global undifferentiated state, total attention, and a feeling of being merged with the external object. We concentrate when we worry, try to fix the stalled car, or work on our income tax returns. We are absorbed when enjoying movies, music, sex, or other diversions.

Like Stephenson, other theorists have viewed play in terms of absorption and diversion. For example, Dutch scholar Johan Huizinga, whose book *Homo Ludens* is considered a classic in the field, described play as "standing quite consciously outside 'ordinary' life as being 'not serious' but at the same time absorbing the player intensely and utterly."[3] Likewise, J.S. Shivers, a major figure in the American recreation profession, wrote:

In analyzing what recreation is, it is found that only one condition is necessary by which unity or harmony is brought about. An intense absorp-tion must seize the individual's attention so that everything outside of whatever he is participating in loses its significance for the period of time in which his whole attention is engaged. This can never be a piece-meal affair; it is either all or nothing. In losing himself, the individual finds himself.[4]

Or more to the point, in losing his *self*, the individual finds his *experience*.

Stephenson aptly described the absorbed commuters as "deadly silent." Absorbed people do not talk; if they did, the spell would be broken because talking involves interaction and the activation of self-awareness. Absorbed people also tend to be relatively expressionless and motionless. The term *fascination* is often used synonymously with absorption, and one of its meanings is "to hold motionless by capturing attention."[5] Thus, absorbed individuals often have a "zombie" appearance which constitutes the "absorbed look." If you have ever turned around during a movie to look at the spectators, you have seen absorption reflected in the staring eyes and motionless bodies. In other cases, absorption is associated with a slouchy posture, glazed eyes, and the nose in a book. Absorbed individuals are oblivious; they usually have to be called back to reality by exasperated family members reminding them that it is time to eat or sleep. Other people often get annoyed when they see individuals in the absorbed state, which seems so impractical and unnatural. Our cultural mores stress that people should be up and about, pursuing the business of living.

But appearances are deceiving about the intensity of the absorbed state. While the demeanor is bland, absorbed experience can be intense. Although immobilized — in fact, because he is immobilized — the absorbed person is capable of an intense involvement that is harmoniously experienced and free of distraction. This can be so complete that the person seems to be on another level of existence, in another world psychologically.

Absorption as Hypnotic Involvement

In a sense you are hypnotized whenever you see a good show and forget you are part of the audience, but instead feel you are part of the story.
— *Andre M. Weitzenhoffer and Ernest R. Hilgard*

In the absorbed state, the organism has an expanded capacity for experience. A striking demonstration of this is seen in hypnosis which, researchers now believe, is absorbed attention. When hypnotized, the human being is at his most suggestible, and as a result, just about every possible kind of effect can be produced in experience. Mere suggestions of stimuli, as of sight or sound for example, will be experienced vividly as though they were actually present.[6] Many of the experiences typically induced in hypnosis go against logic: insensitivity to pain, forgetfulness, perceptual disturbances, loss of sense of identity. These are effects a person could not produce on his own. However, they are possible when control of attention is totally surrendered to an external stimulus, which in this case is the hypnotist.

Can it be that the old enigma of hypnosis has been finally solved by modern investigators? Maybe there are no final answers, but research conducted in the last twenty years has greatly sharpened our understanding of this strange phenomenon. At least at this stage of our knowledge, experts in the field are explaining hypnosis with concepts like absorbed attention, "imaginative involvement" and "role absorption."

At first glance, hypnosis appears to be a social process or a communicative situation: a forceful hypnotist dominates a passive subject. This, however, has not been a useful conception, and it has not been supported by research. For example, studies have *not* found that good hypnotic subjects are easily dominated; they are not particularly compliant, or psychologically weak. Nevertheless, this continues to be the popular notion of hypnosis. Investigators like Ronald Shor have urged that we must change "the conception of hypnosis as a technique of obliging people to do what the hypnotist wants them to do."[7] To counteract such views, modern-day practitioners will preface hypnotic induction with a statement such as the following: "First, the important thing here is what you do, not what I do. Secondly, please don't try to make anything happen. Just let things happen."[8]

If hypnosis is something that neither the hypnotist nor the subject does, then what is it? Apparently, it is a unique attentional state that occurs under the right conditions but cannot be willed or forced. This kind of attention is not evident in everyday life, but it is a capacity the organism possesses and uses in dreaming and in awake absorbed states.

After years of fruitless research to identify the personality characteristics of hypnotically susceptible subjects, a significant finding gradually emerged. A number of studies showed that individuals who are good hypnotic subjects admitted to having a lot of hypnotic-like experiences. Basically, these were absorbed experiences. This finding suggests that individuals who are easily absorbed are easily hypnotized. In surveys, these individuals responded positively to questions such as the following:

- Have you ever become so absorbed in listening to music that you almost forgot where you were?[9]
- Have you ever been completely immersed in nature or in art (for example, in the mountains, at the ocean, viewing sculpture, paintings, etc.) and had a feeling of awe, inspiration, and grandeur sweep over you so that you felt as if your whole state of consciousness was somehow temporarily altered?
- Have you ever been so strongly in love with somebody that you somehow felt that your own self was fading and you felt at one with the beloved person?[10]
- When you dance, do you feel that the music and the mood are being expressed through your movements, while you yourself fade into the background?
- While watching a movie or show do you sometimes become so involved that you feel yourself participating in the action?[11]

In 1975, Spanos and McPeake wrote that "investigators of widely differing theoretical orientations" are converging toward the view "that hypnotic suggestibility is related to subjects' tendency to become 'involved' or 'absorbed' in everyday imaginative activities such as reading a novel, watching or acting in dramatic productions, and the like."[12] As noted earlier, story-enjoyment is the epitome of absorbed experience. In their book on hypnotism, Barber, Spanos and Chaves pointed out how responding to hypnotic suggestions is comparable to story experience.

> The processes involved in responding to test suggestions — for example, suggestions for limb rigidity, anesthesia, age regression, amnesia, etc. — are similar to those present when a person is reading an interesting novel or observing an interesting motion picture. When reading an interesting novel, a person thinks and imagines with the communications from the printed page. To the extent that he becomes engrossed or involved in his imaginings, he does not have contradictory thoughts such as "This is only a novel" or "This is only make-believe." Instead, he experiences a variety of emotions while empathizing and "living with" the characters.[13]

Thus, being hypnotized is a matter of getting absorbed in the suggestions of the hypnotist. The initial step in getting absorbed is to withdraw attention from oneself and one's surroundings; ideally, absorption occurs in a quiet or sheltered place (e.g., a theater), or at least where there are no demands on one's attention. Similarly, in hypnosis, the first request is that the subject close his eyes, thus shutting out the surroundings and focusing all attention on the words of the hypnotist. An attempt is then made to weaken thinking and internal processing by suggestions of relaxation and sleep. The good hypnotic subject is someone who can let go and get totally absorbed in the instructions of the hypnotist; he does not question or evaluate, but immediately makes the hypnotist's instructions his own. The hypnotist presents his suggestions in vivid word-pictures that tend to capture attention and are easy to identify with: "Imagine your hands are two pieces of steel that are welded together so that it is impossible to get them apart." With such an image at the center of total attention, and with no other thoughts to contradict it, the experience of "hands welded together" becomes for the moment the only reality the subject knows.

> A feeling of rigidity is produced in the hands when the "good" subject clasps them tightly and contracts the muscles. As he then thinks and imagines with the suggestions, he focuses on the rigidity that is already present. In order to unclasp the rigid hands, it is necessary to remove the muscular contractions by relaxing the hands. However, the "good" subject does not relax the hands; instead, he continues to focus on the rigidity that is present and does not take them apart until he is told that he now can relax them.[14]

It seems that the hypnotist functions mostly as a guide to help the subject get absorbed. Apparently, with some training the subject can do it all on his own. Self-hypnosis seems to be a genuine phenomenon; there is evidence that subjectively and behaviorally it is comparable to hypnosis induced by another person. [15]

If the hypnotic state is absorbed attention, then it should also be comparable to other total attentional states such as meditation. This connection has been supported by research. One study took phenomenological and physiological measures of subjects during meditation and the hypnotic state and found no differences between the two. [16] Investigators are beginning to realize that both states require the same kind of mental orientation, which some have called "sustained, nonanalytic attending." [17]

Tellegen and Atkinson conducted a large scale investigation into the nature of hypnotic susceptibility. Using many questions from earlier studies on hypnotic-like experiences, they devised a new research questionnaire which also elicited information about topics thought to be related to hypnosis, e.g., trust, sleep, impulsiveness, optimism, etc. This questionnaire was administered to a large number of subjects, together with some standard personality scales and measures of hypnotic susceptibility. Factor analysis showed that the principal component in the research questionnaire was what the authors called *absorption*. When this factor and the other personality measures were correlated with hypnotic susceptibility, only absorption was related to a significant degree. Tellegen and Atkinson defined absorption in this way:

> Absorption is interpreted as a disposition for having episodes of "total" attention. . . . This kind of attentional functioning is believed to result in a heightened sense of the reality of the attentional object, imperviousness to distracting events, and an altered sense of reality in general, including an empathically altered sense of self. Only absorption was consistently correlated with hypnotizability. [18]

It is interesting to note that most of the extremely absorbing diversions have been compared to the hypnotic state in one way or another. In a book entitled *LSD, Marijuana, Yoga, and Hypnosis,* Theodore X. Barber discussed the similarity of drugged and meditational states to hypnosis. [19] Additional support for this view came from a study conducted by Spencer Sherman. He hypnotized a few "excellent" subjects into a very deep trance state in order to see what the hypnotic experience would be like without the usual behavioral suggestions from the hypnotist. What these subjects reported was similar to the cosmic experiences that characterize deep meditation and altered states of consciousness; in some cases even EEG patterns were changed. [20] In what is considered the classic psychological study of mysticism, James Leuba wrote in 1925, "The first step of the Christian mystical method is in substance the first step of the hypnotic method; it begins with the fixation of attention upon some thought or external object in order to circumscribe mental activity." [21] Ortega y Gasset argued that the mystical state, and the more common experience of falling in love, are basically hypnotic conditions.[22] Freud made similar observations about being in love.[23] Finally, this whole topic was treated in excellent fashion in a book by Josephine Hilgard, *Personality and Hypnosis*. With data from interviews and questionnaires, Hilgard showed that hypnotizability is related to a capacity for absorbed involvement in various entertainments, religious and aesthetic experiences. Hilgard, who is a psychiatrist-psychologist, based her conclusions on extensive investigations conducted at the Laboratory of Hypnosis Research at Stanford University.

> What we found out was that the hypnotizable person was capable of a deep involvement in one or more imaginative-feeling areas of experience — reading a novel, listening to music, having an aesthetic experience of nature, or engaging in absorbing adventures of body or mind. This involvement is one of the things the existentialist is talking about when he speaks of the breaking down of the distinction between the subject and the object of his experience; it is what those seeking expansion of consciousness mean by their all-embracing experiences; it is something like Maslow's peak experiences. . . .
> If we were to define this involvement, to distinguish it from its nearest relatives such as enjoyment of, or interest in, an activity, we would have to stress the quality of almost total immersion in the activity, with indifference to distracting stimuli in the environment. The often observed narrowing of attention in the hypnotized subject implies something like this.[24]

Hypnosis itself is not the subject of this book, but it is highly relevant to its purpose. Hypnosis is accepted in scientific circles as a demonstrable phenomenon, and the finding that it is actually based on absorbed attention gives credence and legitimacy to the concept of absorption. Absorbed attention is not generally recognized as being different from everyday consciousness. Most people probably believe that getting absorbed is simply an intense kind of attention, much like concentrating on work or a personal problem. Actually, absorption is a completely different orientation, and hypnosis shows how different.

Does it seem unbelievable that hypnosis can make a subject insensitive to pain, forgetful of his identity, or blind to other people nearby? Yet the same effects are produced by watching a movie, for example, when we not only tolerate but enjoy the normally painful emotions of fear and grief. Likewise, when absorbed in the movie we forget who we are and feel that we have become the hero, all the while being unaware of the people sitting around us. Usually, hypnosis has been viewed as the doorway to mysterious worlds. But here, hypnosis leads in the other direction: back to normal existence, to show what is possible in play and diversion.

Mental Relaxation

Mass entertainments like novels, movies and television are often criticized because they exert a "hypnotic effect" on people. In view of the data just presented, apparently this is no mere figure of speech. But what is usually meant by this criticism is that these entertainments do not stimulate the mind, but lull and relax it. This, too, is true.

Absorption, as well as hypnosis, is dependent on a relaxed mental state, which means that self functions, especially evaluative thinking, must be suspended. Thus it is necessary to suspend critical thinking during our entertainments if we want to get fully involved in them. In other words, absorption demands a trade-off; what we sacrifice in the cognitive area, we gain in experience. We cannot have it both ways. It is the very suspension of mental functioning that makes the person more suggestible, open and capable of expanded experiencing.

Mental relaxation is not just a matter of having peaceful thoughts. It is an anti-cognitive condition, an identifiable phenomenon. On the EEG it is identified by the presence of alpha waves, which, according to reports, are experienced as "a general calming down of the mind — where you stop being *critical* about anything."[25] As one investigator said, hypnosis "eliminates all spontaneous processes in consciousness.... Consciousness is limited to the idea-content given by the hypnotist."[26] And what William James said about hypnosis is also true for absorption:

> It is characterized by *the absence of any conflicting notion in the mind.* Either there is nothing else at all in the mind, or what is there does not conflict.... Ask him [the hypnotic subject] what he is thinking about, and ten to one he will reply "nothing." The consequence is that he both believes everything he is told, and performs every act that is suggested.[27]

The phenomenon of mental relaxation has received little theoretical attention in psychology, but it was discussed in a scholarly book well known to most psychologists: *Plans and the Structure of Behavior* by Miller, Galanter and Pribram. These theorists referred to mental activity as "inner speech" and the making of "Plans" which act much like computer programs. Mental relaxation was discussed in a chapter on "Relinquishing the Plan" — a process that is most evident in the natural course of falling asleep, and in hypnosis.

> The hypnotized person is not really doing anything different, with this exception: the voice he listens to for his Plan is not his own, but the hypnotist's. The subject gives up his inner speech to the hypnotist.
> It is not sufficient to say merely that a hypnotized subject is listening to Plans formulated for him by the hypnotist. Any person watching the pair of them at work would also be listening to the same Plans but would not feel the

same compulsion to carry them out. What is the difference between normal listening and hypnotized listening?

It is assumed that a waking person hears the suggested Plans and then either incorporates them or rejects them in the planning he is doing for himself. But a hypnotized subject has stopped making his own Plans, and therefore there can be no question of coordination, no possible translation from the hypnotist's version to his own. The hypnotist's version of the Plan is the only one he has, and so he executes it. The basic assumption here . . . is that he must execute *some* Plan all the time. Of course, the subject is capable of elaborating the Plan that the hypnotist gives him, just as he would normally supply the tactics to elaborate some strategy of his own. But the hypnotist's Plan takes precedence over any Plans of his own.

So the question becomes: How does a person stop making Plans for himself? This is something each of us accomplishes every night of our lives when we fall asleep. Stopping is not always easy, as anyone who has suffered from insomnia will attest, but most of us manage to do it without too much difficulty. It would be natural to suppose that the same procedure would work when a person wanted to turn off his own inner speech in order to become hypnotized. He would try to create the same conditions under which he usually falls asleep. He would make the room dark and quiet. He would sit or lie down in a relaxed, comfortable position. . . . The person might try to stop thinking about his own Plans by giving his inner-speech machine something dull and stupid to do, like counting sheep or concentrating on some small detail. He would try to discourage himself from thinking fitfully of what is going to happen next, what people will think of him, how long he has been here, where he is in relation to other objects in the room, etc. He would, in short, try to relax and stop talking to himself. And that is exactly what the standard hypnotic procedures ask him to do. In hypnosis, however, he does not fall asleep, because he finds that there is a substitute Plan provided by the operator's voice, and so the operator's Plans begin to be played out on the subject's nervous system as though they were his own.[28]

One of the implications of this analysis is that the organism is not likely to be physically active during mental relaxation. Activity requires organized interactions with the environment, which in turn are dependent on processing Plans and codes. In other words, being active requires evaluative thinking, reality testing, and other self functions. Physical activity would thus be incompatible with relinquishing one's Plan or relaxing mentally. There are exceptions, which we shall study in Chapter 11; but the general principle seems to be that *mental relaxation is directly correlated with physical relaxation and body immobilization.* This immobilization of the organism is seen in all kinds of relaxed conditions, such as drowsiness, autogenic and progressive relaxation procedures,[29] hypnotic induction, and in absorbing spectator entertainments. In all these cases, the person stops moving, looking about, and interacting with people. In general, the absence of purposeful action implies the absence of purposeful thinking; the absence of external behavior implies the absence of internal processing. It makes sense that the organism could relinquish its executive function only to the extent that it immobilized itself. Therefore, the passivity that many scholars object to in our spectator entertainments is really a necessary condition for attaining the mental relaxation so highly valued by adults seeking relief from the demands of everyday life.

By way of contrast, it should be noted that while activity is incompatible with mental relaxation, emotional arousal is not. It is possible to be emotionally aroused and mentally relaxed at the same time, and this kind of relaxed arousal typically occurs in absorbed states. Unlike our actions, arousal occurs reflexively and requires no evaluative thinking. It has often been recognized that emotional experience is independent of, and even diametrically opposed to, cognitive functioning.

Suspending the Master Codes

> The mystic, like the lover, attains his abnormal state by "fixing" his attention upon an object, the function of which is, for the moment, simply to withdraw attention from everything else and permit a vacuum of the mind. — *José Ortega y Gasset*

Anybody who has taken up meditation or some other relaxation program knows how difficult it is to break out of the everyday orientation. Even though we withdraw from the world into some quiet place, it is often difficult to quiet the mind, especially if we are troubled. It is difficult to stop thinking and talking to ourselves. The widespread use of alcohol and tranquilizing drugs, which relax us mentally, highlights the fact that people need help in breaking out. Although we are hardly aware of it, everyday consciousness is a tough and binding condition of the organism; it resists being relaxed. To understand its tyrannical nature is to appreciate the possibility of mental relaxation and play.

Everyday consciousness is ruled by an invisible system of codes and programs. Although we seem to live and think spontaneously, there are actually internal programs that exert ironclad control over everyday attention, organizing and integrating all psychological activity. The organism has thousands of physiological codes that regulate its internal environment, and probably as many psychological codes that regulate its relations with the external environment. Just as the heart is programmed to pump blood, so the brain and nervous system are programmed to process the organism's business with the world outside.

Everyday consciousness is the psychological state for conducting the business of living, i.e., doing all those things necessary for health, comfort, social relations, and other needs. We might do it well or poorly, but we are all literally forced by the nervous system and society to conduct this business. We have to feed ourselves, obtain shelter and in general compete with other

humans for valued resources. In becoming socialized we are programmed
with habits and codes that make us take care of these tasks. No matter what
a person's station in life, it is almost certain that his consciousness is normally
taken up with processing such programmed activities. And the term *business*
is an apt metaphor for it all, since this processing is serious and work-like.
It has a demanding quality that leads to hurrying. There is always an agenda,
conditions are competitive, and accounts are kept on how well we do. Failure
to keep up with the business of living leads to adverse consequences. At first,
we might experience guilt and be subjected to criticism from family and
friends. But continued neglect would result in the loss of family, friends,
employment, and even life itself. Complete neglect of the business of living —
to the degree, for example, that alcoholics sometimes neglect it — would make
one an outcast and lead to institutionalization.

There is nothing new in the notion that everyday activity is ruled by internal programs. To a large extent, this is what psychology is about. The areas
of learning and personality study how the organism acquires and integrates
internal dispositions. Modern advances in neurophysiology show conclusively
that all input and output of the organism are routed through these central,
mediating structures, which function much like computer programs.[30] Well-
known British neurologist J.Z. Young wrote that "the brain operates in certain
organized ways that may be described as programs, and the actions of these
programs constitute the entity that we call the mind of a person."

> I propose to say that the lives of human beings and other animals are gov-
> erned by sets of programs written in their genes and brains. Some of these
> programs may be called "practical" or physiological and they ensure that we
> breathe, eat, drink, and sleep. Others are social, and regulate our speaking
> and other forms of communication, our agreeing, and our loving or
> hating.... Perhaps the most important programs of all are those used for
> the activities that we call mental, such as thinking, imagining, dreaming,
> believing, and worshipping.[31]

In his monumental work *The Act of Creation,* Arthur Koestler presents
similar ideas but uses the word *code* instead of program.[32] A code is a built-in
set of rules for behaving in some patterned way. A code can be any kind of
psychological disposition: habit, attitude, need, role, etc. Unlike
psychologists who tend to emphasize the differences among these dispositions
and give us a fragmented view of personality functioning, Koestler emphasizes
the structural similarity among all dispositions — i.e., they are all encoded instructions to the organism — and he looks at how they make up the organism's
adjustive processing system. In that system, codes are switched on as the need
arises. The processing is hierarchically organized in a system of master codes
and subcodes, allowing for both stability and flexibility in personality.

The most dramatic evidence for code control is found in a skill like handwriting. When a person wants to write a sentence, he has only to think of the words, and the writing seems to flow out of the pen — obviously controlled by some code in the brain that swiftly translates thoughts into finger movements. When writing words, one does not have to consciously remember how to form each letter; the code does it automatically. Koestler wrote that "all coherent thinking and behavior is subject to some specific code of rules to which its character of coherence is due — even though the code functions partly or entirely on unconscious levels of the mind, as it generally does" (p. 42).

The psychological codes are not triggered in blind stimulus-response fashion but operate in the context of an overall processing system. Since we can do many things at one time — think, act, talk, look, hear, feel — at each level codes are firing to pattern our responses so that they are consistent with the organism as a whole and with the demands of the environment. The priorities are set by a few master codes that keep the processing organized. The master codes function like a central relay station, directing the traffic among specific subcodes that consist of actual skills, habits, motives, etc. The strength of any code is relative, depending on its standing in the entire system. Thus the so-called force of habit is attenuated by the overall system within which it operates and to which it is subordinate. It is estimated that there are ten thousand million nerve cells in the human cerebral cortex,[33] making possible endless combinations of master codes and sub-codes, operating much like a human computer. This processing system is more like the functioning of electronic circuits than chains of stimulus and response. In fact, recordings from the brain indicate constant patterned electrical activity. This activity undoubtedly reflects the systematic firing of codes that are always processing physiological and psychological adjustment.

The complexity of this code processing is reflected in attention, which in everyday life is multi-directional, yet at the same time hierarchically organized. Everyday attention maintains a focal point at the same time that numerous peripheral areas are monitored. Attention moves about ceaselessly while awake, and the relation between focus and periphery is constantly changing in an orderly fashion. There is also continuous selectivity as the manifold informational bits that bombard the senses are sorted out, some to be heeded, others to be blocked out of consciousness. In even the simplest situations these multiple functions go on. Take for example driving to work. Our eyes attend to the road and traffic conditions; our hands and feet control the mechanics of operating the car; we may be listening to a passenger in the car who is talking to us; and still in our mind we may be thinking about a reply, or even pondering some problem that we have to face at work. (Such divided attention, of course, stands in sharp contrast to absorption, where attention is total.)

Overseeing the entire psychological processing system are master programs. These are generalized codes that keep the organism on track as it conducts its daily life. The master codes give us the sense of being purposeful and self-aware. Without them we would be disoriented, bundles of habits and subcodes without direction. The system of master codes can be conceptualized in terms of the business of living, which, reduced to basics, involves an *organism* interacting with the *environment* in an *evaluative way*. Thus we might postulate that there are three interrelated master codes, one for each of these elements.

• *Self*. Undoubtedly the most important code in the human computer is what is usually recognized as the rule of life, namely, to look out for oneself. Self is the first principle; it is our most basic frame of reference. This master code sets the priorities in processing: The first question asked of all input is how it relates to oneself. This code guarantees that the organism will always take account of itself.

• *Reality orientation*. This second master code governs our interactions with the environment. From the moment a person wakes up to the time he goes to sleep, he is occupied with the external environment — moving from one place to another, handling objects, talking to people, adhering to schedules, making plans. This code mediates sense of space and time, monitoring our ever-changing relationship to external objects. This code not only keeps the organism oriented to the external environment, but, as we shall see later, it defines and in a sense constructs reality.

• *Evaluative processing*. Finally, there is a master code which complements the other two; it is a generalized set to evaluate the interaction between self and reality. Like all effective systems, the organism has a built-in program for self-correction. This is the function that makes comparisons with standards and then initiates corrective action through problem-solving, reasoning, etc. The functioning of this master code is most evident in thinking or inner speech; in the everyday stream of thought we find ourselves continually making judgments, comparing, criticizing.

These master codes function in an interrelated way to call out and coordinate specific subcodes in the processing system. There is no higher mechanism in the psychological life of the organism. What we call self or will is just an aspect of these programs in the human computer.

Master code processing varies in intensity, depending on the conditions. It is diminished when conditions are routine or relaxed. On the other hand, it is intensified when the organism is being tested or threatened, i.e., when there is business to do and some action is required. If for some reason the subcodes cannot meet the test, then we see more evidence of the master codes as the action reverts to the control stations. For example, if while driving to work something happened to disrupt the routine processing of the situation, then we would see evidence of the master codes "taking charge" to reorder the priorities and correct the problem. If we got hit by another car, had a flat tire, or came upon a roadblock or a blinding snowstorm, the normal processing of driving would be interrupted. We would instantly become much more self-conscious and ego-involved (self code); we would conduct an intense search of the environment (reality code); and we would find ourselves thinking intently about solving the problem (evaluative code). Although the master codes are operative during most of waking existence, they are most clearly evident in stressful conditions when the business of living is intensified.

Neuropsychologists who study brain-behavior relationships have found evidence of master codes in cortical functioning. For example, Lezak used the term "executive functions" to refer to certain supramodal abilities that are apparently mediated by the frontal lobes.[34] Executive functions consist of self-awareness, decision-making, and the ability to initiate, modulate, and stop behavior. This conception is similar to our notion of controlling computer programs that determine the firing of specific subcodes and mediate our basic orientations toward self and reality. "The executive functions," Lezak wrote, "consist of those capacities that enable a person to engage in independent, purposive, self-serving behavior successfully" (p. 38). Apparently, damage to the frontal lobes would disrupt the master codes but would leave intact the subcode system. Lezak cites an example of such a case and shows what existence would be like without the executive functions. The patient, who had been a professional before his brain injury, could now work only at a menial job under supervision. His intellectual, cognitive, and motor abilities were intact, but "initiating, self-correcting, and self-regulating behaviors were severely compromised" (p. 39). The patient could handle routine but nothing that required judgment or decision-making. In general, this man was passive and unquestioning; he did not have short-term plans or long-term goals. Similar effects are seen in prefrontal lobotomy, which in the past was a surgical treatment for highly distressed psychiatric patients. These patients, before treatment, displayed symptoms of excessive, unremitting master code functioning. Prefrontal lobotomy disrupted the master codes, toning down the business of living and bringing relief to the distressed patients.

In the intact brain, master codes normally become functional as we awake, and they are suspended as we fall asleep. They are also suspended in mental relaxation and absorbed states. It is possible for subcodes to be activated during absorption, but only directly by the external stimulus—not through the master code processing system. For example, the patterned movements of dancing are controlled by the music, not by evaluative processing from the inside. Likewise, when we are absorbed in reading a novel or watching a movie, specific subcodes are firing to translate the print or the screen images into meanings. However, we do not interact with the novel or movie as business; we do not need self-referent priorities, a reality orientation, or evaluate processing. Instead, we remain relatively motionless, become suggestible, and let the story take complete control of attention.

It should be noted that because they are necessary for survival, the master codes are never eliminated in an absolute sense. Their control of attention is merely held in abeyance. The organism always has the ability to retake control of attention if that is necessary. If, while we are absorbed, the phone rings or we get hungry, then master code processing can be switched on to take care of the business, breaking the absorbed spell. Even in sleep, when consciousness seems to be extinguished, the organism apparently maintains some attentional processing at a "pilot-light" level so that it can be reactivated if the need should arise. In these cases it might be said that the master codes are idling but are out of gear with self and reality.

It is when the master codes are out of gear that one is likely to see the deadpan look of the absorbed. In everyday consciousness, when the master codes are processing interactions with the environment, the organism has an animated appearance. Eyes look about the surrounding environment, posture has a set to it, movements reflect inner motivations. Normal external appearance develops out of — and is expressive of — master code processing and the interactions with the environment. Likewise, in absorption the "blank" look reflects "blank" master codes. During absorption, a person can have intense and moving experiences without the normal outward signs of emotional arousal. To be sure, while absorbed we might laugh or cry, but for the most part the eyes remain fixed and facial features impassive. The "vacant expression of the eyes" so characteristic of absorption was noted by Charles Darwin in his classic study *The Expression of the Emotions in Man and Animals.* [35] Darwin observed that movements around the eyes generally reflect mental activity. But when a person is absorbed or meditating, there is "almost complete relaxation of certain muscles of the eyes," and the "eyes appear vacant," all of which is strong indication of "mind absent." In other words, the vacant look shows that absorbed experience develops independently of the master codes, i.e., the mind.

But if, in absorption, we temporarily suspend these codes that are so vital to everyday functioning, what happens to experience when they are suspended? That is the topic of the next chapter.

Chapter 3

The Enjoyments of Being Absorbed

Poetry and drama, everyone will agree, provide experiences
which are richer than real life. — *William Stephenson*

When we are absorbed, we continue to be awake and experiencing — but
in a different mode, with qualities that are not experienced in the psychological
arrangement of everyday life. A reorganization takes place that puts us on
another plane of existence.

In this reorganization, what is mediated by the master codes slips to the
background of consciousness, and what was in the background comes to the
fore. It seems as though we are psychologically turned inside out — from self
to nonself, from multiple interaction to total attention, from a thinking and
processing creature to an experiencing one. In some ways, absorption is not
only different from everyday consciousness, but the opposite of it.

This reorganization of experience can be described as a figure-ground
reversal. All perceptual experience is organized into figure and ground.[1] The
figure refers to what stands out in the perceptual field, what is perceived to have
an identity distinct from the rest. The *ground* is the area behind the figure.
Psychology textbooks demonstrate figure-ground organization by presenting
trick pictures which make it easy for the two elements to be reversed. One
such picture appears to show a white goblet on a black background. However,
when one refocuses attention on a specific part of the picture — the black area
along the stem of the goblet — the background suddenly takes shape and
becomes a figure: face-to-face human profiles, formed by the shape of the black
areas along the stem of the goblet. With the emergence of the new figure, the
original goblet shape seems to disappear and becomes the background.

Since figure-ground organization is imposed by the central nervous
system, it is probably characteristic, not only of perceptual experience, but
of the entire field of consciousness. And as in the case of the trick pictures,
the figure-ground reversal of consciousness is brought on by a major shift in
attention.

Everyday consciousness contains a number of broad dualities that are

33

organized on a figure-ground basis. The most important is the self-object dichotomy. In everyday life, self is the central and continuing experience; the object is less important, experienced as peripheral and transitory. The self is "here" while the object is "out there." In absorption, however, this relationship is reversed. Sense of self fades to the background while some object of fascination comes vividly to the center of total attention. As we shall see, other dichotomies, such as thinking *vs.* feeling, are also organized in terms of figure-ground, and in absorption are reversed in a similar manner.

Such figure-ground reversals provide us with the greatest possible contrast and diversion. Not only is perception different — *we* are different. If human existence does indeed have a pattern of alternating between work and play, it must be made possible by some fundamental shift in consciousness. If we could not make this psychological flip-flop, if we could not reverse the self-object and other dualities of existence, then there would be no difference between play and work, art and life, dream and reality.

Feeling a Different Identity

What absorbs me, that I am, rather than mine own self. — *Meister Eckhart*

Getting out of oneself is a fundamental reversal of existence because most of the time we are very much *in* ourselves. Everyday consciousness has a persistent self-orientation, though it may not be readily apparent, just because it is always there. Some might argue that we really attend to things in the environment, not ourselves. Vision and hearing, the main sensory channels, are oriented to the outside. However, while external stimuli have a role in controlling attention, there is a more powerful determinant in the organism itself, in the form of a master code. Here is how Gardner Murphy described the role of this master code in everyday life:

> Whatever the self is, it becomes a center, an anchorage point, a standard of comparison, an ultimate real. Inevitably it takes its place as a supreme value. . . .
> But the self is not only an aspect of all experience and a standard for all experience; it contributes to the *quality and form of all experience*. Each person, each thing, each idea is in some degree my own, in some degree external to me; and by virtue of that subtle process of interpenetration which characterizes all associations, each person, thing, or idea becomes touched with the brush of my own selfhood. . . .
> A large proportion of the individual's perceptual and motor activities are concerned rather directly with his own body . . . with seeing and hearing *oneself*. A person cannot open his eyes without supplying the object viewed with a fringe of face, chest, hands, and arms; he cannot speak about the most impersonal thing without hearing his voice, both through the outer air and

through inner bone conduction. . . . As he adjusts the eyes to see or turns the head to hear, the proprioceptors serve to make the activity a self-activity. . . .

. . . No matter how quickly one shifts his focus in reference to each new external event, the activity stream is ordered in terms of the expected or desired outcome of each activity for the self. . . .

The self is a perceived object; when not clearly perceived, it can still be dimly perceived. And when not even dimly perceived, a set may be maintained toward it, a readiness or disposition to respond to it as to anything else which lies near at hand and to which adjustment must be made. In all perception there are elements which in themselves are unnoticed, yet make up vital parts of the total. In the same way, the self may be an unnoticed part of the continuing life picture.

Thus the more closely we look at the matter, the more probable it appears that most human adjustments are in some degree adjustments not to an external situation alone, but to a perceptual whole of which the self is a part, a self-in-situation field.[2]

It is a truism in psychology that perception involves a self-object interaction.[3] In the 1950s the "new look" school of perceptual research demonstrated that perception is not totally objective and representative of the external world, but biased by self-related motives.[4] Maslow further declared that the attention allocated to external objects is only partial, just what is necessary for the purpose of tagging and identification.[5] He referred to this rapid and cursory kind of attention as "rubricizing." Thus our perception is greatly attenuated and filtered by self-referent codes in the organism. We do not experience the object itself, but what it means to our purposes. While an endless array of objects move in and out of attention, the self-factor remains constant and dominant.

In absorption, this entire self-process is abated. Self is no longer "a center, an anchorage point." Diminished self-orientation is what people remember most about the absorbed state. For example, when Maslow asked subjects to describe their experiences while enjoying certain kinds of entertainment like art, music, and stories, he found their reactions to be *"ego-transcending, self-forgetful, egoless."*[6] Similar terms were used by Stephenson to describe the more mundane experience of reading the newspaper: "It is not just a joke to say, as many a housewife has, that her husband loses himself in his newspaper." Stephenson pointed out the nonself aspects of such an experience.

What indeed are we to mean by being self-involved? I find it necessary to distinguish two meanings for our purpose. To see one's photograph unexpectedly in the newspaper is definitely self-involving in the sense that it matters to us, as self, to our sense of pride, conceit, or the like. But when one is absorbed in doing something, like reading a newspaper intently, all sense of self is absent; afterwards you may say how much you enjoyed it, but at the time there was no self-reference, no pride, no vanity, no sense of oneself, no wish, no being-with-anything, no intrusion of the self upon the news. . . . It is more like being in a trance than being in touch with reality."[7]

The loss of self-feeling that occurs in absorption is not experienced directly. In fact, to try to become aware of it is to have self-feeling. It is only afterwards, when we compare the absorbed state with everyday existence, that we realize how unaware of ourselves we have been. This realization is most compelling as we make the transition back to everyday consciousness. When we set aside the novel or walk out of the movie theater, there occurs a re-emergence of self—a quality of experience we realize has not been there for some time.

Loss of self-feeling is a negative aspect of absorption, i.e., it is something subtracted from consciousness. There is also a positive side wherein something new is added. In getting absorbed, we do not just lose ourselves; we lose ourselves *in something*. Some object of fascination comes to the fore, usurping all attention from our sense of identity. Instead of being our everyday selves, we seem to merge and become *one-with* the thing in which we are absorbed.

The most common example of being one-with is identifying with the hero of the story. It is also the pleasing sensation of being carried along by music, and in sexual experience it is the feeling of being fused with the loved one. It is also the culmination of spiritual experience, as when the mystic feels "consumed" by the supernatural being. This feeling of being one-with is a condition of intense involvement that can occur only in the absorbed mood, when the self-barriers are down. It cannot occur in everyday consciousness, where there is a strong self-object dichotomy.

There is little doubt that being one-with constitutes a genuine phenomenon. It has been recognized by many scholars in different times. Referring to it as a "sense of union," William James reported many instances of it in *The Varieties of Religious Experience*.[8] Similarly, Walter Pahnke, in his study of spiritual experience induced by psychedelic drugs, identified one of the main effects of such an experience as the feeling of "unity" or "oneness."[9] Being one-with is comparable to what the Freudians refer to as the "oceanic feeling of oneness."[10] Donald Hebb took note of the "feeling of otherness" that can occur in conditions of sensory deprivation, i.e., when the person is immobilized and cut off from the environment.[11] Probably the best-known formulation of this absorbed effect comes from aesthetics theory and the notion of "empathy," especially as defined by Theodor Lipps. Empathy is the feeling of participating in the art object by an inner imitation of its form and movement. "The more I am absorbed in the contemplation of seen movement," wrote Lipps, "the more involuntary will be the imitation. . . . I feel myself performing this movement in the other's movement."[12] Modern research has supported Lipps' notion of "inner imitation." Muscle-tension studies show that spectators who are intently watching the graceful movements of athletes or dancers often kinesthetically "mimic in a minute way" their action patterns.[13]

However, missing in these concepts is the idea that being one-with is usually an enjoyable experience. In naturally occurring absorption (not hypnosis), the experience of being one-with represents the culmination of being attracted to some entertainment. Being one-with is pleasing; one feels enchanted, possessed. This was demonstrated in a study which asked subjects to describe their typical reactions to pleasurable situations. It was found that one of the stages in enjoying pleasure is a psychological "merging" with the pleasure source, being absorbed into it.

> This is apprehended as a strong pressure to merge with the pleasure source, to absorb it or be absorbed by it. Attention and interest are withdrawn from external reality, the "self" is entirely concentrated on and lost in the pleasure. Despite the fact that this is difficult to formulate introspectively and for communication, quite a few in this sample indicated their awareness of it by such phrases as "to absorb," "to become part of," "completely lost in it."[14]

In the duality that characterizes everyday existence, the self is primary while the object is secondary. But when we become absorbed in the object, this order is reversed. The object gets all of the attention and thus acquires the significance that the self previously had. As Tellegen and Atkinson wrote in discussing the self-dissociation that occurs in hypnosis: "Objects of absorbed attention acquire an importance and intimacy that are normally reserved for the self and may, therefore, acquire a temporary self-like quality."[15] In absorption, the object takes on all of those qualities that Gardner Murphy assigned to everyday self—"a center, an anchorage point . . . an ultimate real." On the other hand, everyday self becomes secondary. Thus, if during the absorbed state we are reminded of ourselves, it is often with a feeling of looking back or down on a distant, remembered self. All of this is implicit in Maslow's analysis of "egoless" states, which, he wrote,

> can be object-centered rather than ego-centered. This is to say, that the perceptual experience can be organized around the object as a centering point rather than being based upon the ego. . . . It is possible in the aesthetic experience or the love experience to become so absorbed and "poured into" the object that the self, in a very real sense, disappears.[16]

Being one-with constitutes a temporary alteration of identity, at least in terms of how identity is structured in attentional experience. It is a different way of being, structured by an external object rather than by an internal code. Thus, being one-with represents a reversal of our most basic human condition: the duality of self-object. The compulsion to be aware of self, as something separate from the environment and from other people, represents a landmark both in the development of the individual and in the evolution of the species. Developmental psychologists like Piaget have pointed out that a crucial stage in psychological growth is the emerging awareness of self as separate from the surrounding world.[17] It is also believed that the ability to make the self-object distinction was crucial in the development of the human race. In his book on lore, Edmonson speculated that animal became human and encultured by way of language. The first language distinction, made probably in paleolithic times, was the recognition that self is different from what is out there. Edmonson wrote: "What the 'Southern Apes' invented was ego. . . . We may therefore hazard the guess that the original expression of truly human awareness was the metaphor *I:you.*"[18]

All of this points up the fact that the identity reversal that occurs in the absorbed effect of being one-with, although it may seem brief and elusive, constitutes a fundamental kind of change. Perhaps this is why humans hunger for this experience, as Aldous Huxley pointed out.

> Introspection, observation and the records of human behavior in the past and at the present time, make it very clear that an urge to self-transcendence is almost as widespread and, at times, quite as powerful as the urge to self-assertion. Men desire to intensify their consciousness of being what they have come to regard as "themselves," but they also desire — and desire, very often, with irresistible violence — the consciousness of being someone else. In a word, they long to get out of themselves, to pass beyond the limits of that tiny island universe, within which every individual finds himself confined.[19]

Spellbound in a New Reality

> I first read "Treasure Island" when it was new and I was fourteen. I read it again — certainly for the fourth time — this last week. And I am nearly sixty now. But the old spell held. The door knocker could rattle and the telephone could jingle — and be hanged to them both. I was away. I had weighed anchor. — *James O'Donnell Bennett*

Absorption also makes us "forget everything"; it makes us feel "detached from the everyday things," and so we seem to be "taken out of ordinary consciousness." Maslow obtained reports of such changes in his study of special enjoyments, and he concluded that in these states "there is a very characteristic disorientation in time and space. It would be accurate to say that in these moments a person is outside of time and space subjectively."[20] In absorption, therefore, we also lose sense of everyday reality, as well as sense of self.

Just as self is a relative and changeable perception, much the same is true of reality. Although physical reality stands absolute, our experience of this reality, our sense about what is real, is relative and changeable. With the radical reallocation of attention that occurs in the absorbed state, it is possible in a genuine psychological sense to break out of everyday reality.

As noted earlier, reality is not directly perceived, but filtered and reconstructed by internal codes. In his book *The Construction of Reality in the Child,* Piaget showed that sense of reality is not given but it built up slowly by internalizing the rules of how the environment works.[21] This kind of learning eventually results in a master code system that keeps the organism interacting with the environment in an organized way. Ronald Shor, a psychologist who made extensive contributions to hypnosis research, used the term "generalized reality-orientation" to refer to this master code system. "The usual state of consciousness," wrote Shor, "is characterized by the mobilization of a structured frame of reference in the background of attention which supports, interprets, and gives meaning to all experiences."[22]

What modern research has shown is that our reality orientation is not fixed but rather is a variable function. Ornstein described it as a "personal construction," and he reviewed the literature showing that it can be easily disrupted.[23] Hilgard pointed out that the reality orientation has to be maintained by constant monitoring of the environment, and that if this is stopped, as in hypnosis, then the result is unrealistic experience.

> The amount of reality testing that goes on in ordinary life is overlooked because it is so familiar, but once it is called to attention it is easy to notice how frequently people check their orientation by squirming, scratching, looking around, noting the time, adjusting clothing. The "stimulus-hunger" that Piaget and others have noted is in part this need for a contact that maintains the location and boundaries of the body in its relation to the environment of things and other people. This reality testing is reduced in the hypnotized person, partly as a result of the manipulations by the hypnotist. . . . Reduction of reality testing leads to the acceptance of reality distortions.[24]

The purpose of hypnotic induction procedures is to nullify the normal reality orientation, making possible an altered state of consciousness. Ronald Shor wrote that "any state in which the generalized reality-orientation has faded to relatively nonfunctional unawareness may be termed a trance state."[25] In hypnosis, as in all absorbed states, the reality orientation fades away as the person withdraws his attention from his environment, stops thinking evaluatively, and surrenders control of attention to some external agent. Inability to do these things keeps the reality orientation functional and so prevents hypnosis or absorption. "It is significant," wrote Robert White, "that one of the commonest complaints of unsusceptible [hypnotic] subjects is that they could not forget the situation as a whole, could not stop thinking. . . . Such comments . . . imply that the frame of reference has refused to contract, that in spite of external circumstances there remains an internal alertness to 'other considerations' which is the opposite of drowsiness and the enemy of successful hypnosis."[26]

Interestingly, even though the generalized reality orientation is suspended and we feel detached from the everyday world, it is possible to develop a new psychological reality based on what is at the center of absorbed attention.

The reality code is a mechanism for allocating attention to multiple points. When it is suspended, attention is consolidated to a single point. Whatever image is at the center of this unitary state is likely to be experienced in a vivid way, seeming very real. One reason for this convincing experience is that there is nothing to contradict or compete with the trance image. "Any object which remains uncontradicted," wrote William James, "is ipso facto believed and posited as absolute reality."[27]

Another reason the trance image is likely to be experienced as very real is the intensity of attention. There is an inverse relationship between the number of attentional targets and intensity of attention. It is generally believed that "the greater the number of objects to which our consciousness is simultaneously extended, the smaller is the intensity with which it is able to consider each."[28] The opposite of this principle would apply here: With only one object in consciousness there would be a much more intense allocation of attention — and, thus, a more vivid perception. This was demonstrated empirically when Spanos and McPeake found that the more absorbed and involved their hypnotic subjects were, the more likely they were to rate their hypnotic experiences as credible and involuntary.[29] For example, inability to bend the arm resulting from hypnotic suggestion was perceived as a "real" occurrence — i.e., something that happened on its own — only by those subjects who were intensely absorbed.

Most of the points we have been discussing here are embodied in Maslow's concept of "total attention." It is important to note that total attention does not mean attending to the total environment, but rather that all of attention has been allocated to one point. Contrasting it with everyday ("rubricizing") attention, Maslow pointed out that

> the percept is exclusively and fully attended to.... What I am trying to describe here is very much akin to fascination or complete absorption. In such attention the figure becomes *all* figure and the ground, in effect, disappears, or at least is not importantly perceived. It is as if the figure was isolated for the time being from all else, as if the world were forgotten....[30]

"Realness," then, or the experience of reality, can be produced by an intense, single-minded attentional state. And, paradoxically, this experience can occur only after we have stopped processing everyday reality. In this manner do we exchange one reality for another, a switch that ideally should occur in all play. When it does, there is often a feeling of being in another world. This switch represents another enjoyable reversal, much like the one discussed earlier, where being one-with replaced everyday self. Here, a new realness replaces everyday reality.

This reversal explains why unrealistic artifacts such as stories and art can become very convincing when we get absorbed in them; in the end, they often seem more real than the world about us. Classical music can evoke inner un-named realities in people who cultivate this diversion. The absorption produced by psychedelic drugs can make objects more luminous and significant than we find them in everyday life. During the time that we are involved in a movie, the shadows on the silver screen can convey realities that seem more important than the one we left outside the theater.

On just a logical basis, art and entertainment should be weak and unrealistic experiences. After all, we have to turn away from the physical world to engage in them. Also, the things that entertain us are mere figments of the imagination. They are not inherently a part of everyday life, which presumably makes things real and important. Therefore, art and entertainment should seem less real, less significant.

But of course, just the opposite is the case. Art and entertainment do not always engage us, but when they do, they come alive and create their own worlds. This is because the experience of realness is not dependent on the presence or absence of concrete objects, but rather on the intensity of our attention.

The sense of realness that develops in the absorbed spell, therefore, has nothing to do with how realistic the entertainment is or the extent to which it mimics the real world. Nor does it have anything to do with fantasizing or using imagination, in the usual meaning of these terms. Imagination, i.e., merely picturing something in our thoughts, could never explain the power and conviction that can characterize absorbed experience. Besides, in watching a movie (for example), there is no time to use imagination or fantasy; all that we can do is attend and experience. Neither do we make a conscious attempt to "make-believe." The sense of a new reality is not the result of some mental activity, but just the opposite; it is due to mental relaxation and total attention.

It should be emphasized that exchanging one reality for another is ideally the goal of all recreation. However, instead of being accomplished psychologically as is done in absorption, the exchange is often brought about in a physical way by utilizing different activities and locations. Physical reality can be altered by changing space and time; social reality, by altering rules and roles. Most of the amusements and sports that make up conventional recreation attempt to manipulate these factors to create a physical or social reality different from the everyday kind. For example, sports often take place in unique settings (e.g., ball diamond, tennis court), and the activity is speeded up to intensify experiencing. If not confined to a playing area, sports can stimulate a sense of new reality by being distanced in some environment such as in the woods or mountains (hunting, mountain climbing), or in the air (parachuting, hang-gliding), or on ice or snow (skiing, ice-skating). Water seems to be the favorite environment for outdoor sports, offering swimming, diving, surfing, scuba diving, skin diving, fishing, water polo, water-skiing, canoeing, sailing and motor-boating.

Although its activities are highly circumscribed by rules, sports sometimes permit behavior that is discouraged in everyday life. Some sports permit individuals to violate normal safety precautions and to take personal risks that would not be tolerated in the workplace. In some sports it is permissible to kill animals or be violent with other human beings. Sometimes it is acceptable to view another individual as an opponent who is to be defeated, humiliated, and in some cases physically attacked. While all of this danger and conflict is controlled by rules, still sports allow us to go beyond the limits generally accepted in normal living. In this way they offer the participant a different reality.

Exchanging physical or social reality is also what we do when we eat out, or vacation in faraway places. These too are diversions, stepping "sideward into another reality" by changing the physical or social stimuli. Today, these kinds of diversion are very much in evidence when we look at where adults play. As a result of modern affluence and technology there has been a phenomenal movement of recreation away from the home, a tendency to separate it from everyday reality. Surveys now show that after television, the most popular leisure activity is "getting out."[31] Recently there has been increased utilization of discrete recreational environments such as the night club, beer garden, bowling alley, beaches, mountain resorts, campgrounds, historical sites, ocean cruises, touring programs and a variety of amusement, state and national parks. Likewise, the statistics on tourism show there has been a great upsurge in both foreign and domestic recreational travel. Since mid-century, international tourism has become "the number one item of international trade," and in this country tourism ranks as one of the top three leading industries in forty-six of the fifty states.[32] There is no doubt that the need for diversion is what stimulates all this travel. As one marketing research analyst asserted:

> The greatest reason for [recreational] travel can be summed up in one word, "Escape." Escape from the dull, daily routine. Escape from the familiar, the commonplace, the ordinary. Escape from the job, the boss, the customers, the commuting, the house, the lawn, the leaky faucets.[33]

In general, then, it seems that all recreations attempt to divert us, to replace everyday reality with one that is more exciting. Absorbing entertainments attempt to accomplish this by changing the psychological determinants of reality, which are attentional in nature. Other recreations, such as sports and social get-togethers, attempt to accomplish this by changing the physical determinants of reality, which consist of space, time, rules, and roles. Although it would seem that changing the physical determinants should result in a more complete diversion, the final test is always our experience. Being in a different setting does not always make us feel different; in fact, our troubles often follow us wherever we go. The diversion effect may be more reliably brought about by changing the psychological determinants; there, experience is fashioned, and so can be more directly acted upon.

High-Quality Experience: Relaxed Arousal

Although we often use the terms synonymously, *self* and *experience* represent different domains in human existence. Self is found in the codes and habits associated with identity, role, social interaction, reality testing and evaluative thinking—all of which make up the business of living. Experience, on the other hand, is what makes us feel alive. Experience occurs when there is arousal and emotional activation of the organism. Experience is not just sensation or consciousness but a feeling of being animated by something significant.

Self is embedded in our thoughts, inner speech and the "reflected appraisals" from others. Physiologically, self is mediated by the forebrain and the left hemisphere, especially the speech center. Experience, on the other hand, is mediated by the deeper centers in the brain, and in some ways the right hemisphere. Experience can vary in terms of intensity and quality. Intensity is reflected in the overall arousal level of the organism; it can be measured in the vital signs such as brain waves (EEG), heart rate, and breathing, which speed up when the organism is aroused.

While intensity of arousal has been widely investigated, psychologists have not taken much note of the quality of arousal. Quality is determined by the extent to which experience is enlivening and vitalizing. Low quality experience is found in those emotions that are stimulated by threat to self, e.g. anxiety, fear, hate, shame. Such arousal is unpleasant and experienced with a feeling of being threatened or trapped. Low quality experience is also found when the intensity of arousal remains low for long periods of time, as in monotonous conditions. Prolonged repetition dulls experience and makes the organism listless, apathetic, and depressed.

The two factors of self and experience are out of balance by the time adulthood is reached. Once the organism is socialized, self is the dominant factor and experience is secondary. In the process of becoming civilized we learn to overrule the private flow of experience and let ourselves be governed by verbalization, reason, social pressures, and the general demands of reality—all aspects of self. The fact that delay of gratification and tolerance for frustration are so necessary for successful living shows that experience generally takes a backseat to self. Many psychologists have pointed out that self actually has an inhibiting effect on experience. What are usually referred to as "ego defense mechanisms" are really self-referent habits designed to suppress, distort, or otherwise neutralize emotional experience. Typically, mental health workers have denounced the suppression of experience that goes on in everyday life, but perhaps suppression is necessary if we want to conduct the business of living in an efficient manner. Over-attending to experience would distract us from coping, adjusting, meeting standards, and being productive. After all, what is needed in the business of living is evaluative processing, a strong sense of self, and realistic activity — not a flowering of experience.

Because of the dominant and suppressive effects of self, everyday life generally yields low-quality experience. Much of the arousal experienced stems from self-related problems and so tends toward unpleasant emotions such as tension, annoyance, and boredom. When positive arousal does occur, it is often experienced in a distracted way. Many scholars have noted that the practical nature of everyday life is inimical to rich experiencing. Freud wrote that "the meagre satisfaction that [man] can extract from reality leaves him starving." Philosopher Irwin Edman wrote that "ordinary experience, that of a practical or instinctive compulsion, is at once restless and dead."[34] America's foremost philosopher, John Dewey, pointed out that day-to-day life is "humdrum" and "slack," and that the experiencing of it tends to be continually disrupted and distracted. This "leaves many a person, especially in this hurried and impatient human environment in which we live, with experience of an almost incredible paucity, all on the surface. . . . What is called experience," he wrote, "becomes so dispersed and miscellaneous as hardly to deserve the name."[35]

The only way experience can flourish to its full enlivening potential is to make it dominant over self. Only by negating the self factor can we remove the suppressive and distracting influences that impair experiencing. This, of course, is brought about in our absorbing entertainments. We temporarily reverse the normal imbalance of self over experience, setting up conditions to suspend the former and enhance the latter. The result is high-quality experience — enlivening, flowing, harmonious and enjoyable.

This condition — when self is down and experience is up — can be described as "relaxed arousal." This sounds contradictory because arousal seems the opposite of relaxation. But in this case, the term refers to aroused experience that occurs when the mind is relaxed, or more specifically, when the self and evaluative functions are suspended. Relaxed experiencing, therefore is a combination of things that do not normally go together — mental relaxation combined with intense experiencing. When arousal is high in everyday life, both mind and body are activated, and evaluative thinking increases as do the physical functions. But apparently it is possible to activate the one and not the other. In the safe and nonself condition of absorption, there is no need for evaluative thinking; thus only the body is aroused with emotional experience. One theorist defined play as "arousal seeking,"[36] but more to the point, it is the seeking of relaxed arousal. In itself, much arousal would be anti-recreational.

Again and again throughout this book we will come upon certain experiences that just do not fit the traditional model of emotional arousal. They contain contradictory qualities and can be explained only by some such concept as relaxed arousal. This is seen, for example, in the mellow intensity of getting high on alcohol or recreational drugs, or in aesthetic experience which is somehow sensuous and abstract at the same time. Another contradiction that is hard to understand in terms of the usual ideas of emotion, but is easily resolved with the concept of relaxed arousal, is the phenomenon of enjoying negative emotions, which we routinely do in the course of story entertainment.

In everyday life there are many situations that are disagreeable and so we avoid them — uncertainty, loss of control, being fooled or misled, violence, humiliation. Much the same is true of distressing emotions such as anxiety, anger, or shame; in everyday life they are irritating and even painful, primarily because they involve threat to self and are meant to prod the organism into some corrective action. But when these emotions are aroused by a story — when self has been suspended and so cannot be threatened — then we can magically tolerate, even enjoy, these aversive stimuli. The fact that we can actually enjoy such distressing emotions is proof positive that the self is not there during the story, and as a result the arousal is "relaxed," i.e., without ego-involving implications. The emotions may disturb, but instead of threatening us, they are exciting and so serve to lock us ever more tightly into the story spell.

One of the chief reasons people return to stories is to have their experience expanded in this way, to feel what they cannot feel in everyday life. In the relaxed condition of the story, it is possible to fully experience the dark side of life — fear, hate, revenge, irrationality, death. When such experiences are upon us in "real" life we are in no mood to savor them. Yet this negative side of life is of great interest to people simply because it is an inherent part of human existence, and stories give us full access to it because self has been suspended. As DeVoto noted, "Fiction is our license to meet disaster on more favorable terms than reality permits."[37]

The purpose of art and entertainment is to develop experience fully. "It is one of the chief functions of the artist," wrote Irwin Edman, "to render experience arresting by rendering it alive."[38] This is not so much a matter of intensity of arousal, but of breadth, depth, and quality of experience. The absence of self-involvement in absorbing entertainments permits experience to be a thing unto itself. It does not develop out of some emergency, nor is it a processing emotion aimed at resolving some frustration. The relaxed arousal found in absorbed experience is not instigated by inner speech, but by inner imitation, which allows us to resonate fully with the object of fascination. The experience develops in a relaxed and suggestible condition that is most conducive to expansion of consciousness, enriched with intuitive and unconscious associations usually inaccessible to us. In the absorbed state, it is possible to have a flow of feelings, unchecked by distractions or evaluative thinking. Thus, there is a run-through of natural, cathartic cycles of feeling and association. There is a build-up and release, a flow and follow-through. John Dewey described such discrete and time-limited responses as having "*an* experience," which is usually made possible by art and entertainment.

> We have *an* experience when the material experienced runs its course to fulfillment.
> In such experiences, every successive part flows freely, without seam and without unfilled blanks, into what ensues.... A river, as distinct from a pond, flows. But its flow gives a definiteness and interest to its successive portions greater than exist in the homogenous portions of a pond. In an experience, flow is from something to something. As one part leads into another and as one part carries on what went before, each gains distinctness in itself....
> Because of continuous merging, there are no holes, mechanical junctions, and dead centers when we have *an* experience. There are pauses, places of rest, but they punctuate and define the quality of movement. They sum up what has been undergone and prevent its dissipation and idle evaporation.... In a work of art, different acts, episodes, occurrences melt and fuse into unity, and yet do not disappear and lose their own character.
> In a distinctly esthetic experience, characteristics that are subdued in other experiences are dominant; those that are subordinate are controlling.[39]

William James made similar observations about experiences that occur outside the everyday life. He, however, was concerned more with the depth of experience than with its unified nature. Absorbed experience is likely to seem more meaningful because it tends to involve early impressions and unconscious associations. James referred to such effects as a "deepened sense of significance," which, he recognized, "sweeps over" us in the enjoyment of scenic beauty, art, music, literature, and even alcohol. He also pointed out that when such experience occurs it tends to take us out of the routine; thus, he described it as a rudimentary kind of mystical state, a first step toward altered consciousness.

> The simplest rudiment of mystical experience would seem to be that deepened sense of the significance [of something] ... which occasionally sweeps over one.... Effects of light on land and sea, odors and musical sounds, all bring it when the mind is tuned aright. Most of us can remember the strangely moving power of passages in certain poems read when we were young, irrational doorways as they were through which the mystery of fact, the wildness and the pang of life, stole into our hearts and thrilled them. The words have now perhaps become mere polished surfaces for us; but lyric poetry and music are alive and significant only in proportion as they fetch these vague vistas of a life continuous with our own, beckoning and inviting, yet ever eluding our pursuit. We are alive or dead to the eternal inner message of the arts according as we have kept or lost this mystical susceptibility.[40]

The business of living requires that we be informed, in control, rational and realistic. But in the reversals of art and entertainment, experience is dominated by opposite qualities which are thoroughly enjoyable — "strangely moving power," a sense of "eternal inner message."

Though normally we avoid ambiguity, contradiction, and the unknown, art and entertainment often use these very elements to capture attention. In everyday life when we do not know, we think and try to figure things out; in absorption, we simply attend more closely. In absorption, the elements of contradiction and mystery invalidate our normal codes and make them obsolete, allowing us to slip into an intuitive, receptive mode. These elements heighten the sense of awe and puzzlement that is so important to absorption. Although there is not much verbal enlightenment, there is intuitive illumination. Absorbed experience often has the strange combination of knowing and not-knowing, the feeling of being puzzled by a mystery and yet having some kind of knowledge about it.

In her analysis of intuitive feelings, Frances Clark pointed out that this kind of experience occurs best when self is submerged in the object.[41] Intuitive experience results from identifying with things, not from intellectualizing about them; from total attention, not rubricized perception; from inner imitation, not inner speech. One could speculate that the suspension of the master codes probably opens up neurological tracts that are unavailable to reason and reality. This process would stir up dimly remembered events, shadowy images, moods, intimations — a whole complex of associations irrelevant to everyday processing, but one that enhances aliveness and the historical continuity of the organism. Although these intuitive associations are experienced as a vague sensing of things, they are nevertheless felt with force and conviction, serving to enrich every kind of absorbed experience. It is for this reason that absorbed experience is often described as "deep" or "inner" or "spiritual" or as having special significance.

Absorbed experience is also often described as "sweet," apparently because it is at once relaxing and enlivening. It is not surprising, therefore, that the individuals and objects that absorb us usually inspire feelings of fondness and almost romantic attachment. In this regard, a curious observation was made in a recent psychological study.[42] This was a meditation study, and for several weeks the subjects spent half an hour each day absorbed in a blue vase. After the study was over, the subjects reported they had come to have a fondness for the vase. After staring at a vase day after day, one would think, the subjects should have been bored to death with it. Instead, some said they felt an emotional attachment to it and would miss it.

The unusual reaction of these subjects may have relevance for how we all feel about the people and things that absorb us. We come to love them. Most people have sentimental feelings for certain actors, or they have favorite television programs whose characters seem near and dear, or they become attached to a certain kind of music which they play at every opportunity. "It says something about the nature of movies," wrote Pauline Kael, "that people don't say they like them, they say they love them."[43]

It has always been inexplicable to social critics why the public seems to over-value entertainers or star athletes. Not only are they paid salaries that seem disproportionate to their contribution to society, but they are adulated. They have fan clubs, get special attention from the media and retain their aura of glamour even when their personal lives are flawed. We have a cool and distant respect for political leaders, inventors or great doctors, but a warm affection for the likes of a Humphrey Bogart or a Katharine Hepburn. A special few such as Rudolph Valentino or Elvis Presley have become demi-gods in the public mind.

All of this is not as irrational as it seems. Entertainers are makers of absorption; they have some fascination value that absorbs the rest of us. Absorbed experience is inherently enjoyable, and we love the people and objects that make the experience possible. Therefore, the fame and fortune accorded to performers is not excessive; it simply reflects the value that people put on absorbed experience. We have never really appreciated how valuable and important these experiences are. They are, after all, the sources of adult play. Entertainers do contribute — not to the workaday world, but to the domain of play, which, as we have seen, is of increasing importance in modern existence.

The status accorded to these producers of absorption constitutes something without parallel in everyday life. For example, nothing is more important than food and money; they gratify our most basic needs, yet we do not regard these objects with any special fondness. Normally, people do not get sentimental about food, nor do we glamorize cooks, chefs, or waitresses. Behaviorists refer to money as a "generalized reinforcer," and it is indeed a powerful reward. Money is the key to survival and comfort. However, except for the occasional miser, nobody gets sentimental about money. We all try to get as much of it as we can, but far from being endearing it is seen as a necessary evil. How different from our feelings for the makers of absorbed experience!

It must be admitted that everyday life has its enjoyable moments, but these tend to be of an extrinsic nature — achievement, material gain, and various kinds of ego-gratifications. These undoubtedly nourish us; in fact, they are psychological staples — the meat and potatoes of life. Absorbed experiences are of a different order; they usually come afterwards, like the dessert. They nourish by delighting us. They are "sweets" for the psyche.

Chapter 4

Story Enjoyment

Would'st thou divert thyself from Melancholy?
Would'st thou be pleasant, yet be far from folly?
. . . .
Would'st thou be in a Dream, and yet not sleep?
Or would'st thou in a moment laugh and weep?
Wouldest thou lose thyself, and catch no harm,
And find thyself again without a charm?
. . . .
O then come hither,
And lay my Book, thy Head, and Heart together.
—*John Bunyan*

If there is such a thing as a universal recreation, it must be story entertainment. No other diversion is so well loved. To speak of people enjoying stories has an old-fashioned ring to it, as though this might have been a popular diversion sometime in the past. Actually, however, there is more story entertainment going on today than at any other time in history. Stories are a staple of our daily entertainment fare, and they come in all shapes and sizes to suit every kind of taste. The universal popularity of stories is disguised by the fact that we have so many different words for them. For example, when we talk about the movies or the theater, we are really talking about stories. Television, too, is a story medium. Broadway, Hollywood, and book publishing are all founded on the story.

The essence of diversion is found not in games or sports but in story entertainment. This is the ideal of play — absorption, pure and simple. The story is undoubtedly the greatest invention for diverting attention from the business of living so that cares are forgotten, a new reality materializes, and the person comes alive with harmonious experience and new identities. For most people there is no better way to break out of everyday life than to get inside a story.

Long before there were tranquilizers and talk-therapies, the great tradition of story entertainment brought mental relaxation and glowing experience to troubled lives. It is especially when life numbs us with boredom or sleeplessness or distresses us with pain that we turn to stories. It is said that in France during World War I, soldiers returning from the trenches "would, however weary, seize on any kind of book or periodical" for diversion.[1] In World War II, soldiers in the South Pacific would sit in the rain to watch movies. During times of economic and social distress people flock to the movies, as they did during the great Depression, and as they do today in India.[2] Stories are an attentional antidote for the sick and disabled. The modern patient has books and television; in ancient times there was storytelling. In his text on ancient medicine, Guido Majno stated that the earliest record of medical care came from Homeric Greece. When a wounded soldier was carried off the battlefield, "the first attentions that he received in the [barracks] were a seat, lots of storytelling, and a cup of Pramnian wine."[3] The son of Alexandre Dumas was told by a French surgeon: "All our hospital patients recover or die with one of your father's books under their pillow. When we wish to make them forget the terror of an approaching operation, the tediousness of convalescence, or the dread of death, we prescribe one of your father's novels, and they are able to forget."[4]

The Story Spell vs. the Illusion of Reality

> We do not go to literature merely to find the forcefully iterated
> confirmation of our own petty and limited selfhood, but to know, in some
> sense, the whole range, the gamut of human feeling. —*John Stevens*

Although story entertainment is an effective and universal diversion, one would never know it from the stereotype that most people have about stories. Implicitly in the popular mind, and explicitly in much that is written about narrative literature, there exists a conception of stories so narrow and misleading that one wonders why anyone would want to bother about them.

This stereotype asserts that a story is not an object in its own right but merely a representation of something else. According to many critics, stories are supposed to create an illusion of reality. They are judged, not by their consequences, but by their antecedents—not by how they enhance our experience, but by how well they copy reality. It follows that when reading or watching stories we should attend to them much as we do any other object or event in reality—i.e., process them intellectually. But since the story is only an imitation, our experience of it will be weak. Words typically used to describe story experience denote its secondhand status: "vicarious," "fantasy," "imaginative," "make-believe," and "as if." The inescapable conclusion is that story experience is only a watered-down version of real life. For stories to be judged worthwhile, critics demand that they have special linkages to reality. Thus, stories can be redeemed by having artistic merit, social significance, or a message or by being thought-provoking.

This is actually a primitive conception of stories, derived largely from the perspective of working life. It is a conception suited to tribal cultures where stories were indeed used for workaday purposes, i.e., to teach lessons, convey moral precepts, or pass on the group's history. One might expect a similar view in totalitarian societies where story entertainment is often used to advance ideology. But in most of today's societies, stories have been free to develop solely for entertainment. There are other institutions and methods to take care of education, religion, history, and politics. Therefore, we need a rationale that looks at stories not as tools, but as play objects. A very different view emerges when stories are conceptualized in terms of play.

A story does not have to represent reality or contribute to our reality adjustment. In fact, it is a story only to the extent that it diverts us from reality. The story is a device for diverting attention and inducing contrasting experience. It derives its power and credibility, not by mimicking reality, but by mustering total attention. In other words, it must create an absorbed *story spell* in the reader or observer. A story is not entertainment if it is processed with everyday attention; it comes to life only in the state of total involvement. While it is true that the content of a story is based on reality, it is far from being a copy of that reality. The story is constructed along lines that maximize experiencing. It must follow certain rules, but the rules of experience, not of reality. This is why stories can be very unrealistic yet credible to our experience, as is the case with fairy tales, science fiction, or ghost stories. As one scholar noted in discussing the unrealistic aspects of Shakespeare's plays, "The strange coincidences, remarkable discoveries, and wonderful reunions are unimportant compared with the emotions of relief and awe that they inspire."[5] In the domain of play, reality is only the means to the end of harmonious experiencing. While the story content is loosely derived from reality, the experience is of a different order. It occurs in the absorbed state and is characterized by all those reversals discussed in the previous chapter.

Story effects are not illusions. An illusion is a deception or a misperception. To say that the story gives an illusion of reality implies that the imitation is so good that the person believes he is perceiving the real thing, as though he has been deceived into believing something is real. But the realness that develops in a story is not based on trickery. Nobody is actually deceived when involved in a story; there is no misperception as such. The effect of the story is not based on beliefs about reality but on experience and attention. Tyrone Guthrie made some of these points in a discussion on the role of the stage director. He said the director's job is not to create a representational illusion of reality, but rather to

> interest the members of an audience so intensely that they are rapt, taken "out" of themselves. You may say that if they are taken "out" of themselves, then they must be taken "into" something else, and, logically, that "something else" is the imaginary world of the play. Agreed. But is this absorption the

same thing as illusion? I do not believe so. You can be absorbed listening to music, quite without illusion; you can be absorbed by a great painting without supposing that what it depicts is real; you can be absorbed by a novel without the illusion that you are yourself David Copperfield or Huck Finn.[6]

Absorbed attention is almost synonymous with story entertainment. In his book *The Dynamics of Literary Response,* Norman Holland reported on a survey that he took among college students and faculty, and the results are pertinent here.

> I have asked a number of subjects to describe their feelings when they are engrossed in an "entertainment," a detective story, a murder mystery, science fiction, television, or a simple old-fashioned fun movie. They speak of "escapism, a feeling of joyful unreality, lack of any worry" or "involvement— at its best a motion with the work." "I am gathered up, carried along, and unaware of being a reader, viewer, etc." "I lose track of time." "I am attentive and absorbed, unaware of surroundings except those in the book or show; for example, when I am watching good T.V., I don't see the knobs or floor or anything else."
> . . . This reaction to entertainments is not confined to naive subjects. A group of university professors of English report as their reaction: "Total anesthesia," "Absorption," "A sort of drugged or fascinated absorption in the events as they unfold." "The continuum goes from totally absorbed (cinema) to fairly distanced, self-conscious hunting for something (non-fiction). Fiction can go either way (rarely a blend though)." "Varies but usually I'm completely absorbed—even by crude stuff."[7]

The degree of attentional involvement described in this survey is comparable to the effect of hypnosis. As was discussed in an earlier chapter, modern researchers use story involvement as a paradigm for hypnosis. Josephine Hilgard's book on the connection between hypnosis and absorption contained a chapter on reading involvement. Her research showed that not all reading involvement is related to hypnotizability. Reading didactic or scientific material is not. Rather, hypnosis is approached in the kind of reading "in which the very 'being' of the person is swept emotionally into the experience described by the author." After having the experience of hypnosis and knowing what it felt like, here is how two of Hilgard's subjects commented on its similarity to story reading.

> "Hypnosis was like reading a book. . . . It's stronger in a way than reading. When I get really involved in reading, I'm not aware of what is going on around me. I concentrate on the people in the book or the movie and react the way they react. The intense concentration is the same in a book or a movie or in imagination as it is in hypnosis. Reading a book can hypnotize you."

"If it's a new author, I read two or three pages slowly, then I pick up speed (if the author's good) and am not aware of turning pages or of things around me. When I'm reading Faulkner, everything fades except what he's saying — I start living with a book — I'm more identified with Faulkner in the emotion and expression and totalness. I come out to meet him. It's as though nothing else is important. The room has faded — you separate from everything else. It's just the book."[8]

If story enjoyment is hypnotic experience, then story writing is hypnotic induction. This is the thesis of an interesting little book entitled *Hypno-Fiction* by A.L. Schafer, who argues that the technique of writing fiction is primarily a matter of hypnotizing the reader. Words are not used to develop thoughts; recall that thinking is antithetical to absorbed attention. "If you want to make your reader 'think,'" wrote Schafer, "turn instead to essays." The writer of fiction should use words to capture attention, "hallucinate the senses," and arouse feelings; "make them feel, see, hear, taste, and smell." In other words, stimulate experience. This is accomplished by means of vivid, picture-making language, and words that arouse conditioned reactions. Most writers would probably agree with these recommendations, which are certainly consistent with the often-quoted dictum of novelist Joseph Conrad: "My task which I am trying to achieve is, by the power of the written word, to make you hear, to make you feel — it is, before all, to make you *see*."[9] From all that we have said about story experience, it seems that Schafer has hit on an insightful connection in comparing fiction writing to hypnotic induction.

A hypnotist communicates his suggestions to his subject in specific, vivid, sense-stimulating words and symbols, with an authoritative voice allowing no contradiction and concentrating the attention of the subject without distraction. In the same way, the writer of Hypno-Fiction, writing with an authoritative style, uses specific, vivid, and sense-stimulating words, concentrates his reader's attention upon the characters, scenes, and story.[10]

Literary scholars have long recognized the importance of hypnotic susceptibility in story involvement. They did not call it that, or course, but such a function is implied in the notion of "the willing suspension of disbelief." This principle admonishes the person to clear his mind of all preconceptions so that he can get involved in the story and enjoy it to the fullest. As Holland pointed out, people automatically make such an adjustment when they get set to enjoy a story: "Somehow, even before the curtain rises, even before our eyes have run over the screen credits or the first line of a poem or story . . . we adopt some odd mental stance or 'set' in which we are willing to accept all kinds of unrealities and improbabilities."[11] Suspension of disbelief is really the suspension of evaluative thinking and master code processing; it is comparable to the suspension of the generalized reality orientation which, as noted earlier, is a precondition for being hypnotized. The suspension of disbelief makes us suggestible, and it encourages total attention and the development of the absorbed spell.

At the beginning of a story, it is likely that evaluative processing is suspended only partially. We retain some of our personal standards, which determine whether we like the story or not. If it passes this initial test, the story takes increasing control of attention, and processing is correspondingly weakened. The more absorbed we get, the more suggestible we become. In this altered state, we might accept things that would be rejected in our everyday frame of mind. As DeVoto pointed out, this is a boon for story writers.

> If a novelist has a good enough story — if the events are absorbing enough, vivid or powerful or arresting, for the maintenance of his illusion — he need have little else and especially he need have little technical skill beyond that of narrative. If the story is good enough, the reader will show a tolerance for inner illogicalities, contradictions, and disparities, and even for emptiness, that contradicts everything the theorist of technique asserts.[12]

Part of what makes it easy to suspend disbelief is knowing that the story is not true; we are absolved of all responsibility to treat it as a reality object and so have license to suspend the master codes. This condition, of course, follows from what we have said about mental relaxation in general: The organism can relax only in a safe situation where there is an assurance that no demands will be put on the processing system. "It is precisely our knowledge that we are dealing with a fiction," wrote Holland, "that enables us to experience it fully."[13]

However, truth or fiction is only part of the issue here; the larger question is whether the story is business to us. If it is not, and most fiction is not, then it is easy to suspend the master codes and get fully absorbed. But we can also become absorbed in true stories as long as they are not business to us; this would include many nonfiction categories such as history, biography, adventure stories, and of course the daily newspaper. On the other hand, even fiction can be business to us, making absorption difficult. For example, if the story was about somebody who had a disease that we were concerned about getting, then anxiety and threat would be aroused, making it difficult to suspend processing and self-referent thinking.

Is it possible to think evaluatively and still get involved in a story? Probably not. Nevertheless, some literary scholars advocate such a half-and-half approach, which ideally should give us the best of both worlds — an intense story experience together with a critical evaluation of it. This approach is usually recommended as the best way to appreciate literary masterpieces. Scholars of literature disdain absorption because they rightly recognize that it is a mindless state, which they feel is acceptable for light entertainment but unworthy for appreciating the complexities of a masterpiece. Thus, Bacon and

Breen, oft-quoted authorities on literature, recommend being "half in life and half out of it" when reading. According to them it is possible and desirable to combine evaluative thoughts with experiencing, "to entertain thoughts in close company with feelings or emotions."[14]

This approach may sound good on paper, but it does not make much psychological sense. Thoughts *about* a story would contradict its realness, and one could never feel totally involved. As noted earlier, absorption is the antithesis of evaluative processing; any attempt to mix these opposite orientations is doomed to failure. The half-and-half approach is like officiating at a game and playing in it too. This cannot be done in sports and neither is it feasible in story entertainment.

If one wants to maximize experiencing, then the thinking should be done before or after reading the story. This would be true even in the case of great novels and plays which are, first and foremost, great stories and should be enjoyed as such. "No amount of technical analysis, no self-conscious devotion to style, can ever obscure the primary fact that the purpose of fiction is to tell a story."[15] And that story will come alive only in the rarefied atmosphere of the absorbed state. The other elements that are found in narrative art — symbols, ideas, personal and universal meanings — can best enrich our experience through prior study. If the individual is well cultivated in literary art, he does not have to engage in a lot of intellectual analysis when enjoying the narrative masterpiece: "Just as the fisherman, in playing his steelhead, makes physical adjustments which are not preceded or accompanied by trains of discursive thought, so the perceptive reader of a book can follow the development of a literary situation without rationalizing all the formal and material tensions."[16]

It is odd that literary scholars think it desirable to be psychologically half in and half out of the story, because otherwise every attempt is made to keep the story separate from reality. Scholars have long insisted that the story space is a special domain that must not be violated by intrusions from everyday life. In an earlier era, critics abhorred the practice of authors who in the middle of a novel would address comments to the "gentle reader," or interrupt the story with lengthy essays about social ills. A good example of the separation of story and reality is the separation that is strictly maintained in the theater between stage and audience. Holland discussed a case of a play that violated this separation. Because it stimulated self-referent processing, the audience was unable to get absorbed in it.

I was privileged to see one of the early performances of a play by A.R. Gurney, Jr., *The Rape of Bunny Stuntz.* Mr. Gurney gave his play the format of an occasion like a P.T.A. meeting, though part of his point was that the subject of the meeting never became explicit. It was just another meeting of the kind middle-aged suburbanites seem to get drawn into. When you walk into the theater the houselights are half on and the stage contains simply a speaker's table, a cashbox (evidently for receipts or something), a few papers, a chair. The heroine, Bunny, comes to the table and addresses the audience exactly as though it were the P.T.A. (or whatever) that had come to one of its regular business meetings.

As soon as this situation became clear, one sensed all through the audience a tightening and edginess. Gradually, this wore off, but at the outset the atmosphere of tension was almost palpable. On asking members of the audience after the play, I found that others had felt as I did: they were afraid they would be called on to do something, to speak or second a motion or vote in response to the events on the stage. And the tension relaxed only when it became clear that, because of Bunny's distractions, the meeting was not going to be a meeting, but a play. We were not going to have to do anything ourselves.[17]

Another personal recollection, this one of a story spell rudely shattered by the unexpected intrusion of reality, shows again how incompatible the two domains are. As reported by DeVoto, this incident occurred at the end of a puppet show which dramatized several episodes from *Don Quixote*. DeVoto found the show "enchanting," and indeed the man who performed it, Tony Sarg, is considered a master of his art.

But at the end he did a shocking thing:
The puppets hung suspended in their last tableau. The stage was fully lighted and it was as big as the world. One's pleasure still ran clear; the illusion was untouched. But suddenly from behind the backdrop that so truly suggested a landscape in Spain an enormous foot appeared. A leg followed, a leg the size of an oak log. Then Mr. Sarg in his awful entirety was before us, a giant bent double who smiled and waved a vast hand in answer to the children's cries. The illusion had been so strong that for a moment he was as big as Og the king of Bashan, who slept in an iron bedstead nine cubits long. But he beckoned the realities in with both arms and abruptly was just a life-sized man, and Don Quixote and Dulcinea and their companions, lately alive, were now small, ridiculous dolls, the poor puppets that Cervantes' puppetmaster had called them in the novel.
One disliked Mr. Sarg. For the surprise of children, whom we may treat here as the readers of novels who have the simplest hearts, he had sinned against his art. There had been Spain, castles, the bemused knight, his mistress, his squire, and ho! such bugs and goblins finally drowned in laughter as would make any theater alive. But now there was just a litter of miniature stage lumber, some hanged figures, and disgust. The producer of the illusion had destroyed it by stepping into it.[18]

There is magic in the transformation of "miniature stage lumber" and "some hanged figures" into an enchanting world of castles and fabulous people. But such magic is due, not only to the art of the puppeteer, but also to the story spell that develops in the spectator.

The Fallacy of Vicarious Experience

The fact that such unlikely figures as puppets — and muppets and cartoon characters and folklore animals — can be the basis for viable stories refutes the old notion that the purpose of the story is to give us a slice of reality. At one time in England, puppet shows, with stock characters and situations much like the modern television sitcom, were the rage in story entertainment.[19] On September 21, 1668, Samuel Pepys made this entry in his famous diary: "To Southwarke-Fair, very dirty, and there saw the puppetshow of Whittington, which was pretty to see; and how that idle thing do work upon people that see it, and even myself too!"[20] Like Pepys, we can only marvel at the power of the story to move us and engage our experience. Experiencing is the *raison d'être* of stories.

It is still a commonly held belief, however, that story experience is but a pale version of everyday emotions. Supposedly, real experience comes only from real life. Thus story experience is supposedly weak, all in the imagination. The technical term here is *vicarious,* meaning that the experience comes to us, not directly from reality, but from "imagined participation" in some substitute. The term vicarious has always implied a lower order of experience because the reactions are derived from things that only symbolize or reenact one's own life.

To refer to an experience as "vicarious" implies that there can be genuine experience only when the self is interacting with the physical reality. However, recall that self and experience represent two independent domains; experience without self is not only possible, but often superior.

Furthermore, the notion of vicarious experience is based on an outmoded concept that physical reality is known to us in some direct and unbiased way. The truth of the matter is that neither the physical nor the social reality can be apprehended absolutely. As discussed in an earlier chapter, all input into the organism is filtered by perceptual codes so that what we call reality is actually a "personal construction."

In other words, if vicarious means "felt or enjoyed through imagined participation in the experience of others,"[21] then the term applies to all experience. Because so much of workaday life is social in nature, we are always participating in the experience of others. Social reality is largely a matter of symbols, inferences, and shared assumptions, all of which enter our constructions of the "real."

Human beings have but one arousal system, as effectively activated by symbolic or "artificial" stimuli as by physical ("real") stimuli. Thus the experiences that occur in the midst of a story are just as genuine as those that occur in everyday life.

To be sure, the quality of experience can vary greatly, but not because it is "weakened" by fictional stimuli. Rather, it is more likely to be impaired by monotonous conditions, and by evaluative and self-referent sets that distract us from the full realization of our feelings.

The adverse effects of such evaluative sets on experience was dramatically demonstrated in a study that had subjects look at a movie in different ways to see which was most conducive to arousal.[22] The movie was a documentary about work accidents, some of which were depicted in bloody detail. Skin conductance and heart rate were monitored continuously throughout the film as physiological measures of arousal. Three groups saw the film, but before they did, each received different information that was designed to create a particular viewing "set." The first group was told that the accidents depicted in the movie were staged with the help of trick photography, and that the movie was fictitious. In the second group an attempt was made to induce a viewing set for "intellectualization," i.e., for evaluative thinking. These subjects were told that throughout the movie they were to "reflect" on it and analyze the interactions that occurred from the point of view of a scientist. Finally, there was a control group where no attempt was made to manipulate the viewing set. As might be expected, this group showed the highest level of arousal while watching the film. However, the "fiction" group showed significantly higher arousal than the "intellectualization" group. This suggests that emotional involvement is not impaired by knowing that something is fiction, but it *is* inhibited by evaluative thinking. The Kreitlers discussed this study in their monumental work *Psychology of the Arts* and concluded that "awareness of the artificial features of a filmed event and knowledge about the fictitious character of a story, even if enhanced, do not prevent emotional involvement to the same degree as an analytic attitude, similar to the one often adopted by art critics and professional reviewers."[23]

There is only one conclusion to be drawn from this study: It is not good to think during story entertainment — it weakens experiencing and emotional involvement. It is no wonder that novels and movies which make us think are not usually successful as general entertainment. Likewise, it is not surprising that television viewing, a very popular diversion, has the reputation of being a "mindless" activity, which incidentally has been supported by research. Interviews with people who had just watched a story on television indicated that not much thinking had been going on; for instance, they could not recall many details of what they had just seen. Also, it seems that television viewing is processed primarily with the right hemisphere of the brain, which is the non-cognitive side.[24] Critics leap on such facts as proof that the general public is too lazy to think and prefers low forms of entertainment. Such criticism implies that our entertainments should always be viewed with a set for intellectualization. However, simply by being fiction, entertainments give us permission to relax mentally and turn off the "computer" for a while.

There is little doubt that stories stimulate intense experience. We have all probably recognized the signs of it in ourselves — feelings of emotional involvement in the story. Sometimes there are physical signs of arousal such as laughing, crying, squirming, tensing, chills. "All novels are adventure stories," wrote DeVoto; "they deal with strange occurrences in a strange world, occurrences that raise your pulse-beat and make your breath catch with suspense."[25] It is not surprising, therefore, that emotional themes are a vital ingredient of the successful novel, as one study found.[26] Best sellers and poor sellers were compared on the degree to which they emphasized various elements like characterization, plot, romanticization, action, or emotion. The presence of emotion in a novel was the single best predictor of its popularity.

Empirical research has supported the fact that physiological arousal is stimulated when we get absorbed in stories. This was demonstrated in one study that had subjects listen to a tape-recording of a short mystery story by Ellery Queen.[27] At the same time, the subjects were monitored for tension by electromyographic recordings taken from the forehead, chin, and forearms; presumably, minuscule changes in facial and bodily tension would reflect changes in involvement. At the beginning of the study the subjects were told to relax and listen to the tape as if it were a radio program; it was emphasized that this "was not a test of intelligence, memory, or the like." The story was only ten minutes long, and the subjects listened to it three times, with a five-minute break between each presentation. The results showed that a significant buildup of tension occurred during each presentation of the story. Although the tension levels were somewhat lower as the story was repeated, still it is surprising that they developed so systematically with the progress of the story, even when it was presented for the second and third times. The tension levels were significantly higher than those obtained from a control group who listened to an excerpt from Kant's *Critique of Pure Reason*.

Some other empirical observations along this line were based on body temperature as a measure of arousal. This report was prepared by Nathan Kleitman, an investigator widely known for his research on sleep and the physiological cycles in the body.

> In the course of an extended study of the variations in the dirunal body temperature cycle, which required ten oral temperature readings per day, it was found that after attending a two- or three-hour commercial motion picture show the subject's temperature was higher than usual for the particular time of the day. Sitting for that length of time under laboratory conditions almost always led to a distinct fall in body temperature, an expected result of muscular relaxation.[28]

Intrigued by this incidental observation on two female subjects, Kleitman obtained additional measures of body temperature during movies and compared them with readings taken on non-movie days. One subject furnished fifty-five movie temperature readings whose average was 99.59 degrees.

Non-movie temperatures averaged 98.66, or .93 degrees lower. Similar data were obtained from the other subject. Although the difference here appears small, it must be noted that body temperature is a highly stable trait. Kleitman reported that the probability of getting such an increase in temperature by chance would be one in a billion, and therefore he felt that it represented a significant finding.

> In summary, on the basis of occasional data obtained on many subjects, male and female, and through an analysis of multiple readings on two female subjects, it appears that attending motion picture shows, though looked upon as "relaxation" in the sense of escape from the humdrum reality of existence, *is by no means relaxation in the physiological sense.* On the contrary, although the spectator remains in a sitting position for two or more hours, the subject-matter of the film evokes an increase rather than a decrease in muscle tension which manifests itself in a highly significant rise in body temperature of one-half to one degree F. (p. 508)

Kleitman is calling attention here to the phenomenon of relaxed arousal. As implied in his quote, the organism can be behaviorally relaxed in the sense of being immobile and unexpressive; this is mental relaxation. On the other hand, it can be in a state of intense arousal, as reflected in the elevated body temperature. As we have already observed, this paradoxical state is the characteristic condition of the absorbed spectator.

The relaxed mentality of the absorbed person primes him to resonate and react fully, which greatly augments the overall experiencing in a story. This condition makes possible the unconscious and multilayered meanings that abound in story entertainment. "It is only by temporarily losing ourselves," wrote Holbrook Jackson, "that we may hear those inward intimations which are often awakened by a book and are its best reward." Arthur Koestler has described how stories stir up a broad swirl of remote associations that enhance experiencing:

> When you read or listen to a narrative you travel like a barge towed by a tug. But in each case the progress of the boat causes ripples on the lake, spreading in all directions — memories, images, associations; some of these move quicker than the boat itself and create anticipations; others penetrate into the deep. The boat symbolizes focal awareness, the ripples on the surface are the fringes of consciousness, and you can furnish the deeps, according to taste, with the nasty eddies of repressed complexes, the deep-water currents of the collective unconscious, or with archetypal coral-reefs. When thinking is in the tow of a narrative, focal awareness must stick to its course and cannot follow the ripples on their journey across the lake; but it is their presence all round the horizon, on the peripheries of awareness, which provides resonance, colour, and depth, the atmosphere and feel of the story.[29]

This is the "deepened sense of significance" that William James listed as the first aspect of mystical experience. These "memories, images, associations" come from old experiences that are no longer connected to the master code processing system. They contain traces of outgrown roles and emotions, impressions about the way things used to be, forbidden fantasies, and infantile impulses. Because the requirements for conducting the business of living are continually changing, especially as we move from childhood to adulthood, new codes and processing circuits come into being. The old ones cannot be ejected from the brain, so they are bypassed in favor of the up-to-date programs. The old ones are still in the computer, but they have low priority. In fact, the master codes may actively inhibit these old associations, which would only distract and confuse the organism in going about its current business. Thus, everyday consciousness has no access to the old, which exists outside the orbit of the master code processing system; there is no way to stimulate it or attend to it in the everyday frame of mind. But although this old experience cannot serve as a guide for living, it is the basis for unconscious associations; because it still carries significance for the organism, it can enrich experiencing, provided that the master codes are suspended.

Another reason why stories tend to arouse strong experience is that they can be specifically designed to be objects of fascination. They are constructed in such a way as to capture attention and intensify arousal. For example, in a movie a particular scene can be staged for maximum effect on our reactions, depending on what the director wants us to feel. Through the use of attention-getting color, close-ups, dramatic detail, and fast action, the movie literally forces us to see and feel in a particular way. This really amounts to breaking up our everyday perceptual patterns and expanding consciousness. "Hypno-fiction" can do the same. In everyday life, our master codes edit reality in order to maximize efficiency, need-satisfaction, comfort, survival — and in so doing they subordinate and dissipate experience. Fiction edits reality in order to maximize experience.

As noted in the last chapter, sports and other physical recreations attempt to alter reality to intensify experience. Much the same is true of stories, which symbolically manipulate time, place, rules, and roles to achieve certain effects. For example, space and time are more fluid in stories; we are not absolutely embedded in them as in everyday life. Time is usually condensed; blocks of dead time are omitted. Time can be reversed, as in flashbacks, or brought to a standstill in an extended examination of a critical moment. In spite of such changes, stories still convey a convincing sense of reality, as Nicoll noted about movies: "The sense of reality lies at the foundation of the film, yet real time and real space are banished; the world we move in may be far removed from the world ordinarily about us."[30]

In a story, space is always different from the narrow orbit of everyday life. Stories are usually about faraway places, high life or low life, behind the scenes, inside the very minds of people. In stories, the rules and roles are

different from what most people know. To spark interest, stories often change
the relations between sexes, age groups, and social classes. In a story, there
is always more freedom of action, more adventure, more excitement, more
violence, more sex — and happy endings. There is no sense of routine. Story
characters are also different from the people most of us deal with. They talk
more, are more witty, glamorous, and heroic. What Bosanquet said about
comedy would probably apply to all stories to some extent: "In strong humor
or comedy you have to endure a sort of dissolution of the conventional world.
All the serious accepted things are shown you topsy-turvy. . . . You must feel
a liberation in it all; it is partly like a holiday in the mountains or a voyage
at sea."[31]

It is a minor circumstance that the story is acted out on a stage or in a
movie. The important thing is the fullness of our experience. It might seem
that to read the story or watch it played out by actors would make it seem
distant, artificial, weak. But just the opposite is true. Total attention brings
it alive as it could never be otherwise. It is indeed bigger — and better — than
life.

> Everyone loves a story, right? Homer sang of windy Troy to eager
> listeners, New York crowds awaited the ship from England that brought in-
> stallments of Dickens' *Old Curiosity Shop,* people still line up for hours to catch
> the latest Bergman film. Novels and movies are repeatedly, if somewhat
> tiredly, described as compelling, gripping, sexy, heart-rending and tragic.
> The trouble is: *they are.*[32]

Being One-With Fictional Characters

Last Tales, a book by Isak Dinesen, contains a short story, set in bygone
times, wherein there is a conversation between a cardinal and an elderly lady.
In answer to a question of hers, he narrates a story. The lady surmises that
the semi-tragic story told by the cardinal is really about himself. She tells him so.

> The Cardinal lifted an ivory paper-knife from the table, turned it between
> his fingers and put it down.
> "Madame," he said, "I have been telling you a story. Stories have been told
> as long as speech has existed, and *sans* stories the human race would have
> perished, as it would have perished *sans* water. You will see the characters
> of the true story clearly, as if luminous and on a higher plane, and at the
> same time they may look not quite human."

The cardinal goes on to complain that the "new art of narration," which
was then coming into existence in the form of novels, puts too much emphasis
on characterization to the detriment of plot and action.

"The individuals of the new books and novels — one by one — are so close to the reader that he will feel a bodily warmth flowing from them, and that he will take them to his bosom and make them, in all situations of his life, his companions, friends and advisors...."

"Oh, Your Eminence," said the lady, "do not speak ill of the new fascinating art of narration, to which I am myself a devotee. Those live and sympathetic persons of the modern novels at times have meant more to me than my acquaintances of flesh and blood. They have indeed seemed to embrace me, and when, reading by candlelight, I have wetted my pillow with the tears of Ellenore, this sister of mine — frail and faultful as myself — seems to have been shedding my own."[33]

This little exchange tells us in a nutshell why stories are enjoyable and entertaining. First, it has to do with the story being "luminous and on a higher plane"; in other words, a new world seems to devleop, and it is made luminous by total absorbed attention. In addition, there is a feeling of having a different identity as we lose ourselves in the characters of the story. The fictional character becomes a reality — a presence that overshadows our own.

Nothing so well illustrates the extremes to which people go in identifying with fictional characters than the fact that they actually cry in response to the characters' sorrows. In everyday life, crying is always recognized as a sign of extreme distress, and it always elicits concern and sympathy from others. And yet it is not unusual for people to cry while *enjoying* a story. Why? Irving Singer answered the question this way, analyzing the crying that might occur when a character in a stage play dies:

> The hero dies, and you begin to weep. Now for whom are you crying? Surely not for the actor: you know that as soon as the curtain falls, he will scramble to his feet and prepare for a great ovation. Is it then the character in the play? But there is no such person. You are fully aware that Hamlet (at least Shakespeare's Hamlet) never existed. How can his death, which is purely fictional, sadden you? Yet it does, more so perhaps than the death of real people you may have known. What happens, I think, is that you respond *as if* the actor were really Hamlet and *as if* Hamlet really existed. The "as if" signifies that although you *know* the actor is only acting and Hamlet only fictitious, your imaginative involvement causes you to express feelings appropriate to real people.[34]

It seems that an interesting question is being posed here, but the answer is disappointing. This explanation falls back on the old stand-by of "imagination" and "as if"; in effect, it says that we make believe and adopt the illusion of the story. We pretend that Hamlet is real, and so we cry when he dies. The problem comes when we try to explain why his death should sadden us more than the death of real people — just as it is hard to explain why Dinesen's lady feels that fictional characters are more important to her than "acquaintances of flesh and blood."

These issues clear up when we view story response in terms of absorbed attention. Mere mental processes like "imagination" and "as if" cannot explain the convincing and forceful experience typical of story entertainment. Such an experience can be produced only by absorbed attention and is more a matter of stimulus and response than of imagination; if only Hamlet stimuli are being attended to, then Hamlet is real, and when he dies, presumably we cry. The principle laid down by William James on this matter bears repeating: "Any object which remains uncontradicted is ipso facto believed and posited as absolute reality."[35]

We might ask, who is it that the absorbed theatergoer perceives on stage when he watches John Gielgud play Hamlet? It depends. If the theatergoer were shaken from his absorbed spell and asked that question, there would be no doubt about the reply; he knows cognitively that he is watching Gielgud play the role. On the other hand, if we could somehow ask the question without breaking the absorbed spell, the answer would be different. If the person were totally absorbed in the drama, had stopped attending to self and the surrounding world, and especially had stopped attending to thoughts or stimuli that would contradict the story or indicate that it was made up, then *Hamlet* would be on the stage. And when he died, it would genuinely sadden the theatergoer.

In the movie *Barry Lyndon* a little boy disobeys his father and takes a ride on a horse that was to be his birthday gift. While riding alone through the fields, the boy is thrown off the horse and is fatally injured. He lives long enough to be returned to his parents' side, and dies with his father on one side of his bed and his mother on the other, both weeping profusely while mournful music plays in the background. This scene rarely leaves a dry eye in the house. But the spectators are not so much crying *for* the dying boy, who is a very minor character in the story; the movie has built up little involvement in him. Rather, the spectators cry along with (one-with) the weeping parents, the principal characters. One does not have to talk about imagination or "as if" to understand the reaction here. It was not a matter of pretending that the boy was real and pretending that he was dying. Instead, the stimulus configuration of parents-and-dying-child was the only thing in the attentional field, and so it was experienced as real. Given only this stimulus, and nothing to contradict it, the spectators naturally respond with an emotional reaction like crying.

Usually in a story, we do not cry for someone, but with someone. When we cry, it is usually late in the story, after an absorbed state has developed fully, and we are completely one-with the characters. Just coming upon a sad scene, without the involvement and prior story preparation, would probably leave us cold, even if it were a tear-jerker of the first order. In other words, crying is most likely to occur after we have become suggestible and open. It reflects the extent to which people let go, suspend social codes, and react spontaneously when they are involved in a story. Also, since crying is much more common in childhood, it is an indication of the extent to which old experience is being reactivated during story entertainment.

Crying in a movie rarely gets so uncontrolled that we have to go out to the lobby to compose ourselves. That is to say, it does not violate the attentional spell we have for the story. That spell is paramount, and all reactions occur within its confines. Nor is crying in a story so distressing and painful as in everyday life. It tends to have a bittersweet quality, so that overall it is still a part of the entertainment.

Crying and enjoying distressful emotions in a story can be understood only in the context of the attentional spell. If story entertainment were based on everyday reactions, then our involvement in it would weaken when aversive emotions were aroused. But just the opposite is the case: Aversive emotions usually make the story spell more binding. It is when the villain arrives on the scene, frustrating or frightening the other characters — and through them, us — that the plot thickens, along with our enjoyment. The story spell, of course, remains supreme, embracing both the positive and negative aspects of the tale. We maintain the story spell for the villain and his actions, and we are probably one-with him more than is generally realized. It is likely that the Freudians are right in asserting that even the foulest villain strikes a responsive chord at least at an unconscious level, gratifying some childish or destructive impulse.[36] Thus, stories involve us on both sides of the conflict. The conflict is us; we are one-with the whole thing.

In general, then, the story is simply an invention for enriching and expanding experience. Like every other invention, it advances the human being beyond his primitive condition. Story entertainment is an advance in experiencing in the same way that vehicles improve our ability to move. In the primitive condition, we move our bodies by walking or running. But humans have devised better ways of moving; they invented devices like the automobile, the train, the airplane. Stories are similar devices, only they produce better *experience*. They edit reality for what is most captivating and emotionally involving. This editing process does not mean that the product is less real and less important. Nobody says that a car ride is vicarious walking, or that cars are unrealistic because they do not mimic walking. A car ride is recognized as a superior way of moving. In the same way, stories can give us experience that is superior to most of the everyday variety, where existence tends to be routinized or continually disrupted and distracting. A story is like a machine that dispenses complete, more intense experience. This machine extracts the ego-involvement, compresses and intensifies experience in the absorbed spell, and then turns out new realities.

Chapter 5

Ever More Absorbing Stories

Neither illiteracy nor adversity, poverty of mind nor penury of culture,
can deprive people of literature. Song and story, myth and Märchen,
are universals among mankind, and indeed have been taken as criteria
whose possession separates man from the beasts. — *John Greenway*

In general, there has been little recreational development down the ages.
The conventional recreations we have today consist of the same simple activities that humans have always enjoyed. Games, social get-togethers, dancing, or watching shows, for example, do not permit much variation. Many
sports played today were known to the people of ancient times.[1] Only a limited
number of situations are conducive to recreational experience, and these were
only modified, not improved, in different cultural settings. Even major "new"
diversions of the twentieth century like recreational drugs and meditation are
simply revivals of what people have done in earlier times.

Only in story entertainment have there been developments on a scale
comparable to the great advances that have occurred in transportation, construction, energy, and other areas of working life. Two trends stand out: The
inventions of writing, printing, broadcasting, and movie-making have led to
increased production and consumption of stories; and they have made stories
more absorbing.

Early Developments in Story Entertainment

The first kind of story entertainment came from the *telling* of tales. The
rich folk literatures that have survived show that tribal people had an almost
passionate love of storytelling. In fact, the folktale is the principal artifact of
prehistoric times; "no product of human culture has been collected more avidly
than the folktale."[2] However, like the other tribal artifacts — the hovels, the
flint tools, the clay pottery — the earliest folktales are primitive devices. They
are short and fantastic stories that were told in ritualistic situations which

emphasized group consciousness rather than personal experiencing. It was the nature of tribal society that everything served the group's goals, even entertainment.[3]

Storytelling may still be the most common entertainment when seen from a worldwide perspective. As one scholar noted, "When the whole earth is considered, including all those people who do not have writing, even now a majority of men and women on the earth are still using folk literatures since it is the only kind they know."[4] But all development in this form of diversion has moved it away from social and ritualistic situations so that a story can be enjoyed as a thing in itself.

The invention of writing made stories visible and permanent, and it gave them an independent existence. The story was cut free from social function and even reality, allowed to develop as a device of entertainment and as the creation of one particular individual. Thus fiction was born.

Writing also switched the story from the auditory to the visual mode, from the storyteller's voice to the page of a book. In a way this amounted to a move from the periphery to the center of attention. Hearing is mostly a monitoring mechanism; although it is a sharp sense, it does not sustain focused attention very well. (Maybe this is part of the reason why folk tales are so short and simple.) Most of the time it is vision, not hearing, that determines what we attend to. Thus, once the story entered the visual field, it acquired an enhanced status in human attention. In effect, by making the story visible, writing opened the doors to sustained absorbed experience.

Throughout fifty centuries of ancient civilization, the handicraft of writing was used to produce and preserve literature, but it did not contribute much to the widespread consumption of it. The invention of the printing press changed that. In less than 200 years, printing became publishing, a major industry that turned out low-cost reading materials. This made possible an unprecedented distribution of stories. Historians tell us that with this sudden availability of books and periodicals, there was a "rage to read," and that people learned to read even without the benefit of formal education.[5] Reading was discovered as a source of diversion.

Printing led to novels, which represented a major improvement in story entertainment because they were more conducive to sustained absorbed experience than briefer, simpler forms such as the folktale or the Romance story. Their length and complexity made possible a greater buildup of involvement. In novels, events are dramatized with the use of dialogue so that there is a feeling of being there, rather than being told about something. Liberal use of hypno-fiction, i.e., using words to "hallucinate the senses," arouses emotional reactions.

There is yet another reason why novels represented a revolutionary development in story entertainment. Novelists had discovered how to write about people as fascination objects, in a way that the reader could feel one-with them. Primitive stories also depicted people as fascination objects, but in crude and extreme ways. Folk tales were about humanoid creatures (gods, giants, animals, elves, etc.), while the superhuman stars of ancient and medieval epics were either fabulously heroic or fabulously villainous. In either case, it is impossible to feel one-with such story characters because they are so unlike ourselves. In these early stories, we are carried along by the action, much as we get absorbed in an exciting newspaper account. But we do not get involved in their characters, who are usually one-dimensional.

Novelists, on the other hand, have succeeded in giving us what is truly fascinating about people—their personalities, emotions, and personal relations. By illuminating this side of their characters, writers emphasized their humanity, making it easy for people to feel one-with them. Novels transport us to another life, which we share more intimately than we ever could share someone's life in reality. In her book *Imagining a Self,* Patricia Spacks discussed the process of feeling one-with the characters in novels. She pointed out that fictional characters "exist for us because they are perceived more confidently than we can perceive ourselves. The structure of cause and effect that contains them makes more sense than the haphazardness of real life."[6] Just as an action story allows us to experience danger and adventure without the unpleasantness that these entail in reality, so also the novel makes it possible for us to experience the presence of its characters since we are not inhibited by worries of what they will think, or what we should say, or similar social concerns. When novels came into being, they offered a new and more intimate way to experience people; it is no wonder that the title of many early novels was simply the name of its main character.

The Movies

> The dark theatre, the bright hypnotic screen, the continuous flow of images and sounds, and the large anonymous audience in which we are submerged all contribute to a suspension of self-awareness and a total immersion in the events on the screen. —*Michael Roemer*

The culmination of the two historic trends in story entertainment—increased accessibility and increased absorption—was reached in the twentieth century with the coming of movies and television. Arriving first on the scene, movies transcended and made obsolete the distinction between oral and written literature. At least in terms of story entertainment, the more meaningful distinction now is between *verbal* and *visual.* Verbal stories would include all oral and printed narrative. Visual stories are stories that we watch.

This distinction is important because it helps to explain the major step-up that has occurred in story absorption. As noted earlier, attention is more easily focused and sustained by vision. Since movies (and television, which we shall discuss shortly) are fully pictorial — rather than being made up of notational figures as is the printed page of a novel — they are powerfully visual and more absorbing. The page of a novel is attention-getting not for itself, but for what it symbolizes. The movie is attention-getting for itself — for the flow of lively, colorful, and moving images it presents.

Verbal stories are read or listened to. Attention must first be focused on the words, which then have to be decoded and pictured in the imagination before we can experience the story. This makes verbal story experience dependent on reading and imaginative skills — mediating processes that are absent in visual stories. Since some attention must be devoted to reading the words, all of it cannot be allocated to the story itself. Also, since verbalization is at the heart of evaluative processing, there is a risk of stimulating such mental activity, which is antithetical to intense experiencing.

In contrast, visual stories are dramatized, not narrated. We seem to be an eyewitness to the events, so there is a feeling of being inside the story. In addition, the visual story is not under our control. It seems to happen as an independent event. Reading a story, we can stop the action, proceed slowly, or reread passages so that the overall experience is somewhat self-directed or self-related. But a movie moves along at its own clip; the images are served up on the screen, and for our part we can only attend and react. There is no need to do any mental elaboration. This direct quality of the visual story is exactly the effect that novels strive for but can only approximate because they rely on symbols. Swedish director Ingmar Bergman made the point that movies are different from verbal narrative, not only in their form, but also in how they are experienced:

> Film has nothing to do with literature; the character and substance of the two art forms are usually in conflict. This probably has something to do with the receptive process of the mind. The written word is read and assimilated by a conscious act of the will in alliance with the intellect; little by little it affects the imagination and the emotions. The process is different with a motion picture. . . . The sequence of pictures plays directly on our feelings.
>
> Music works in the same fashion; I would say that there is no art form that has so much in common with film as music. Both affect our emotions directly, not via the intellect.[7]

Although movies contain dialogue, this verbal element is subordinate to the visual image. It is interesting to note that for their first twenty years movies were "silent," and still they were a popular entertainment. The content of much movie dialogue is trivial, while what is interesting is conveyed nonverbally — for example, through gestures and facial features.

Take these lines from *Marty*. They are spoken in a dance hall during the first encounter between a lonely man and a lonely girl. She says: "I'm twenty-nine years old. How old are you?" And he answers: "Thirty-six."

On the stage or the printed page these lines would fall ludicrously flat. But on the screen, when spoken by performers who can make every detail yield a wealth of meaning, they instantly convey — as they would in life itself — a complex web of feeling: the girl's fear that she might be too old for the man, her need to come right to the point, her relief when he turns out to be older, and finally a mutual delight that their relationship has crossed its first hurdle.

Film thrives on this kind of intimate detail, for the camera reports it so closely that nothing essential is lost to the eye or ear.[8]

Recent insights about the unconscious, right hemisphere functions and nonverbal communication suggest that there is a visual-intuitive mode of experience that is separate from the verbal-rational mode.[9] Certainly our earliest impressions come from experiences in our pre-language years, and therefore are formed in terms of visual associations. The Hungarian critic Bela Balazs felt that movies tap into this deeper side of human nature, which is often neglected in our highly verbal culture.[10]

The stage play is basically a verbal story; its visual component is weak since it is distant from the audience and confined to a narrow stage area. Most of the audience sits too far back from the stage to see the facial expressions of the actors. Thus, the play has to express everything verbally; in fact, most of the action in the play consists of people talking about situations. Although the stage play is dramatized, it is restricted to showing people as they talk and move around. The movie, on the other hand, has a stunning capacity for visual portrayal. Instead of talking about situations, it *reveals* them. It can show the sweep of landscape, or capture minute detail, or even trick us with special effects. It can give a close-up of an actor's face, forcing us to experience the emotion depicted there. For example, who can ever forget the visual impact of this scene?

> In the final climax of *The Bridge on the River Kwai* ... we *see* the anguished bewilderment of the Colonel, played by Alec Guinness, as he realizes what is actually occurring; and this reaction goads him to the final enigmatic action which blows up the bridge. The intention behind this final act remains ambiguous, but the dramatic moment is the Colonel's realization of his terrible dilemma, which realization we read in his face. On the stage, this mental process would have to be projected in speech. On the screen, where nothing is so eloquent as the silent image, any utterance would be fatal.[11]

The movie actor does not need the grand gestures of stage acting. He does not have to project himself; he can afford to be natural, spontaneous, and intimate. The movie screen will make him bigger than life and project him into the center of the spectators' attention. Furthermore, the fact that we are attending to a screen image rather than a live actor is an advantage as far as story involvement is concerned, making it easier to suspend those evaluative and social codes that we always maintain in the presence of people. As Pauline Kael writes:

> Movies — which arouse special, private, hidden feelings — have always had an erotic potential that was stronger than that of the live theater. Enlarged so that they seem totally ours, movie actors are more purely objects of contemplation than people who are physically present. Since they're not actually there on the stage, speaking, rushing off to change a costume, we can fantasize about them with impunity; by etherealizing the actors, film removes the constraints on our imaginations.[12]

To describe movie characters as "objects of contemplation" is to point up the non-everyday kind of involvement that occurs in the absorbed state. This involvement makes their *felt* presence even more complete than their physical presence would be. The same point was made by British novelist Elizabeth Bowen:

> To get back to my star: I enjoy sitting opposite him or her, the delights of intimacy without the onus, high points of possession without the strain. This could be called inoperative love. Relationships in real life are made arduous by their reciprocities; one can too seldom simply sit back. The necessity to please, to shine, to make the most of the moment, overshadows too many meetings. And apart from this — how seldom in real life (or so-called real life) does acquaintanceship, much less intimacy, with dazzling, exceptional beings come one's way. . . . Directly I take my place I am on terms with these Olympians; I am close to them with nothing at all at stake. Rapture lets me suppose that for me alone they display the range of their temperaments, their hesitations, their serious depths. I find them not only dazzling but sympathetic. They live for my eye. Yes, and I not only perceive them but *am* them; their hopes and fears are my own; their triumphs exalt me. I am proud for them and in them.[13]

When the movie machine was invented, people believed that it would simply be a tool for making a record of stage plays. But the movie had a unique potential of its own. It is an absorbing medium in itself — independent of story content. The direct nature of visual experience; the combination of dark theater and luminous screen; the movement and flow of images; all these make possible a reversal of everyday life that is reflected in Kafka's comment on movies: "Sight does not master the pictures, it is the pictures which master one's sight. They flood consciousness."[14]

To a large extent, the movie theater itself shapes our psychology for the time we are in it. The theater is a recreational environment that changes our orientation. Not only does it cut us off from our day-to-day environment, it also immobilizes mentally and behaviorally. At no time in everyday life do we sit so still in a chair, staring straight ahead for some two hours. At no other time while awake do we spend so much time in darkness and quietness, or sit so close to other people without interacting with them. Immobility, darkness, quietness, and social isolation — these are the conditions conducive to mental relaxation and meditation. To be sure, the theater environment attains these conditions imperfectly; nevertheless, there is an effect on the organism. The theater conditions of darkness and quietness deprive us of input, which weakens master code processing, making our attention susceptible to external control.

In the muted theater environment, the large and luminous movie screen has a magnetic effect on attention. It takes control and absorbs completely. Not only does it present the visual images, it makes them bigger and brighter than normal. These qualities — large size and intensity — are considered to be among the most potent determinants of attention.[15] Other things being equal, the bigger and more intense the stimulus, the more it captures attention.

Although size and intensity are important, however, it is really the movement of the images that makes this medium so absorbing. Inherently interesting, movement makes a stimulus dynamic and suspenseful. "Our eyes are involuntarily attracted to movement," wrote one psychologist, "in much the same way as the moth is attracted to a flame."[16]

Movie directors have used movement in very subtle and complex ways, not just to capture attention but also to define our involvement. By moving the camera around, directors continually change our perspective, thereby manipulating our perception.

> A movie can tell its story . . . as though we are actually dreaming it; it can force us to identify with its chosen moods and people. The camera, by moving around, subtly invites us to embrace one character and exclude another — to look up and feel awe of a noble man or fear of a villain; to look down and feel contempt or pity. A sidelong glance of the camera alerts us for trouble — a right-to-left pan . . . invests people and places with a spooky feeling.[17]

In a movie, not only do the people and objects move, but we the viewers also seem to move. Ours may be the more significant "motion" because it adds greatly to our experience of being inside the story. A close-up moves us in close. If two characters are talking and we get a shot of one and then the other, there is a feeling of being nearby or between them, looking at one and then the other as they speak. "The value of such fluid screen activity," wrote Lewis Jacobs, "lies in its ability to impart a quality of immediacy, actuality, and increased physical participation."[18] Also, the motion of the camera seems to bind us emotionally. A certain kind of *motion* of the camera gives rise to a comparable *emotion* in the viewer; for example, "when the camera tracks forward swiftly (as in, say, a musical number) the spectator often feels a mild exhilaration, as if he in his seat were gliding effortlessly through the action. There is a general sense of well-being, of dynamic excitement."[19]

A movie scene can be shot entirely from the perspective of one of the characters, a technique that almost literally makes us one-with the character. We see as the character sees; the camera puts us in his shoes, or to be more precise, in his visual experience. In his discussion of the subjective camera, Herbert Lightman gave a dramatic example of the power of this technique.

> In the film *The Lodger* . . . one sequence concerned the murder of a dowdy London charwoman who had stopped by at the pub for an "arf 'n arf" before going home. Because of previously established motivation, the audience knew that the killer was waiting in her little shack. But when the camera followed her into her room the murderer was not once shown. Instead, the woman started to remove her clothes, whirled about as she heard a sound off camera, and registered fright when she realized that she was not alone. At this point the camera subjectively assumed the point of view of the killer. The frantic charwoman, directing her attention straight at the lens, backed slowly away; while the camera, simulating the lurching gait of the killer, began to close in on her. Terrified, the woman cowered against the wall as the camera lumbered ever closer, ending up in a stark close-up of her frenzied face. When the fade-out came, the killer had not once been shown, and yet the audience had had the unique jolting experience of having directly participated in a murder.[20]

Does such a movie scene stir up genuine, gut-level emotions, or are the reactions merely in the imagination? Psychological studies have consistently shown that movies do produce significant arousal. In most of the research, arousal was measured by rating scales[21]; however, one study utilized physiological indices to determine changes in arousal. Periodic blood samples were obtained from eight male subjects while they viewed four films: a suspenseful film by Alfred Hitchcock, a pornographic film, a documentary, and a control film. Blood samples were drawn to obtain a measure of serum-free fatty acid and cortisol levels, which are elevated when the organism is emotionally aroused. The results showed that significant arousal had occurred during the Hitchcock and pornographic films but not during the others. It was reported that the films had a greater effect than even the stress of fixing the catheter needle in the vein of the arm in order to obtain the blood samples. In their discussion of the results, the authors emphasized that the emotional reactions were to a large extent dependent on the absorbed involvement of the subjects.

> This study demonstrated that carefully selected motion pictures shown in a setting designed to maximize their impact can evoke measurable changes in psychological state of sufficient intensity to be associated with activation of the pituitary adrenocortical and autonomic nervous systems. . . .
> The success of the experimental films in evoking changes in both the psychological and physiological variables was to some extent unexpected. . . .
> The artistry with which the film is produced and more specifically the extent to which the subject is engaged appear to be crucial variables. . . . It is likely

that the method of presentation enhanced the films' effect. Distractions were minimized by having subjects sit alone in a sound-attenuated chamber. A large image was projected on a curved screen so that the subject was immersed in the film.[22]

In the introduction to her book *Reeling,* movie critic Pauline Kael unabashedly celebrated the sheer emotional power of the movies.

> There's a reason for that "Wow!" which often seems all that a person can say after coming out of a movie house. So many images, sounds, and awakened memories may contribute to the film's effect on us that often we can't quite sort out what we think about the way we've been moved. We're not even sure sometimes if we liked it, but we certainly *felt* it....[23]

Movie experience is about as far as one can go in absorption without drugs or prolonged training in meditation. After movies, the next step is hypnosis itself or psychedelic experience.

Television

> There is no better brain-washing than a daytime soap opera.
> — *Marya Mannes*

Television is usually called a "communications medium"—a term that implies it is used primarily for informational and educational purposes. Scholars view television as a social institution, and expect it to be serious and enlightening.

Actually, television has turned out to be a favorite recreational object. On any particular day about 50 percent of adults watch it, more than participate in any other recreational outlet.[24] Television is basically a gigantic toy for inducing adult play experience. After all, people watch television during their leisure hours; they are generally absorbed when watching it; and about 80 percent of television time is devoted to entertainment. (Much of television news would fall in the entertainment category; just as newspaper reading is absorbing, so is watching the news, which is usually made up of interesting stories that have no relevance to ourselves.) Only about 20 percent of television time is made up of "serious" programs designed to be thought-provoking or instructional.

In a book that was highly critical of television, Jerry Mander reported that people have told him they find television boring but have to watch it anyway.[25] Such views seem to confirm that whatever the content, the luminous screen is very absorbing in its own right. This is what Marshall McLuhan probably meant when he said that "the medium is the message."[26]

In other words, the primary effect that television has on us comes by virtue of the absorption and mental relaxation induced by the screen. The content is only a means to this end. In a way, this is true of all story formats; their function is to provide relaxation and experiencing, not cognitive enlightenment. When television functions as a recreational object, which is most of the time, one would expect it to be light, frivolous, and unrealistic — all characteristic qualities of play. The person who called television "a wasteland" was judging it by the standards of workaday life, and so was making an irrelevant statement.

The program content of television needs only one quality: Like the medium itself, it should be absorbing. It is not surprising, therefore, to find that about one-half of all television time is devoted to stories — movies, soap operas, sitcoms, serials, dramas, even cartoons. This amount has remained fairly steady over the years, comparing the programming of the 1960s[27] with that of the 1980s. Half of television time adds up to an astonishing amount of story entertainment every day. Currently, in a typical viewing area that might have fifteen channels, each broadcasting about nineteen hours daily, there would be about 150 hours of story entertainment every day. Whereas a movie theater might bring one story to a neighborhood in a week, in a similar period of time television brings hundreds of stories, all easily accessible in the home.

Actually, television tends to make all of its content story-like. Usually, whatever appears has been carefully edited to make it attention-getting. The term "program" implies the same characteristics as "story" — organization, central theme, and the resolution of some question. Like stories, programs collapse time to eliminate what is uninteresting, and they give multiple views to create a sense of movement, contrast, and excitement. At the everyday level, most human actions are not very interesting; thus, when a live event is being telecast it is covered with numerous cameras so that the director can select the most interesting shot. Sometimes canned audience laughter and applause are used to boost the excitement.

The other fifty percent of television content is made up of such programs as talk shows, games, variety, the news, and various kinds of issue-related and self-improvement programs. While most of these purport to present some significant discussion, all would be greatly diminished without the visual image. We seldom realize how important it is to actually see the person speaking, even if it is just television's infamous "talking head." Like the movie actor, a person on television can be an object of contemplation. We can stare as we never do when actually face-to-face with people. Since we cannot interact with the people on the screen, we are free to get absorbed in them, to get immersed in the human face as a thing in itself. Especially when ordinary people are shown on news programs or talk shows, television makes it possible for us to see the nonverbal story that usually goes on underneath the chatter; we can see the fidgeting, the twitch in the eye, and how people behave when they verbally joust with each other. In addition, Irving Weiss claimed that much of daytime television has a sensual quality which can be appreciated if we "ungrudgingly accept whatever is on . . . in that ideal way in which you would look at paintings in a museum, without caring who painted or is supposed to have painted what."

> For what gradually rises to the surface, as the disinterested viewer can observe . . . is the sub-drama of the human face, voice, and gesture—the source and estuary of all sensuality short of the act of love itself—mixing self-betrayals and revelations more intricately and rapidly than one ever finds them in real life. We could not possibly observe the process of human interaction fully if we were dramatically concerned ourselves.[28]

Just as the microscope opened up a new visual world for scientists, so television opens up new worlds and perspectives to its viewers. By the mobility of its cameras and the editing of its images, television allows us to see what we could never see on our own. For example, no one sitting in the stadium could ever see a football game the way television presents it. Like theatergoers, spectators in the stadium see the game as a weak and distanced image. But a televised game is a different experience. Because the camera allows us to see the sweat and the struggle, we participate in the intensity of the game. We are close enough to see the skillful movements of the athletes, and the tension in their faces. By slow-motion replays our visual capacity is magically extended, allowing us to savor excellent plays. The stadium spectator sees only end results—teams moving up and down the field. On television, we see the process of the game. No wonder surveys show that most people prefer to watch sports on television rather than at the stadium.[29]

Television allows us to experience an event more fully than if we had actually been on the scene. Probably the best example of this new kind of story involvement was television's coverage of President Kennedy's assassination and funeral. One of the many surveys concerning this event conducted in-depth interviews to determine how people reacted to the television coverage. The conclusion: "The reasons people spent much time watching television are to be found in the uniqueness of the coverage. Neither radio nor newspapers could match television's facility for realism and psychological proximity." The report goes on:

> Television created an extraordinarily deep sense of participation in the flow of events, as these comments, representative of about three-fourths of the sample, indicate:
> ". . . . It brought you there as if you were one of the close spectators—closer than had you been on the street watching what was taking place. Each time it took you into the rotunda you felt as if you were one of the people passing in review."

"Just as things happened, they were right there, bringing everything to you at the moment. It was better than being there; you could see more than you could if you were there, I'm sure."

"I don't know how you could beat watching it and drawing your own conclusions. You couldn't possibly in print describe more thoroughly to me what I saw. . . . I don't think anyone [could] give me the same mental picture as having seen it."[30]

At the time that Kennedy was assassinated, Tom Pettit was an NBC correspondent in California, and he was immediately dispatched to Dallas to help with the television coverage. Recalling that weekend, Pettit essentially agreed with the television viewers just quoted. Pettit was a member of the huge crowd present when assassin Lee Harvey Oswald was led to the police station and when he was suddenly and fatally shot, an event that was broadcast on live television nationwide. Pettit wrote:

The eye of the live television camera peered into the confusion and transmitted the first images of Oswald. . . . Television viewers probably saw and heard more than the reporters in that mass-media gauntlet which Oswald was forced through to get to the interrogation room of the Dallas Homicide Bureau. . . .

Oswald's voice was barely audible in the room. But it was heard on television, and most reporters got their quotes from the audio engineers. . . . Oswald was brought down. He walked through a basement office. . . . I was looking directly into Oswald's face. Within seconds he had been shot. He crumpled to the pavement. I kept on talking [on the air] as well as I could. There was unbelievable confusion and excitement. . . . Viewers who saw the events as they happened, and on the videotape playback a few minutes later, saw more than I did. Although I was just a few feet from Oswald, I did not see the actual firing of the shot.

Pettit concluded:

People who watched the events in Dallas on television probably saw more than those of us who were there. Television almost always permits people to see things more perceptively than they could if they actually were at the scene of an event, because cameras and microphones create an extension of the senses. When events are happening in several places, television coverage permits the viewer, in effect to be in more than one place at the same time. People who spent many hours at their television sets had a more comprehensive account of what was happening than the individual correspondents, who were isolated while covering the individual threads of the story.[31]

Although Kennedy's assassination was fact and not fiction, we experienced the televised event as story involvement. Tom Pettit on the scene undoubtedly experienced it with everyday, work-oriented attention, coping as he was with jostling crowds, deadlines, delays, and distractions. But the television viewer, free of all of this, sitting in the comfort of home, was able to experience the thing fully.

It seems likely that the television screen will be the springboard for future recreational developments. So far we have had primarily stories on television, but already there are video games and music videos. According to some, the unique elements of video games — participation and movie theater qualities — may be the seeds for futuristic home television viewing. Apparently, the technologies are already available for wall-size, flat panel television screens and for three-dimensional television.[32] On the distant horizon, Alvin Toffler sees the home television theater becoming more participatory, designed for losing everyday self in vivid and total experiencing. "Recreational industries," he wrote, "will grow, as the whole nature of leisure is redefined in experiential terms."

> Simulated and non-simulated experiences will also be combined in ways that will sharply challenge man's grasp of reality. In Ray Bradbury's vivid novel, *Fahrenheit 451,* suburban couples desperately save their money to enable them to buy three-wall or four-wall video sets that permit them to enter into a kind of televised psychodrama. They become actor-participants in soap operas that continue for weeks or months. Their participation in these stories is highly involving. We are, in fact, beginning to move toward the actual development of such "interactive" films with the help of advanced communications technology. . . .
>
> But the great psych-corps of tomorrow will not only sell individual, discrete experiences. They will offer sequences of experiences so organized that their very juxtaposition with one another will contribute color, harmony or contrast to lives that lack these qualities. Beauty, excitement, danger or delicious sensuality will be programmed to enhance one another.[33]

Today, most people feel that television is involving and hypnotic enough — no need for four-wall sets. Because of its hypnotic capability, many believe that television is close to being the most powerful cultural force in modern society.[34]

Television, in fact, reflects the ascendance of diversion in our affluent civilization. It epitomizes the new work-and-play relationship — mild work and extreme play. Television is not like traditional recreation; it is not something that happens for a brief period at the end of the day. Television broadcasts continually, day and night, on numerous channels. It is an alternate reality that is always accessible — instant absorption. Never before has play experience been so easily available. What is more, television's power to shape our culture has reversed the tendency of workaday values to intrude on and dominate play. Television represents a case where play intrudes on and threatens workaday life.

It seems that many of the concerns that people have about television are really about this changing relationship between work and play. They are worried that play values are superseding work values, and so they insist that television be more serious and realistic. For example, Jerry Mander belabors the point that television emphasizes exciting and attention-getting elements; he complains that it completely controls experience, that it dims thought processes, that it discourages social interaction, and that it is unrealistic.[35] He is right, of course; television does have these characteristics, like all entertainments, but like all entertainments, its effects are only temporary. Television is a diversion; it is *supposed* to be mentally relaxing and to arouse experiences that are different from everyday life.

Although television is being broadcast continuously, it is still only a brief respite for most working adults. It is play, diversion—not a way of life. And although there is grave concern about too much television viewing, there is no indication that the work of the world is not being done because people are glued to their sets. In fact, even in the recreational field television has not been as disruptive as some alarmists would have us believe. In his book *The Age of Television,* Bogart assessed the impact of this new entertainment on other recreations. He found no significant changes in established recreational patterns. Although television is obviously leading the recreational field, it is not crowding the others out. People still read; they still go to movies, football games, museums, and art galleries; they still play bridge and chess; and more than ever they are camping, hiking, and jogging. Like a good diversion, television expands experience, not only immediately, but also afterwards as it stimulates new interests. "TV has given, and gives, massive exposure to aspects of the culture that were formerly the province of the few," wrote Leo Bogart. "People want to see for themselves, and to enjoy for themselves, the things they have seen on the picture tube."[36]

The pervasive monotonies of modern mass existence demand some easily available source of contrast and variety. Television satisfies this need. There is no doubt that it does so for the millions of people who have a surfeit of leisure or are incapable of other recreations—the unemployed, the elderly, the sick and disabled, the shut-ins. As leisure time increases for all, television plays a vital role in maintaining the work-and-play rhythm of existence.

> For television will not go away; it is embedded in the culture now.... Those who would deny that it has been a boon to individuals in their private lives can be brushed aside: there is simply no question that television has answered the most desperate of human needs, the need for escape from boredom, escape from self. Traditionally, heaven has always been seen as a place of pretty continuous entertainment. For those multitudes who cannot escape through their work or their reading or the experience of art, television has been about as close as they could hope to come to a heaven on earth.[37]

Chapter 6

Recreational Drugs

For until this morning I had known contemplation only in its humbler,
its more ordinary forms ... as a rapt absorption in poetry or painting
or music.... But now I know contemplation at its height. —*Aldous Huxley*

Absorption can be induced physiologically by taking a drug. Some drugs
affect the brain in such a way as to weaken those centers responsible for the
self factor, while strengthening those responsible for the experience factor. In
other words, these drugs produce mental relaxation together with a "high" in
experiencing, i.e., relaxed arousal. Since this is basically a recreational effect,
these drugs are called "recreational." For adults such drugs are a major source
of absorbed experience and recreational feeling.

Alcohol, marijuana, cocaine, and the psychedelics are the principal drugs
that induce varying degrees and qualities of absorption. These so-called intoxicating or mind-altering drugs are "as ancient as social man,"[1] but since the
mid-twentieth century there has been renewed interest in them.

The drug most used and abused by the human race is a recreational
one — alcohol. People have consumed more of this drug than all others combined, including medicinal drugs. In the United States, it is believed, about
70 percent of the adult population uses alcohol at least monthly; on the
average, each of these drinkers consumes roughly three gallons of some
alcoholic beverage a year.[2] A number of countries, such as France and Italy,
have higher rates of alcohol consumption than the United States.[3] In the Near
East and Asia, where alcohol is forbidden or difficult to obtain, marijuana is
the main recreational drug. It is estimated that marijuana is used by 350
million people worldwide, which amounts to 9 percent of the earth's population.[4] At various times and places of the past, it seems, the use of these and
numerous other intoxicants was even more prevalent than today.[5]

Such widespread use of recreational drugs cannot be attributed to vice
or mental illness. Rather, it reflects the human condition, especially as it per-
tains to work and play. It suggests that recreational experience does not always
come easily for adults — that the grip of workaday life is difficult to break, and

that conventional recreations are often inadequate. Drugs apparently provide a much-needed boost to recreational experience, notwithstanding their numerous disadvantages. Because drugs do act quickly and effectively, people come to rely on them.

Getting High

There seems to be a prevailing belief that individuals who take intoxicating drugs do so in order to obtain some "secret, unspeakable pleasure."[6] Why else would these drugs be so tempting, even addictive, to so many people? Why this "pursuit of intoxication" if it does not bestow on the drug-taker some pleasure not otherwise available?

Yet there is nothing more naughty in intoxication than the gratifications all people obtain in recreation. These are the pleasures of mental relaxation, enhanced experiencing, and a feeling of being different — all qualities consistent with our humanity and our recreational needs. Because of the biochemical reaction of the drugs, these experiences are likely to be more forcefully induced; but although getting high may be a more intense experience, qualitatively it is similar to other kinds of relaxed arousal.

When one is high or intoxicated, attention is not captured away by some specific object of fascination. Rather, thinking and attention are just more passive, and seem to flow along with whatever image is available. Unlike other absorbing entertainments, drugs do not give us something to attend to, and so people often seek external stimuli to match their inner experience. The stimulus most often used to potentiate drug experience is rhythmic music. Another agreeable stimulus is the sociability of being with other people who also are high. Both kinds of stimuli are found in settings where people go to get high, e.g., the typical bar or the pot party.

In the past, apparently the high was often associated with religious experience — being one-with images of the divine. Religion has always embodied figures from on high, making it a natural match for the expansive feeling of being high on the drug. Huxley reminds us how strong the connections were between drugs and religion in many cultures of the past.

> Alcohol is but one of the many drugs employed by human beings as avenues of escape from the insulated self. . . . To go beyond the limits of the insulated ego is such a liberation that, even when self-transcendence is through nausea into frenzy, through cramps into hallucinations and coma, the drug-induced experience has been regarded by primitives and even by the highly civilized as intrinsically divine. Ecstasy through intoxication is still an essential part of the religion of many African, South American and Polynesian peoples. It was once, as the surviving documents clearly prove, a no less essential part of the religion of the Celts, the Teutons, the Greeks,

the peoples of the Middle East and the Aryan conquerors of India. It is not merely that "beer does more than Milton can to justify God's ways to man." Beer *is* the god. Among the Celts, Sabazios was the divine name given to the felt alienation of being dead drunk on ale. Further to the south, Dionysos was, among other things, the supernatural objectification of the psychophysical effects of too much wine. In Vedic mythology, Indra was the god of that now unidentifiable drug called *soma.* Hero, slayer of dragons, he was the magnified projection upon heaven of the strange and glorious otherness experienced by the intoxicated. Made one with the drug, he becomes, as Soma-Indra, the source of immortality, the mediator between the human and the divine.

In modern times beer and the other toxic short cuts to self-transcendence are no longer officially worshiped as gods. Theory has undergone a change, but not practice; for in practice millions upon millions of civilized men and women continue to pay their devotions, not to the liberating and transfiguring Spirit, but to alcohol, to hashish, to opium and its derivatives, to the barbiturates, and the other synthetic additions to the age-old catalogue of poisons capable of causing self-transcendence.[7]

The high of drug use is enlivening and seems to put us in touch with something more significant, even something spiritual. Thus recreational drugs are typically used to offset ennui. Noted educator Paul Nash offered this in explaining excessive drug use:

> One of the most fruitful ways to examine the drug "problem" is by means of the boredom/adventure/risk/peak-experience continuum. When I look at the life histories of people who have become addicted to drugs, especially hard drugs like heroin, the factor that almost invariably jumps out at me is the intolerable boredom of their pre-drug lives. If life offers little of interest, nothing to "turn me on," no prospect of being better tomorrow, drugs promise a change from the dullness, some unpredictability, the adventure of the unknown (at first), and perhaps even a peak experience.[8]

Psychological research tends to support this view. For example, in a study of over 600 college students, Segal and Singer correlated scores for drug-alcohol use with the results of a variety of personality tests. Analysis of the data showed that drug users were not particularly anxious individuals. Rather, they had a low tolerance for boredom and were "constantly striving for new experiences or stimulation derived from *external* sources."[9] These findings are in agreement with psychiatric concepts and observations. It is not the anxiety-ridden neurotic who is likely to use alcohol or drugs, but the personality disorder who is easily bored by conventional activities and needs a lot of excitement in his life. All of this tends to underscore a point made earlier: When everyday life seems mild and monotonous, there is a need for extreme diversion to bring about variety.

The enjoyable nature of a high is probably the root cause of addiction. There is a direct relationship between addictiveness and the intensity of the high, which in turn is dependent on how quickly and forcefully the drug can take effect in the body.[10] For example, drinking alcohol has only a mild addictive potential because the drug must first pass through the stomach, which delays and dissipates its effects. On the other hand, snorting a drug or injecting it directly into the bloodstream leads to a very intense high, so that this method of drug administration is very addictive. Surprisingly, most investigators have dismissed the power of the high, attempting to study addiction in terms of such factors as social influence, metabolic defect, personality disorder, and deviant learning conditions.[11] However, at its very core, addiction is not so much a behavioral pattern as a craving for a certain kind of experience that is intrinsically enjoyable; the more frequently and intensely it is enjoyed, the less important everyday life becomes. Eventually the addicted person makes a way of life out of getting high.

There is increasing acceptance of the notion that being high is state-dependent, i.e., that it constitutes a distinct psychological state. When sober alcoholics were asked to rate and evaluate their drunken selves, they viewed themselves as entirely different people — a difference that one investigator characterized as "Dr. Jekyll and Mr. High."[12] When the addicted person is high on a drug, he seems to be cut off from his sober personality. What is learned and remembered in one state does not transfer to the other. There is evidence that the longer the history of drug taking and the larger the dosages, "the greater the dissociation between the intoxicated and the sober state."[13]

Repeated and excessive use of recreational drugs apparently makes absorbed experience so irresistible that eventually the addict's entire life is reoriented around it. Drug addiction seems to represent a major and often permanent rearrangement of the psychological states in the organism. Addiction destroys the work-and-play cycle, and moves the drug-taker into a permanent state of diversion. While most people are stabilized in workaday consciousness, the addict is stabilized in the states related to diversion: absorption, relaxed arousal, drowsiness, and sleep. His ties with the everyday business of living are impaired; appetite, energy, concentration, social involvement, and sex are all weakened to a significant degree. The addict feels normal only when he is high and in a state of relaxed arousal.

Thus for the addict, the drug experience is not just an impairment of the sober state, but rather an emergent state with its own characteristics which are based on absorption. Research is showing that the alcoholic is normal only under the conditions of relaxed arousal made possible by the drug. When he is sober, the alcoholic feels uncomfortable and unnatural; he tends to behave in a tense, over-controlled, and over-inhibited way. But when drunk, he seems more capable of *experiencing;* he may be more obstreperous and hostile, or more happy and accommodating.[14] In one case study, the investigators observed the interactions between an older alcoholic man and his alcoholic son. When both were sober, there was aloofness, separation, and distrust. But when they were drunk, both behaved more positively; they were warm and honest with each other.[15] In another study, four alcoholics were observed intensely during sobriety and during a period of experimental intoxication. When drunk, all became more assertive, open, affectionate, humorous, and interesting.[16] Such findings led one group of investigators to conclude that the alcoholic "is frequently not drinking to escape reality, but to make contact with it."[17]

Our attempt to understand the makeup and significance of drug experience is not meant to deny the very real problems brought on by drugs. Drunk driving, alcohol-related crime, and the detrimental effects of drugs on health, family, and quality of life, all add up to a serious problem today. This is an exorbitant price to pay for absorbed experience. In a dark way, though, all of this demonstrates the power of absorption.

Actually, drug addiction, although it is very destructive, is not as unique as it seems. Intense and prolonged absorption of any kind is addicting. For example, meditational experience is deeply absorbing, and throughout history monks and religious people have withdrawn from the world, at great personal sacrifice, to make a way of life of this diversion. And as we shall see in the chapters on cultivated diversions, it is not unusual for individuals to develop lifelong absorptions in certain hobbies or pursuits, often to the point of absent-mindedness for everyday activities, and at the expense of family ties and personal comfort. The experience that makes up the drug high is also comparable to that provided by art and entertainment. It seems that addiction does not reflect so much the pathology of personality or social setting, as the power of absorbed experience. Addiction is too much of a good thing — high-intensity absorption over a long period of time — peak experience gone to seed.

Alcohol

Although some people use alcohol chronically and excessively, most use it in moderation like any other recreational object — to relax and divert themselves. Taking a drink provides a quick and easy way to get outside the everyday mold. People almost always drink at social get-togethers in order to feel less self-conscious and more sociable, or on festive occasions to be one with the spirit of the celebration.

Taking a drink does not lock us in an absorbed spell as a good story does, but it moves us in that direction. It is the first step into altered consciousness. Many scholars have recognized this; William James stated it in a grand way.

The sway of alcohol over mankind is unquestionably due to its power to stimulate the mystical faculties of human nature, usually crushed to earth by the cold facts and dry criticisms of the sober hour. Sobriety diminishes, discriminates, and says no; drunkenness expands, unites, and says yes. It is in fact the great exciter of the *Yes* function in man. It brings its votary from the chill periphery of things to the radiant core. It makes him for the moment one with truth. Not through mere perversity do men run after it. To the poor and the unlettered it stands in the place of symphony concerts and of literature.... The drunken consciousness is one bit of the mystic consciousness, and our total opinion of it must find its place in our opinion of that larger whole.[18]

In this passage, James is asserting that taking a drink to get high is not perversion but diversion, an altered state, expansive and uplifting, and similar to the effects of mystic consciousness of classical music or literature. Surely he is overstating the case here; one wonders what a hardheaded scientist would say about all of this. Here are the observations of a modern pharmacologist:

The pervasive change in the central nervous system caused by alcohol gives rise to generalized differences in emotion and perception. This change in functioning of the central nervous system forms the basis for learning different habits, including general modes of emotional expression and specific muscular functions, controlled by differential drug and nondrug conditions. This effect of the drug, as a differential condition, can be expressed in general terms as an altered state of consciousness.

The degree of emotional and perceptual change caused by intoxicating doses of alcohol is probably underestimated. The central nervous system, in accordance with general homeostatic regulation, compensates for any change or abnormality of function. The environmental situation provides a strong element of continuity, obscuring the changes caused by the drug....A simultaneous comparison between the drug and sober states is impossible.

Evidence for the change in state is found in experiments showing that some people describe their mood as being hazy, distant, and withdrawn when intoxicated. This seems to express a feeling of being different. There is a tendency for people to drink in settings that are clearly distinguished from the usual sober situation. Drinking in a bar or restaurant provides a differentiated location. Distinctive ritualistic customs are often involved in social drinking, such as at cocktail parties or when drinking wine with dinner. Such differentiations of setting and behavior help to emphasize the differential drug state although they also obscure the degree to which it is based on the pharmacological effect of the drug.[19]

Alcohol acts on the body in a number of ways to induce an altered state of consciousness. After passing from the stomach into the bloodstream, alcohol is carried to the brain, where it deprives the cells of oxygen, thus partially anesthetizing cortical functions. The effects of alcohol occur first in the forebrain, and then, with increased consumption, they spread to the back of the cortex. As noted in Chapter 2, neuropsychologists believe that the frontal part of the brain mediates the functions related to self and evaluative thinking. The first effect of alcohol, therefore, is to depress master code functioning, which is experienced as decreased self-consciousness and decreased concern about standards. This release from self and standards is partly responsible for the high and the feeling of being more easygoing. Further intake of alcohol affects areas of the brain related to motor coordination, speech, and vision. The result is typical drunken behavior: incoordination, slurred speech, and the like.

Normally, the master codes determine the priorities of the processing system, allocating attention in a divided and multi-directional way. After alcohol intake, processing is not only slower but also less organized. In various research investigations, "tasks of selective or divided attention appear to be particularly sensitive to the action of alcohol, and it has been suggested that alcohol interferes with central information processing."[20] As a result of their studies of intoxicated subjects, Moskowitz and DePry concluded that alcohol makes it difficult to maintain the kind of divided attention normally required for everyday tasks.[21] For example, the drunk driver has difficulty keeping his car properly on the road while responding to traffic signals. The drunken person is unable to hold three or four things in attention at the same time, changing priorities as the need arises. His attention lacks the hierarchical organization that makes possible rapid processing of signals. Alcohol makes attention less discriminating and selective, and moves it toward a global state that is conducive to lulling and emotional experiencing.

EEG recordings from different sites of the brain show that alcohol disrupts normal processing patterns. "Electroencephalogram recordings show decreases in frequency and increases in amplitude of alpha activity. This pattern of large, synchronized rhythms denotes impairment of the differentiated functions that characterize alert brain activity."[22] The alpha brain wave characterizes meditation and other absorbed states. Other EEG findings show that alcohol tends to weaken cerebral dominance. A large dose of alcohol "dissipated the normally greater amplitude in the dominant hemisphere. This may reflect disinhibition of functioning in the normally subordinate hemisphere."[23] In other words, alcohol changes the mode of consciousness from analytical-verbal (left hemisphere) to passive-global (right hemisphere). Finally, there is evidence that alcohol depresses the subcortical center that regulates intensity of attention.

> Recordings in different brain regions indicate that the reticular formation is especially sensitive to the depressant effect of alcohol. Since this structure has the function of mediating attention and suppressing distraction responses, this may account for the disinhibitory effects of alcohol.[24]

The term "disinhibition" has been often used erroneously to explain the effects of alcohol. It is commonly believed that alcohol simply destroys our inhibitions, automatically releasing deep, pent-up impulses that lead to immature and even criminal behavior. The Freudians define superego as that entity which dissolves in alcohol, meaning that conscience and controls tend to melt away when one is intoxicated. This view would seem to be supported by the fact that many crimes are committed in the intoxicated state, and that about half of the prison population is incarcerated for alcohol-related crimes.[25]

However, the central nervous system does not work in this manner. The brain does not contain "brake mechanisms" that hold back unsocialized impulses. Rather, it contains computer-like programs that analyze and organize input. Alcohol does weaken this system, leading to faulty processing, poor judgment, and weak control of attention. There is disinhibition of attention, not of the id. As in all absorbing conditions, intoxicated attention is at the mercy of external stimuli; if they are such as to arouse violence, then violence dominates internal processing. However, there is no evidence that the alcohol itself releases violent impulses. In fact, it seems to have the opposite effect. One investigator noted that "in laboratory rats, alcohol generally depresses various forms of behavioral expression, including sexual, aggressive, and feeding behavior."[26] Similarly at the human level, studies with projective tests seem to indicate that alcohol actually weakens acting-out tendencies.[27]

Since alcohol is used fairly extensively, there would be continuing pandemonium if it destroyed all controls. People would become unfit to live with. Actually, though, because alcohol favors the blurring over of individualistic drives, it makes us feel a part of the whole situation around us; in a social setting we would feel more disposed to mingle with others, to be one-with them. Alcohol is known as a socializing drug, and, other things being equal, this seems to be true. Alcohol does not dissolve superego — it dissolves ego and ego-involvement, i.e., the feeling of being evaluated and on the spot. When we are high, we tend to drop our usual expectations about self and others; we become less fussy, more accepting, and thus more sociable creatures. George Jean Nathan expressed this when he said, "I drink to make other people interesting."

Alcohol also has stimulant effects. For example, in discussing its pharmacology, Barry noted that the "generalized change in the central nervous sytem, caused by the drug, may add a pleasurable feeling of novelty and adventure."[28] Alcohol stimulates adrenal functioning, which produces broad activating effects throughout the body. In itself, increased adrenalin would be experienced as anxiety. But when combined with the partially anesthesized frontal lobes, the result is relaxed arousal and expansiveness. Men often perceive this condition as a feeling of power and strength[29]; however, it appears that alcohol enhances whatever experience happens to be present at the time the person is drinking, rather than always leading to a particular reaction. Drinking might result in a feeling of power in young men brought together in a group, but it might just as easily be a feeling of sociability, belligerence, sentimentality, or a tendency to cry easily.

In their book *Drunken Comportment,* MacAndrew and Edgerton presented extensive cross-cultural data to show that drunken behavior is largely determined by social expectation and definition. People learn from the cultural mores that by taking alcohol they are automatically granted a "Time Out," and will be held less accountable for what they do or feel. They learn that one is "not really oneself" when drunk, and therefore cannot be expected to comply with life's usual demands. Society grants permission for an altered state of consciousnesss to occur, and legitimizes the experience.

> In many societies persons have available to them the option of calling Time Out by producing "an altered state of consciousness" in themselves. Concerning this last mentioned procedure, we would make the following points: (1) while such an "alteration in consciousness" can be brought about in many ways, it is most frequently achieved by the ingestion of one or another presumably psychoactive agent, and (2) alcohol is far and away the most frequently used substance for this purpose.[30]

Marijuana

> Marijuana consciousness is one that, ever so gently, shifts the center
> of attention from habitual shallow purely verbal guidelines and repetitive
> secondhand ideological interpretations of experience to more direct,
> slower, absorbing, occasionally microscopically minute, engagement
> with sensing phenomena during the high moments or hours after one has
> smoked.... I have spent about as many hours high as I have spent in
> movie theaters ... with about the same degree of alteration of my
> normal awareness. —*Allen Ginsberg*

After movies and television, the most notable recreational development of our time has been the increased use of marijuana. This is a significant development because marijuana is not just a replication of alcohol; rather, it is more diverting and represents a definite step-up in absorption. The recreational power of marijuana has been demonstrated by the fact that it has made great inroads into American culture in spite of being an illegal drug.

Prior to 1960 marijuana was unknown in mainstream America. By 1980, however, sixty-five tons of it were being used every day in this country.[31] In that year, 25 billion dollars were spent for marijuana.[32] Each year more of it, in more potent forms, is being smuggled across the borders. Marijuana shipments seized in the 1960s generally contained less than 1 percent THC, which is the active ingredient in the drug. Recent shipments, however, average 3 to 4 percent THC, and in some cases are as high as 10 to 14 percent.[33] Although other drugs are favored from time to time, none has attained the wide acceptance that marijuana has — excepting alcohol, of course. Use of marijuana is no longer an underground practice; many believe that it is close to being legally sanctioned. A recent NIMH report concluded that "cannabis use is more than a fad and may well prove to be an enduring cultural pattern in the United States."[34]

Marijuana comes close to producing the standard version of the absorbed state. After smoking marijuana, a person starts to have that spellbound look. It is the look that says nothing much is happening on the outside — no self-expression, no goal-oriented action, no reality testing. But much is going on inside in terms of experience and attention; internally, there is a "luminous haze."

> Often nothing will appear to be happening to the outside observer, aside from a few individuals slowly smoking marijuana, staring into space and, occasionally, giggling at nothing in particular, yet each mind will be crowded with past or imagined events and emotions, and significance of massive proportions will be attributed to the scene, so that activity will be imagined where there is none. Each minute will be imputed with greater significance; a great deal will be thought to have occurred in a short space of time. . . . Time, therefore, will be seen as being more drawn-out.[35]

Like other absorbing entertainments, marijuana requires a particular set and setting to induce its effects. Set refers to the person's readiness to suspend evaluative processing and the generalized reality orientation. Setting refers to conditions that are safe, quiet, and free of distraction.

Set and setting are important for marijuana but not for alcohol. In fact, there is a tendency to take alcohol against the set and setting, i.e., when the situation is not recreational but we want to make it so. Alcohol creates its own time-out; special conditions are not needed to nurse it along. It is precisely when we are too involved in work or ego that we feel a need to take a drink and are helped by it. Alcohol is used when we want to move some experience from the world of work to the world of play — when we want to take the edge off the business luncheon, or to make it easy for strangers to mingle at a party. In this respect, alcohol is like a mild or conventional diversion, mixing work and play. On the other hand, marijuana is best experienced in a situation that is set apart and free of workaday distractions. The difference here is evident in how both drugs are used socially. Alcohol is the means to the goal of more relaxed social interaction. With marijuana, however, the drug experience itself is the goal, and the presence of other people is desired only if they enhance this effect.

The fact that alcohol does not require set and setting but marijuana does reveals an important distinction between the physiological effects of the two drugs. Alcohol does not need set and setting because, as we have seen earlier, its main physiological effect is to depress forebrain functioning. However, set and setting are necessary for marijuana, indicating that this drug does not depress the forebrain physiologically. In other words, the drug user has to do it himself by setting up conditions that do not require master code processing. Studies of the physiological effects of the two drugs bear out these differences. While alcohol is a depressant that affects the cortex and especially the forebrain, marijuana is a stimulant that affects primarily the subcortical centers.[36]

Research now shows that the primary physiological and chemical changes induced by marijuana occur especially in the "deep brain" and the limbic area.[37] This area processes the *experience* component of psychological functioning — the feeling of being aware. Here are centers that mediate arousal, attention, and pleasure. The deep brain is sometimes described as the sensory-feeling area. It is a receiving station that collects "raw" sensory input from all over the organism before it is corrected and modified by the higher centers. The organism's basic emotional complexes are also believed to be in this area. The deep brain likely contains some of the characteristics described in Freud's concepts of id and unconscious, although it is probably much more than just sex and aggression impulses. In infancy, before the forebrain is programmed and takes control, the child functions on the basis of the deep brain and thus is an emotional creature, oriented to pleasure and direct sensory input. The images, associations, and emotional complexes developed during this time are recorded in the deep brain. The adult brain — the forebrain — normally suppresses these old impressions but, as discussed in Chapter 3, they can be reactivated during stories and other absorbed experiences when the master codes are suspended.

Normally the limbic area is subordinate to the forebrain. "The frontal lobe is characterized . . . by its multiple associations with the limbic system," wrote Walle Nauta. "The reciprocity in the anatomical relationship suggests that the frontal cortex both monitors and modulates limbic mechanisms."[38] However, it seems that marijuana, by stimulating the subcortical areas, upsets this balance and gives the upper hand to the limbic area. The forebrain tends to lose control of attention to the sensory-feeling area, making the person more suggestible, self-forgetful and susceptible to sensory fascinations. Some researchers have speculated that drugs like marijuana "may allow the individual to exist at a phylogenetically old mammalian level, literally within the emotional brain itself, free from the conflict which is constant between the old sensory and feeling oriented system and the newly imposed 'civilization brain.'"[39]

The difference between alcohol and marijuana can be further examined in terms of their effects on attention. Alcohol weakens the attentional field, breaking down distinctions and divisions, blurring together figure, ground, and distractions; it produces a global state by leveling out attention. Marijuana, on the other hand, produces a total attentional state by excluding everything except the central focus. Attention is primarily selectivity, so that when marijuana stimulates the neurophysiological center regulating attention, the result is an increase in selectivity. In marijuana experience, the attentional figure seems to stand out vividly, more separated from the ground. In a questionnaire study of marijuana users to determine what reactions were commonly experienced in the drug state, there were numerous reports of heightened selectivity of attention, as indicated in these responses:

> "Things seen are seen more sharply in that their edges, contours, stand out more sharply against the background."
>
> "My visual perception of space around me is changed so that what I'm looking at is very real and clear but everything else I'm not focusing on visually seems farther away or otherwise less real or clear."
>
> "If I am paying attention to some particular part of my body, the rest of my body fades away a lot so the part I'm attending to stands out more sharply."[40]

The different attentional effects of alcohol and marijuana have been demonstrated with electrical recordings from the brain. In a double-blind study, after subjects had been administered social doses of either alcohol, marijuana, or placebo, researchers obtained from them an EEG-derived measure (CNV Amplitude) which is "an objective electrophysiological measure of changes in attentional processes."[41] This measure is high when attention is intense, but low when attention is distracted. Below are listed the mean CNV Amplitude in microvolts for each drug condition:

Drug	CNV Amplitude
marijuana	16.6
placebo	13.9
alcohol	11.5

In this study, the placebo condition represents the level of everyday attention. The results show that marijuana increases the everyday level, while alcohol decreases it. These findings would seem to lend credence to the practice of taking beer to counteract the effects of marijuana. The study also supports the old notion that taking a drink softens the hard edges of life. On the other hand, marijuana sharpens them, but in a way that leads to rich and expanded perception.

> Marijuana's reduction of attention to inputs ... is not a phenomenon of general toxicity, as is the effect of alcohol, with its quite uniform decline in all performance areas. It is, rather, a narrowing of the perceptual field along with a concomitant sharpening of focus in the actor's chosen vector of attention—e.g., listening, seeing, tasting, touching, introspection.
>
> The altered sense of time, I suspect, is both cause and effect of this reduction and sharpening of focus. The listener "knows" music is moving at its normal tempo, yet it seems slow enough (or his perception is now "fast" enough) for him to hear instrumental nuances, pick out notes and watch them blend

into chords, in ways that he never can master in the normal listening state. Effects are analogous in other areas — for example, savoring the component flavors in food, or following the train of ideation in the flow of consciousness. As attention and receptivity become circumscribed, the perceptual field becomes one of discrete tunnels; the capacity to receive, break down, and inspect gestalts ("getting into") is enhanced.[42]

The fact that it stimulates attention and the sensory-feeling area of the brain explains why marijuana has often been referred to as a "sensual" drug. The heart of the enjoyment is sensory enhancement, the enriched experiencing of seeing, hearing, taste, and smell. In the world of marijuana experience, the objects of fascination are those that appeal to the senses — music, incense, psychedelic art, and scenes that offer a play of light and shadow. This sensory enhancement, however, is not due to a lowering of sensory thresholds. Experimental investigators find no evidence that marijuana changes the level of visual acuity or other receptor functioning.[43] Apparently, the "sensory" effect is not mediated peripherally but centrally, with the stimulation of the deep brain. In all likelihood, sensory enhancement is primarily attentional enhancement. Marijuana does not enhance all sensory modalities at once but only one at a time, and the one being attended to seems to take total control of experiencing.

> When you're stoned you're not really listening *to* music, it's like you're *in* the music. I feel sometimes that it's not a record I'm listening to, but that the music is all around me, like I was in the middle of the group playing. And I sometimes hear something new and different when I get into a record stoned, no matter how many times I've heard it before. It's like sometimes I can hear Jimmy Smith's fingernails clicking on the keyboard an instant before I hear the note he's playing.[44]

Although attention is heightened in such an experience, it is not everyday concentration, but absorption. Descriptions of marijuana experience usually make reference to the qualities found in absorption. A self-forgetfulness develops: "I would keep forgetting what I was doing."[45] The basic codes that support personal identity are weakened. The body image may fade, sense of time is altered, and the perception of space and distance is changed. Master codes lose control of attention, impairing functions related to intention, purpose, or goal-orientation. The person stoned on marijuana typically has a problem keeping track of things. He cannot remember what he just said or what he wanted to say; he seems unable to stay on the subject as his thoughts slip away from him. Similarly, he has difficulty reading and remembering what he just read.

Researchers usually describe the effects of marijuana as cognitive and memory impairments. A more accurate assessment, however, would recognize that what appear to be memory and thinking deficits are simply the result of the altered attentional priorities.

> One of the most frequently cited effects of marijuana is its apparent interference with short-term memory. Early attempts to document this effect with controlled research led to inconsistent results. Some investigators found such an effect, but others have not. . . . However, recent studies in this area were based on a more systematic analysis of the processes involved in short-term memory, and these studies have yielded more consistent results. In brief, these results suggest that it is the information and acquisition phases of short-term memory that are most susceptible to marijuana effects, the phases that are heavily dependent on attention. . . . We concluded that when marijuana does affect short-term memory, it probably does so through an interference or change in attention rather than through a direct biochemical action in the memory storage system.[46]

As noted in this passage, marijuana has often been found to have variable and inconsistent effects. This is probably due to the unstable relationship that marijuana brings about between the deep brain and the forebrain. Except at very high dosage levels, the ascendance of the deep brain over the forebrain is tenuous and very much dependent on psychological factors—set and setting. While this drug may have some secondary depressant effects, it does not produce much change in forebrain functioning as measured by the EEG.[47] Because of this, apparently the forebrain can retake control of attention if the external situation warrants it. Longtime users of marijuana claim that they can voluntarily bring themselves down from a high.[48] When they are subjects in a research study, marijuana smokers often complain that having to work on experimental tasks keeps them from getting high; a lab situation is hardly conducive to absorbed experience. It is not surprising, therefore, that a number of investigators have commented on the waxing and waning of marijuana effects—periods of absorption alternating with intervals of realistic attention. Studies have found that the drug sometimes impaired task performance, sometimes had no effect, and sometimes even improved performance. Such variability, which is obviously due to set and setting, does not occur with alcohol, which always depresses the forebrain through biochemical action.

If set and setting are not right, apparently marijuana is not a very enjoyable experience. This is probably the reason why the novice fails to get high in the first attempts to use marijuana. Initial apprehensions about taking the drug might well make it difficult to adopt the frame of mind needed to realize its effects. The more distressed the mental state, the greater the likelihood of a "bad trip." Distress implies intense master code processing and activity in the forebrain. In this case, all of the sensory enhancement stimulated by marijuana would get focused on the distress, heightening it into panic and paranoid concerns. In the bad trip, the forebrain is not neutralized by set and setting.

The Psychedelics

Alcohol is mental lulling; marijuana is absorption; but the psychedelics are sheer fascination.

> About three-quarters of an hour after [taking LSD] . . . a different quality of consciousness came with a rush. Nothing was definably changed, but the room was suddenly transfigured. All objects stood out in space in an amazing way and seemed luminous. I was aware of the space between objects, which was pure vibrating crystal. Everything was beautiful. Everything was right. Each smallest thing was uniquely important yet fitted perfectly into the whole. My little ego seemed removed, and I felt that I saw clearly and purely for the first time in my life. I wept with relief and joy. I felt unworthy of such blessedness. The tears streamed down like a releasing fountain. I felt no tension, no self-consciousness, no self-concern; only an all comprehensive well-being. . . .
>
> As I looked around, the colors in the room became more vivid. The greens and blues were particularly lovely. Each object that I looked at held my fascinated attention. Each had a proper place in this crystal space. The living essence of each seemed ready to break through its clear-cut outline. . . .
>
> We walked around the garden together. It was like walking in Paradise. Everything was composed and harmonized. I felt I had never really seen this garden before. I was enchanted with each plant, leaf, flower, tree and trunk and the earth itself. Each blade of grass stood up separate and distinct, edged with light. Each was supremely important.[49]

This, of course, is a firsthand report of a psychedelic experience, typical of many such reports now found in the literature. It contains the basic ingredients of absorbed experience. Psychologically, this person is outside of everyday reality; the whole scene is new and fresh. There is much evidence of total attention; objects are "vivid" and "luminous." Everything is perceived for its own sake, with no implication for self or practical concern. Everything appears to be meaningful and significant, not for personal reasons, but for the sense of harmony and beauty that pervades all. There is such richness of experiencing that this person is overcome and weeps with joy.

What happens in the brain that makes possible such a luminous vision? Basically, chemical reactions that are similar to those produced by marijuana. LSD, mescaline, and psilocybin are all stimulants that affect the subcortical areas.[50] These drugs are considered the major psychedelics; marijuana, which in large doses acts like LSD, is considered a minor psychedelic.[51]

While the effects of marijuana are sometimes variable and uncertain, there is no question about the impact of the major psychedelic drugs. They lock the person in a spell. They cause deep brain experience to flare up vividly into attention, completely cutting the person off from reality. Although the LSD user may passively know that his experiences are due to the drug, he finds it impossible to control attention. These effects go far beyond those of the usual marijuana high. For example, people who are high on marijuana do drive cars, although this is dangerous. However, a person intoxicated with LSD would not even be able to attempt such a routine activity. The marijuana high allows for some social interaction, as at a pot party. However, psychedelic drugs absorb a person so completely that all social interaction is avoided; in fact, such drugs so immobilize a person psychologically that the protective supervision of other people is usually necessary.

Psychedelic drugs differ from marijuana in another important way. They do have some direct effect on the cortex and forebrain. What little is known about the cortical action of psychedelic drugs indicates that they disrupt the chemical transmission of information from one nerve cell to another.[52] Although each of the psychedelic drugs has a different chemical makeup and a different mode and site of action, in general they seem to interfere with the transmitter agents in the nervous system. This alters the functioning of the cortical programs and constancies that stabilize thinking and perception, resulting in disordered sense of time, space, and identity. Attentional control becomes extremely weak. "I can't shut things out of my mind and everything closes in on me," reported one individual who was high on LSD. "Nothing settles in my mind — not even for a second. It just comes in and then it goes out. My mind goes away to many things that come into my head at once and I lose control."[53] Set and setting are necessary with psychedelic drugs — not so much to realize their effects, since they do act chemically on the forebrain, but to insure a positive experience.

In spite of the loss of mental control, the capacity for sensory-attentional experiencing is greatly magnified. "One of the most emphasized fundamentals in the total complex of the psychedelic or imaginative experience is its quality of absolute absorption: attention. To whatever the subject turns, his whole being is given."[54] This declaration opens R.A. Durr's book *Poetic Vision and the Psychedelic Experience*. Durr goes on to quote a report from the psychedelic literature: "Under the influence of the mushroom, one's power of concentration is far more pronounced than normally. You become deeply absorbed in whatever you may be thinking. There is no external distraction" (p. 3). Attention is totally controlled by the sensory enhancement. "Everything glows with a luminosity of its own, and texture becomes three dimensional. There is a tendency to dwell upon the minute, a fleck on the wall, the grain of a piece of wood."[55] A pharmacology text sums up the absorbing nature of psychedelic experience in this way: "LSD and mescaline in moderate doses have been found to be as potent as hypnotic induction itself in increasing the suggestibility of subjects.... There is enhanced awareness of sensory input often with increased sense of clarity, but diminished control of what is being experienced."[56]

Usually psychological research into drug effects is undertaken to demonstrate some impairment. In a comprehensive study of LSD effects, however,

Barr and her associates adopted an exploratory perspective and were able to document the positive and negative changes resulting from the drug.

> A number of findings with the experimental tasks may be summarized as indicating impairment of active functions (concentrating, directing attention, voluntarily controlling thought images, learning complex materials, maintaining sets, and rejecting distractions), and a general movement toward more passivity (more intrusive thoughts and images, decreased sense of being actively in charge). . . .
>
> We assume that the drug (LSD) does act on the brain in some way that interferes with the voluntary control of attending; deliberate focusing or concentrating becomes more difficult, and attention is more easily captured by fascinating adventitious distractions.[57]

What all of this adds up to is an extreme condition of suggestibility. Psychedelic drugs make the organism hypersuggestible to input from the deep brain. The drug pushes to the limits whatever ongoing experience is present there; the forebrain is not available to correct or modulate the effect. The result can be a heavenly experience or a hellish one, depending on the input from the sensory-feeling areas of the deep brain. If the person can adequately prepare himself for the drug by suspending anxious thoughts, and implementing the necessary set and setting, then the psychedelic experience is likely to be a heavenly one — the epitome of absorption. But if the person is unable to do this, then the experience will be an unwelcome one, a bad trip full of fear and distress. Whether it is a good or bad trip, consciousness is greatly augmented by sensory input that is not usually available. The person becomes suggestible and attuned to the "vibes" and nonverbal cues — i.e., the inherent meaning and significance that exists outside the verbal, everyday modes of interaction. The person has an expanded capacity to react intuitively and in terms of unconscious images, associations, and emotional complexes. This makes the experience seem deep, even spiritual.

The term "psychedelic" seems to be a good one for describing these highly absorbing drugs. Apparently, this word is not derived from "psycho," which means mind (i.e., forebrain). Rather, it comes from "psyche," the Greek word for "breath of life," the animating spirit or principle in the organism.[58] If any part of the brain is *psyche,* it is the sensory-feeling area of the deep brain with its centers for attention, arousal, and experience. "Psychedelic," therefore, refers to that which brings out this vitalizing effect — which these drugs do by stimulating the subcortical centers.

Subjects sometimes report that there seems to be a splitting of the self in the psychedelic state, with one self being outside and observing, while the other self is experiencing. This phenomenon apparently refers to the two domains of self and experience. There are not two selves, but rather, two sources of input — the activated deep brain (experience, "psyche"), and the relatively inactive forebrain (self, "psycho"). In a manner of speaking, the deep brain is passively observed by the forebrain. Such an explanation seems to be consistent with Paul MacLean's concept of the "triune brain," which regards the old deep brain and the new forebrain as different biological computers, each a separate system with its own awareness and characteristics.[59]

The experiences induced by recreational drugs are on a continuum with other absorbed states. William James compared alcohol intoxication to the experience of symphony concerts, literature and mystic consciousness. Walter Pahnke actually produced empirical evidence to show that mystical experience is likely to be a part of the drug effects induced by psilocybin.[60]

The enjoyment of beauty is an absorbing experience, characterized by a sense of awe and total involvement. Psychedelic drugs often absorb people in the beauty that is filtered out by everyday perception. In discussing his experiences with these drugs, Alan Watts stated that "time after time, this unprogrammed mode of attention, looking *at* things without looking *for* things, reveals the unbelievable beauty of the everyday world."[61] In describing his experiences with mescaline, Huxley felt that he must be seeing the world with the fresh perception that only great painters have.[62] The exalted experiences provided by the arts are similar to those provided by recreational drugs.

> To Schopenhauer . . . contemplation was the one requisite of aesthetic experience; a kind of contemplation that enables one to become so absorbed in the quality of what is being presented to the senses that the "Will" becomes still and all needs of the body silent. Drugs reportedly foster this kind of Nirvana and are so used by many today. For Nietzsche . . . man is able to lose his futile individuality in the mystic ecstasy of universal life under the Dionysiac spell of music, rhythm, and dance. The American Indian with his peyote and the modern jazz musician with his marijuana have discovered this kind of Dionysian ecstasy without formal knowledge of aesthetics.[63]

Interest in the psychedelics has waned since the 1960s. Nevertheless, these drugs represent a high-water mark in the modern push toward absorbed diversion and radical play. For awhile, the drug revolution stimulated much experimenting with psychedelics to foster creativity or to cure mental illness. Both ventures have come to naught. Psychedelic drugs can transport us to new worlds as nothing else can, but they do not program the forebrain with more effective codes for conducting the business of living. When the drug experience is over, the forebrain reasserts itself, and its longstanding codes and programs are likely to override any emotional insights that occurred when the person was high.

Chapter 7

The Recreational Value of People

There are moments when the affections rule and absorb the man....
The moment we indulge our affections, the earth is
metamorphosed. — *Ralph Waldo Emerson*

It is generally assumed that being with other people enhances recreational experience. The sharing, the sociable give-and-take, and the good feeling of fitting in — all of this creates a special excitement and significance that seems to be missing in solitary recreation. Expressions like "making merry" somehow suggest the presence of people as a necessary ingredient of enjoyment.

All of this may be true in some ideal sense, but in practice people seem to have a difficult time relaxing with each other. The fact that serving alcoholic drinks is often part of socializing shows that humans have a lot of reservations about letting go with other members of the species. It is interesting to note that nobody has to take a drink to enjoy a movie.

In modern times, the ascendancy of absorbed diversions has pushed social recreation to the background and raised questions about its adequacy. The big new diversions of our affluent civilization — movies, meditation, and to some extent television and marijuana — are basically solitary recreational experiences. Much the same is true even in sexual diversion, as we shall see in the next chapter; today, there is an emphasis on sex as sex, rather than on sex as relationship.

All of this does not mean that people are becoming more antisocial, only that in some cases diversion is preferred to socializing. In the past, people had to make do with each other as sources of recreation, but today there are powerful technologies that efficiently induce diversion experiences. Obviously, people do not always make good recreational objects for each other. There are some exceptions, as in the one-to-one involvements of love and friendship. But in public get-togethers people seem to be instinctively on guard. A story or drug or music is just for mental relaxation, but people constitute a completely different kind of stimulus. People belong primarily to the world of work, not play.

Human Interaction as Personal Business

People are basically business to each other. "What men call friendship," wrote La Rochefoucauld back in the seventeenth century, "is only a reciprocal conciliation of interests, an exchange of good offices; it is in short simply a form of barter from which self-love always expects to gain something." Such a view of human relationship may sound crass and cynical, but modern social scientists agree wholeheartedly with La Rochefoucauld. In fact, his insight about people has been embodied in "exchange theory,"[1] which constitutes the accepted view of human interaction in social psychology today.

The theory holds that social interaction is a kind of business — the bartering of desirable interpersonal commodities. Each partner in the interaction expects to realize a profit, not in terms of money but in terms of qualities that are highly valued in society or are intrinsically pleasing: good looks, status, power, sex, intelligence, charm, success. To be well-endowed with some of these commodities increases one's bargaining power in the interpersonal marketplace. For example, in one study it was found that highly attractive women would accept as dates only men in high-status careers, whereas unattractive women settled for men in lower-status occupations.[2] Thus, in the dating marketplace, attractiveness can be exchanged for high status. Exchange theory asserts that all human interaction is based on such a quid pro quo. Apparently nobody interacts for nothing.

According to exchange theory, human interaction is always being watched and evaluated; accounts are always kept regarding the interpersonal profits and losses. As in commercial business, profits must exceed the debits, which in relationships consist of time, energy, and other resources spent on the partner. If the person feels that he is giving more than he is getting, he is likely to withdraw from the relationship. What about the one-sided relationship that endures even though it seems to favor only one of the partners? Presumably, this would be a case of extending credit to a trusted partner, or paying off past debts, or investing in someone who is a good bet for the future. Some relationships are shaky business ventures, showing little profit to either partner; in such cases, the partners are usually highly evaluative of each other and self-conscious about the relationship. They keep track of what they give and what they get. On the other hand, in some relationships, the riches flow liberally both ways, so that there is no need to mind the books and keep track. Love and friendship are examples of such blessed relationships where the payoffs are so profuse that there hardly seems to be an exchange going on.

Yet there is *always* an exchange going on. Why else would loving relationships cool, and old friendships break up? Why is it that longstanding marriages sometimes end in divorce? Why do parents sometimes disown their children, and family members stop talking to each other? There is indeed an inherent accounting in human relations, one that transcends even family ties and custom. To have viable relations with others, one must be able to pay one's way. Society will make some allowances and extend credit for awhile, but in the long run nothing is free. The accountability of adults is an ironclad rule of social living; this principle has been recently reasserted in reality therapy and in the writings of O. Hobart Mowrer.[3] In infancy, the child is treated to a short period of unconditional love, but after that and especially in adulthood the individual must be able to trade fairly with others, or suffer the consequences.

Clinical observations strongly support the tenets of exchange theory. In fact, "exchange" may be too mild a term; modern scholarship finds that human interaction is competitive and usually characterized by the business of establishing dominance.[4] More than ever before, we are coming to understand the subtle manipulations by which humans use, control, hurt, and defeat each other. Seemingly innocent interactions can reflect underlying maneuvers and ruthless power struggles which today are euphemistically called "the games that people play."[5] No matter how civilized we presume to be, human existence continues to be a struggle, not for survival as in the animal kingdom, but for status, material comforts, and similar advantages. If we fail to manage our interactions adequately, then we are at risk for a whole range of psychological penalties — "put-downs," disappointments, distress, personal defeat — all of which lower one's value in the interpersonal marketplace.

Thus social interaction is psychological work, self-referent and evaluative, meaning that master code processing is involved. There is always a degree of self-consciousness when someone looks at us or talks to us. A set is immediately activated to assume some kind of social role, to organize a coherent response, and usually to make a good impression. Simply talking to another person is public behavior that must meet certain standards, so we evaluate the interaction as it occurs, knowing that the other person is also evaluating it. All of this entails fairly intense processing in the organism. When interacting with other people, it would be almost impossible to forget oneself completely, to the extent, for example, that we do when absorbed in a movie. Sexual interaction may be the only exception to this rule.

The level of business in human interaction has probably been intensified by modern living conditions. Just because there are now more people, living closer together in urban settings, one would expect human relations to be more competitive and contentious. The more competitive the social interaction, the more intense the master code processing, and the more difficult it is to relax. This may be one reason why the value of social recreation has waned in modern times, and in its place people have favored private, solitary recreation as found in the absorbed diversions.

In the past, human interactions were probably less frequent than they are today, with the result that recreational get-togethers made a greater contrast with everyday life. People were more separated physically and socially; prior to the twentieth century most people in the United States lived in a rural environment, with access to only a few social contacts outside the home. With no automobiles, no telephones, no radio, and no television, people were captive to the distances that separated them. In the past, too, role and status distinctions were greater, also tending to separate people. Interpersonal relations were formal, role-bound, and strongly constrained by custom and religious authority. Work and serious purpose dominated most of waking existence.

Under such circumstances, social recreations would be relaxing and highly valued. It would be exciting to get together with friends and neighbors, to talk leisurely, to play games, to set aside the stiff and proper roles. Such sociable activities would make a definite contrast with everyday life, and therefore would be recreational.

All of this has changed in today's world. Affluent society has given us an affluence of social contact. Modern working conditions permit and encourage socializing on the job; most professional and white collar work is entirely a matter of interacting with others. Radio and television have made it possible for the human voice and face to be almost everywhere. The telephone, automobile, and other amenities have greatly extended our ability to socialize almost continually and with a wide range of people. Indeed, modern civilization may have given us too much of a good thing, and thereby undercut its value as a recreational time-out. A person who socializes all day is likely to find nothing special about a get-together that offers only more socializing.

The sheer availability to people in modern times seems to have made social interactions more competitive and relationships more fragile. People are quick to look elsewhere if a particular relationship encounters difficulties; there is a tendency to be more evaluative and less tolerant. In fact, professional counselors encourage such an approach, with a strict application of exchange theory. For example, marriage is treated almost legalistically. Couples are told to define their relationship by contracts that specify what each partner can expect; they are encouraged to control each other's behavior by appropriate rewards, and in general keep account of the exchange.[6] A relationship must pay off or else. This was not the case in the past, when human interactions, especially marriage, were defined and controlled by society; the economics of human relations were tempered by custom and religious values. But the interpersonal marketplace has changed. It has gone from "socialistic" (externally regulated and subsidized) to laissez-faire; that is, the market is free, or at least determined only by the profit motive of the partners and what they can extract from each other. Today, social relations must stand on their own in highly competitive market conditions.

Such factors have had a drastic effect on interpersonal relations — making them less satisfying and less stable. The most obvious indication of this trend is the high divorce rate. The movement toward brief and superficial relationships has been noted by many social scientists. "As we enter the last quarter of the twentieth century," wrote Zick Rubin, "men and women in industrialized societies throughout the world may expect to have more acquaintances, more casual friendships, more fleeting romances, and fewer enduring relationships than ever before in history."[7] Alvin Toffler also commented on the hurried and transitory nature of our social involvements — another aspect of the "throw-away society" that is plagued by relentless change and obsolescence.[8] Christopher Lasch found exchange theory with a vengeance in what he has called our "culture of narcissism." Striving to extract rewards and realize interpersonal profits, modern adults, according to Lasch, are becoming increasingly manipulative and even combative in both their work and "play."

> Americans have not really become more sociable and cooperative, as the theorists of other-direction and conformity would like us to believe; they have merely become more adept at exploiting the conventions of interpersonal relations for their own benefit. Activities ostensibly undertaken purely for enjoyment often have the real object of doing others in. . . .
>
> The search for competitive advantage through emotional manipulation increasingly shapes not only personal relations but relations at work as well; it is for this reason that sociability can now function as an extension of work by other means. Personal life, no longer a refuge from deprivation suffered at work, has become as anarchical, as warlike, and as full of stress as the marketplace itself. The cocktail party reduces sociability to social combat. Experts write tactical manuals in the art of social survival, advising the status-seeking party-goer to take up a commanding position in the room, surround himself with a loyal band of retainers, and avoid turning his back on the field of battle. . . .
>
> Our society, far from fostering private life at the expense of public life, has made deep and lasting friendships, love affairs, and marriages increasingly difficult to achieve. As social life becomes more and more warlike and barbaric, personal relations, which ostensibly provide relief from these conditions, take on the character of combat. Some of the new therapies dignify this combat as "assertiveness" and "fighting fair in love and marriage." Others celebrate impermanent attachments under such formulas as "open marriage" and "open-ended commitments." Thus they intensify the disease they pretend to cure.[9]

Such views may seem exaggerated until one considers the casualties of modern social relations: psychiatric patients. The prevalence of psychiatric problems today is a good measure of how "warlike" social relations have become. One of the achievements of modern-day psychiatry and psychology is the recognition that so-called mental illness is often the outgrowth of the human social condition. In most cases, anxiety, depression, psychosomatic illness, paranoia, and other psychiatric symptoms can be traced to stressful human relations. Clinician-scholars like Alfred Adler, Harry Stack Sullivan, and Karen Horney viewed mental illness in terms of stressful relationships and the problems due to striving for superiority, loss of self-esteem, and feelings of envy. Such notions have been refined and elaborated in the work of Timothy Leary, Jay Hayley, and Eric Berne, who have focused on the reciprocal aspects of human interaction. The contributions of these and many other clinicians have established the principle that psychiatric problems are basically people problems.

In America today, there is a tremendous mental health establishment that involves thousands of professionally trained people, all kinds of treatment facilities and modalities, sophisticated medications, and generous government support. The size of this establishment reflects the high casualty rate of stressful interpersonal relations. It also reflects the failure of conventional social recreations to offset the tensions of everyday business. The unique benefits that once flowed from social recreation must now be obtained elsewhere—from psychotherapists and medications.

A recent development in the mental health field bears witness to what seems to be a failure of social recreation in modern times. In the 1950s, a wholly new psychotherapeutic-educational movement started to take shape with services such as sensitivity training, growth groups, Esalen-type experiences, and a variety of pop psychology seminars and workshops. All of these techniques were aimed, not at the traditional psychiatric patient suffering acute distress, but at people who seemed to be unable to relax with others, with the result that their social relations were all business and therefore unsatisfying. This new kind of patient was usually very effective at work and in the business side of life, but unable to benefit from sociable recreation. He was unable to experience others in a playful way, which is how people become interesting to each other and how friendships and other loving relationships get started. The traditional psychiatric patient cannot work because he is disabled by anxiety; the new patient cannot play because he is disabled by an overriding work or business orientation in his social relations. Attempts to treat the play-disabled patient started with Rogerian counseling. Unlike the traditional therapist, the Rogerian counselor did not have to analyze or diagnose his patient; he did not have to dispense insights to him.[10] All that was required was that he listen in an empathic way, much like a good buddy. The main function of the counselor was to provide "unconditional positive regard"—in other words, friendly understanding and nonevaluative acceptance, which, of course, is what most people get in their friendships. Such therapy has been referred to as the "purchase of friendship."

It is undeniable that human relationships are bonded during play, not during work. Although most interactions are businesslike, relationships take hold only to the extent that we can relax, open up, and enjoy the other person for his or her sake. Just as human personality itself first gets started in the playful world of childhood, so adult relationships—which are extensions of personality — get started in the playful world of sociable recreation. Court-ship, for example, is basically play — a sharing of diversions and enter-tainments. This leads to more intense social play in terms of love and sexual activity. Eventually, out of all of this comes a workable relationship that car-ries on the business of marriage and family. But it all starts in sociable play. And the modern breakdown of sociable recreation must be a factor in the prevalent decay of social relationships. "Today," wrote Toffler, "a vast sociological and psychological literature is devoted to the alienation presumed to flow from this fragmentation of relationships. Much of the rhetoric of ex-istentialism and the student revolt decries this fragmentation. It is said that we are not sufficiently 'involved' with our fellow man."[11]

Sociable Recreation

Ideally, sociable recreation is people getting together for the sheer enjoy-ment of being with others. This is easier said than done. If people simply came together with the avowed purpose of enjoying each other's company, the result would probably be self-consciousness, guardedness, and mild panic. Interact-ing with people is just too hot and businesslike to be approached in such a direct way. Rather, social interaction must always be approached indirectly, with the pretext of doing something else. We get together to have coffee, to dine out, to play cards, to dance, to go shopping. While all such activities have some purpose and enjoyment, the more significant pleasure comes from doing them with other people. The pretext is important because it takes the interac-tion off center-stage, allowing it to be more relaxed. The pretext also supports the interaction by giving it some direction so that people have something to do and talk about.

Throughout history, one of the most popular pretexts for getting people together has been playing games. Games are social phenomena, as Roger Caillois recognized in his classic text on the subject.[12] Kaplan pointed out that games are first of all cooperative ventures; the competition occurs in a context where there is congenial agreement among the players about the rules and roles.[13] Games are sociable events not only when played informally, but also when played as organized and professional sports. Such games attract spec-tators whose contagious good mood usually makes socializing easy. Nor is sociability limited to games of skill; games of chance, such as church bingo, horse racing, and gambling provide the same fellowship. Although the manifest purpose of games is winning, the underlying purpose is to stir up some fun with friendly people. To be a player in a game is to have a ready-made role and interaction which makes socializing less self-conscious.

The somewhat artifactual setup of social recreation — arranging a pre-text, calling a time-out, and using space and stimuli that are different from everyday life—is society's attempt to tone down the forebrain and the master codes. Before a person can relax and disarm himself, the conditions must be relatively free of business and evaluation. Talking about the characteristics of a party as an example of sociable recreation, Jeanne Watson wrote that "people should set aside critical standards, should not pass judgment on themselves or each other."[14] It is only when conditions are nonevaluative, as in Rogerian counseling, that people open up.

To the extent that we can trust certain individuals to be nonevaluative and nonthreatening, conditions are ripe for the development of those "non-business" relationships found among friends and lovers. This is social recreation at its best. Poets and philosophers have often made observations about the nature of friendship, recognizing that such relationships are inherently relaxing, and therefore different from normal social interaction. Katherine Mansfield wrote: "I always felt that the great high privilege, relief and comfort of friendship was that one had to explain nothing." A similar view was held by Charles Lamb, who described friendship in terms of being free to talk nonsense, and having that nonsense respected. And according to Emerson, "A friend is a person with whom I may be sincere; before him I may think aloud." Love and friendship represent respite from the evaluative business of everyday life. Emily Dickinson expressed this when she wrote to a friend: "I felt it shelter to speak to you." Saint Bernard of Clairvaux expressed a similar sentiment: "We find rest in those we love." Here is a Quaker lady writing to a dear friend, and the experience described is close to absorption: "It was such a joy to see thee. I wish I could tell how much thee is to my life. I always turn to thee as a sort of rest and often just think about thy face when I get troubled."

The conditions for relaxed interaction are most often found with people who are similar to ourselves, with whom we are most likely to feel safe from threat and evaluation. Social relaxation and recreation, it would appear, is a highly ethnocentric affair, best accomplished with our own kind. To be like is to be liked. Friendly and loving relations always involve a blending-in process, being close to, a part of. They move us toward the experience of oneness or being one-with that is the end point of all absorption.

Social psychologists consistently find that friends and lovers are highly similar to each other, not only in variables such as age, social class, and education, but also in values and beliefs.[15] Interacting with people who possess traits similar to our own makes it easier to feel kinship. As Zick Rubin pointed out in his book *Liking and Loving,* shared traits make it more likely that people will agree with each other, and so feel free from evaluation and criticism. All of this, of course, holds true for the most intimate of relationships: Marital partners select each other on the basis of similarities, not differences.

Hundreds of statistical studies, dating back to Francis Galton's study of hereditary genius in 1870, have found husbands and wives to be significantly similar to one another not only with respect to such biological and social characteristics as age, race, religion, education, and social status, but also with respect to physical features like height and eye color, and psychological characteristics like intelligence.[16]

It is almost impossible to relax with people who are perceived as being different from ourselves. Prospective friends, therefore, tend to submerge their differences and individualities. "Achievement and uniqueness are both likely to be seen as barriers to friendship, rather than advantages," wrote Watson. "People almost feel obliged to assure their friends of love and acceptance and to pretend that achievement and uniqueness do not exist."[17] On the other hand, friends often solidify their relationship by griping together about outsiders. Such conversation is often a part of relaxed, sociable interaction, as long as its subject is an outsider.

All of this is not to say that friends, families, and sociable groups do not have their differences. But when such differences are emphasized, interactions cease to be recreational. Actually, since interpersonal differences are the rule in human affairs, love and friendship are usually imperfectly realized, and relaxing relations are always at risk. It is no wonder, therefore, that two other popular diversions—alcohol and music—are often used to support recreational interaction. What we have already said about alcohol improving sociability, also applies to music. When there is lively music in the air at a get-together, our social sensibilities are enlivened. There are songs that just put us in the mood to like people, which is why music is so often used to express feelings of love. Music, of course, is the basis of one of the most sociable recreations—dancing.

One kind of sociable interaction does not need alcohol or music—it is intoxicating and lyrical enough. The experience is being in love.

Falling in Love

Falling in love is no more than this: attention abnormally fastened upon another person. —*José Ortega y Gasset*

The term "love" has many meanings; as used here it refers to an intensely romantic state of infatuation. Being in love is not a matter of sexual excitement and pursuit, but simply a longing to be with and one-with the loved one. It is characterized by feelings of self-surrender and an almost naive idealization of the loved one. It usually overtakes a person in young adulthood, and at most occurs only a couple of times in a lifetime. It is often referred to as an immature form of love, but there is no doubt about the reality of this state. It is the kind of love that one falls headlong into, often unexpectedly or irrationally, so that for awhile one feels completely captivated by another person.

It tends to occur suddenly and dramatically, causing a qualitative shift in experiencing, much like a figure-ground reversal. This sudden shift is the reason for expressions like "falling into" and "being hit by" love. For those who do not recall the feeling, here is how it happened to a former British prime minister, no less, who at the age of sixty suddenly fell in love with a twenty-five year old woman.

> I was sitting with her in the dining room on Sunday morning — the others being out in the garden or walking — and we were talking and laughing on just our old accustomed terms. Suddenly, in a single instant, without premonition on my part or any challenge on hers, the scales dropped from my eyes; the familiar features and smile and gestures and words assumed an absolutely new perspective; what had been completely hidden from me was in a flash half-revealed, and I dimly felt, hardly knowing, not at all understanding it, that I had come to a turning point in my life.[18]

Being in love exhibits the characteristics of absorbed experience — total attention, decreased self-feeling, and relaxed arousal. There is a general usurpation of attention by an object of fascination, i.e., the loved one. Couples in love never seem to get enough of each other; if they are not with each other then they are thinking about each other. It was for this reason that Emerson said of the lovestruck young man, "He became all eye when one was present, and all memory when one was gone."[19] This is close to total attention. Lovers do make more eye contact with each other, as demonstrated in a study by Zick Rubin, who found that couples who were judged to be strongly in love spent more time looking at each other than did couples whose love was judged to be weak.[20] This need to have the loved one in the center of the attentional field is comparable to an addiction, according to psychologist John Money. "The person who has fallen in love," wrote Money, "becomes addicted to the love partner — obsessed and preoccupied with the next 'fix' of being together or talking together."[21] As in the case of addiction, the lovers feel right when they are together, but when they are separated they are lovesick. And when they are together they find every opportunity to lose themselves in the egoless experience of smooching. As Freud recognized, the sense of self almost ceases to exist when one is in love.

> Normally, there is nothing of which we are more certain than the feeling of our self, our own ego. This ego appears to us as something autonomous and unitary, marked off distinctly from everything else. . . . [However,] at the height of being in love the boundary between ego and object threatens to melt away. Against all the evidence of his senses, a man who is in love declares that "I" and "you" are one, and is prepared to behave as if it were a fact.[22]

As we have seen in story entertainment, total attention makes objects seem more real and significant than they are. Much the same happens when one is in love; total attention makes the loved one more perceptually salient and important. The loved one is overvalued, idealized, and idolized. "Others often find ridiculous the enthusiasm with which a lover speaks about the one he loves," wrote Lepp. "They know the individual in question to be a completely ordinary person."[23] This fixing of attention on the image of the beloved and ignoring whatever contradicts that perception makes being in love close to the hypnotic state, as Freud pointed out:

> From being in love to hypnosis is evidently only a short step. The respects in which the two agree are obvious. There is the same humble subjection, the same compliance, the same absence of criticism, towards the hypnotist as toward the loved object. There is the same sapping of the subject's own initiative.[24]

Being in love has also been compared with other absorbed conditions, such as intoxication. "Novelists and poets are not completely wrong," wrote Lepp, "when they describe love as being a kind of emotional intoxication. In its intense states it reminds one of drunkenness or of mystical ecstasy. All the other psychological powers find themselves considerably inhibited if not absolutely paralyzed."[25] On the other hand, to Ralph Waldo Emerson the high of being in love was more like a psychedelic experience than an alcoholic one. A hundred years before Huxley claimed that mescaline cleansed the doors of perception, Emerson said that love in a young man "opened his perceptions of natural beauty." Emerson seemed intrigued with the fact that being in love makes the beauty in nature come alive, making perceptions vivid and significant. The man in love, he said, "is a palace of sweet sounds and sights; he dilates; he is twice a man." The sweetheart's "existence makes the world rich." According to Emerson, being in love was a time

> when the moonlight was a pleasing fever and the stars were letters and the flowers ciphers and the air was coined into song; when all business seemed an impertinence, and all the men and women running to and fro in the streets, mere pictures.
> The passion rebuilds the world of youth. It makes all things alive and significant. Nature grows conscious. Every bird on the boughs of the tree sings now to his heart and soul. The notes are almost articulate. The clouds have faces as he looks on them. The trees of the forest, the waving grass and the peeping flowers have grown intelligent; and he almost fears to trust them with the secret which they seem to invite. Yet nature soothes and sympathizes. In the green solitude he finds a dearer home than with men.[26]

In addition to becoming sensitive to the hidden beauty in the world, the person in love finds himself attracted to such things as poetry, sentimental songs, and dancing — all of which match the sense of flow and harmony in him. Being in love just naturally leads many people to write poetry, and has often inspired excellent verse in otherwise mundane poets. The rhythmic arts of poetry and music have been especially effective in conveying the raptures of love. Musical rhythms and lyric imagery seem especially expressive of the walking-on-air, being-in-another-world feeling that is inherent in love's relaxed arousal. In his classic treatise *On Love,* Stendhal wrote: "A rapid waltz in a drawing-room lit up by innumerable candles, throws young people into a state of intoxication which banishes shyness, increases their sense of power and in the end gives them the courage to fall in love."[27]

For all of its color and magic, however, this spell of being in love soon passes, like any other diversion. Being in love is no way to act in the everyday world, where human relations are essentially competitive and business-like. It is a violation of the master codes. Therefore, the romantic spell does not long defy the business side of life, and eventually succumbs to it. If the lovers get married, then their love ceases to be total attention, and instead takes on the business qualities of living and working together; affection becomes a matter of habits, not absorbed experience. But whether the lovers live together the rest of their lives, or separate and never see each other again, the interlude of being in love is looked back on as one of the high points of life. As Emerson said, "The remembrance of these visions outlasts all other remembrances."

Chapter 8

Sexual Experience

Any couple, married or unmarried, may now plan most of
their copulation as recreational. — *John Money*

Romantic love often leads to sexual experience. Sex is certainly a break
from routine, and, as we shall see, the enjoyment of it depends on absorbed
attention. However, sex is no simple diversion; it has many entanglements
with the everyday. In fact, although it has the potential for being supreme
play (pleasurable ecstasy), it also has a serious side and is supreme work
(reproduction). It defines the polar extremes of existence; no wonder that it
has been such a contentious issue in our lives.

From Procreation to Recreation

"Sex above all needs to be more of a relaxed act." — quoted in the
Hite Report on Male Sexuality

In the Judeo-Christian tradition, sex is sanctioned primarily as biological
function and social business, for reproduction and the bonding of marriage.
This "procreational ethic" is embedded in our laws, social mores, child-rearing
practices, and even private experience.[1] Sex is seen as serious business — a not
unreasonable position given the risks of unwanted pregnancy and disease.
Like recreational drug use, sex is a diversion with potentially grave consequences. Even Freud considered it to be a "heavy" in human affairs.

The procreational ethic says that since the purpose of sex is to reproduce
the race, it is permissible only to married couples, who presumably are engaged in procreation. Heterosexual intercourse is the only acceptable outlet;
masturbation and homosexuality are considered perversions. Foreplay should
be brief and should culminate in intercourse. According to the procreational
ethic, sex is the prerogative of the male, and women either cannot or should
not enjoy it. Sexual pleasure consists primarily in the release of tensions, which
occurs in the male orgasm.

In emphasizing the work aspects of sex, the procreational ethic has depreciated those aspects related to play and experience. It makes people squeamish and guilt-ridden about engaging in sexual activity.[2] This negative conditioning carries over even into marriage, where sex is sanctioned. Anxiety makes people susceptible to distractions that prevent total involvement in sexual experiencing. Furthermore, the marital situation itself is the source of many distractions. Sex is likely to suffer in the face of arguments, financial difficulties, in-law problems, pregnancies, noisy children at the bedroom door, and fatigue. And because sex is often perceived as a barometer of the relationship, husband and wife feel obliged to maintain a sexual schedule as a sign of their love. In an article on sex as work ethic, Masters and Johnson pointed out that spouses tend to get into a routine with sex, engaging in it much like other goal-oriented, workaday activities, to the point where boredom sets in.[3] It becomes the work of releasing tensions, rather than the diversion of maximizing pleasure.

There is much data to indicate that the procreational marital situation has not been very effective in satisfying sexual needs. Masters and Johnson estimated that there is some type of sexual inadequacy in about half of the marriages today.[4] In Kinsey's time, although two-thirds of the adult male population was married, marital intercourse accounted for fewer than half of the orgasms (46 percent) experienced by males.[5] In her survey, Shere Hite reported that 16 percent of the husbands admitted to having extramarital sex during the first year of marriage. Of those men married for more than two years, over 70 percent had been unfaithful to their wives.[6] Hite's survey of women also yielded an interesting statistic that is relevant here: Only 30 percent of women regularly experience orgasm during intercourse, but nearly all women who masturbate have orgasms regularly.[7]

For these and other reasons, the procreational order seems to be gradually giving way to an attitude that puts more emphasis on pleasure in sex. This "recreational ethic" champions sex for its own sake, unencumbered by interfering considerations. There is an exclusive emphasis on sensual pleasure, variety, fantasy, and the full gratification of both partners. Advocates of this approach often use the term "cool sex" to describe pleasures that are induced at a leisurely pace, rather than pursued compulsively with orgasm as the only goal. However, the difference between procreational and recreational sex is not just the difference between hot and cool. Sex is arousal, and most would probably agree that the hotter, the better. What is "cool" is the relaxed mental condition and the permissive approach.

"The best modern sex is nonreproductive," wrote Alex Comfort, one of the proponents of recreational sex. "The development of a recreational erotic life needs privacy. Sexual freedom isn't compatible with a childbearing lifestyle."[8] This new ethic asserts that sexual pleasure is the right of all adults — men and women, married and single. Accordingly, women are expected to participate fully and reap the enjoyments of sexual activity, including orgasm. There is an interest in exploring the varieties of sexual expression, including noncoital experiences. Masturbation is no longer considered a health hazard; Albert Ellis has referred to it as man's best friend, and for women it is being recommended as a valuable way of exploring one's sexual responsiveness.[9] Homosexuality is acceptable for both men and women.

While the notion of recreational sex seems like a hedonistic fad, actually it may represent a historic response to the present worldwide problem of over-population. Dr. John Money, highly respected sexologist at Johns Hopkins, wrote that "the idea of recreational sex is not a whimsical irresponsibility of some morally degenerate imagination. Rather it is a technically feasible possibility that has become an urgent moral imperative in a world that is in-creasingly overpopulated and already has begun to experience the effects of overexploiting its ecological resources."[10] In view of such considerations, pro-creation is no longer a mandate to every married couple. If ever there was a time to play at sex — rather than to work at it reproductively — this is it, and society has provided the tools in the form of contraceptive devices, legalized abortion, sterilization, and the acceptance of nonmarital social-sexual relationships.

Numerous other aspects of the modern temper have favored the recrea-tional approach to sex. For example, the women's liberation movement has tried to raise women's consciousness of their own sexuality, rejecting the no-tion that woman's role is primarily that of childbearer.[11] Furthermore, the affluence of modern life makes it likely that sex will be cultivated as a diversion, as it often has been by the wealthy and the privileged. Alex Comfort wrote that "good sex is easier for affluent people who have privacy, contraception, leisure and control over their lives."[12] Bernard Murstein echoed this view in his historical review of sexual mores:

> People can better express their sexuality when they have the leisure time to pursue eroticism. The eighteenth-century French peasant had an enormous work load, and only the aristocracy could devote their lives to leisure. Today's average working person has more free time than ever before, and it is no acci-dent that the preoccupation with eroticism we are witnessing has paralleled this increased leisure.
>
> Yet one of the deterrents to sexuality, today as always, is physical fatigue. The barber on his feet for eight hours, or the housewife whose day is filled with shopping, laundering, house-cleaning, and tending to small children, is often too tired to think of sex. And when they do, their limited energy is very *goal-centered* on the orgasm, without much energy for the byplay that is characteristic of the "erotic." In the future, however, with less physically demanding labor and shorter workdays, more leisure time will be available, and some of it will be devoted to sex activities.[13]

Under the procreational ethic, sex was supposedly just an expression of the bigger realities of love and marriage. But the recreational ethic makes sex independent of marriage and even of love. Love and sex together make the ideal fulfillment, but in some ways that linkage has been detrimental to erotic potential. Love is a tender relationship on the continuum with liking and friendship. It has no particular agenda except to be in the presence of the loved one. Sex is something altogether different.

Sex is an episodic physical process that is localized in the genitals and results in a generalized arousal. It involves a cycle of pleasurable sensations, tension and release. It is possible to have sex with individuals we do not care about; in fact, sex can be associated with hate and violence, as in rape. Sex does not need a human partner; apparently an animal will do for some, or simple pornographic pictures. Sexual excitement is aroused, not by loving feelings, but by specific sexual stimuli such as the manipulation of the genitals, sexy images, or erotic fantasy.

According to Albert Ellis, failure to maintain total attention on sexual stimuli per se is one of the main reasons for weak sexual arousal, especially in women.

> Another common psychological block to sex satisfaction that is frequently ignored in the psychiatric literature . . . is that of simple ignorance. Millions of civilized (and primitive) women, because they have never received any incisive knowledge of the psychology and physiology of sexual response, seem to be completely ignorant of the fact that sexual arousal and satisfaction are not a function of proper physical stimulation alone but are largely a cerebral function — a result of what the individual *thinks* and *imagines* while she is engaging in sex relations. They do not realize that women, in particular, often have to *focus persistently* on sex-love objects and relations while their bodies are being adequately stimulated. When they fail to do so, and focus instead on nonsexual objects and concepts while they are engaging in sex acts, they frequently set up insuperable psychological blocks to satisfaction. If the facts of frigidity were fully known, it might well be found that guilt and shame, although important factors in creating frigidity in many instances, are often less important than a woman's failing, out of sheer lack of sex knowledge and proper training, to try to focus on stimulating things and events when she is having sex relations.[14]

Ellis would have been proud of the women who gave the following replies in the Hite survey when asked what they thought of during intercourse in order to enhance sexual arousal:

> "I concentrate very hard on the inward, outward movement of the penis. And what it looks like as it's going in and out."
> "I concentrate on . . . thinking of what he is doing to me."
> "The concentration . . . must be focused with all your might between your legs — *on the vagina.*"[15]

The close association between sex and love-and-marriage has also created problems for many men whose sexual potency becomes weak or conditional after years of marriage. Typically, this problem might be seen in an older man who is impotent with his wife but capable of being aroused through masturbation or by another woman such as a prostitute. In this case, it seems likely that the "other woman" is simply a fresh sexual stimulus, devoid of distracting reminders of everyday life which the wife represents. Such an inability to perform sexually with a loved one was considered a neurotic disorder by the Freudians, who saw it as an unhealthy separation of love and sex.[16] They theorized that such a sexual block resulted from an "Oedipus complex," wherein a strong maternal attachment causes the man to perceive his wife as mother, inhibiting sexual feelings. It is ironic to note that Oedipus — or at least his countrymen — did not have to worry about such problems because in ancient Greece, as in many other societies, the marriage system actually made a clear separation between love and sex. In ancient Greece, marriage had only a reproductive function. "The wife was regarded as a friend, a housekeeper, a mother of lawful children — but not as a sexual companion."[17] Greek men cultivated their erotic enjoyments as true diversions, outside the bounds of everyday life, with prostitutes and nonmarried women companions. Apparently, this practice was customary in ancient cultures. Bernard Murstein wrote in his historical review of love and sex: "The ancient Chinese, Greeks, and Romans were highly erotic and sensual, but rarely so vis-à-vis their assigned wives."[18]

All around us today is the evidence of changing sexual attitudes: the now common practice of unmarried couples living together, the decline of traditional family units, the phenomenal rise in pornography, the general acceptance of homosexuality, the public discourse on sexuality especially among women, and the rise of a profession of sexologists and sex therapists. Actually, at present there seems to be much confusion regarding sex (see Vance Packard's book *The Sexual Wilderness*[19]), but this is characteristic of periods of transition. As the social and institutional changes fall into place, the foundation will be set for a new orientation. More and more, people are likely to perceive their sexuality as they do their health, education, career, etc.: an essential part of life, to be enjoyed to its fullest.

Absorption and Erotic Fantasy

"Passionate lovers" may be mystics unawares. — *Denis De Rougemont*

It is ironic that the supreme business of the race — reproduction — is achieved when a person is in a state of mind that is anything but business. In other words, when people are sexually aroused, they are spellbound, sometimes outside of themselves in ecstasy. Reproductive business is absorbing.

"Ecstasy," "rapture," "joy," and "passion" are some of the terms often used to describe sexual experience; all of them convey the absorbed feeling of being swept away. Both Maslow and Laski, who have conducted studies on ecstatic or peak experiences, reported that one of the frequent triggers for such states is sex.[20] Using literary material, Colin Wilson showed the similarity between sexual experience and various reported states of ecstasy.[21] In the Hite survey there were numerous reports of sex as absorbed experience. Here is how some of the women described their sexual experiences: "Floating." "My body feels poised, alive, pulsing — glowing, 'high.'" "Somehow it gives me the chance to climb above myself — to wake up from the fogginess of daily existence." "Like being outside of my body, outside of my mind, not really caring what is important to my usual self." "My body runs itself, with no thinking on my part." "During the climax, it feels like everything around me stops existing and I am fully concentrated on this good feeeling which seems to intensely buzz for a while." When sexual involvement is intense, the feeling of being one-with is experienced in terms of mingled bodies, merging physically and genitally. "If the man is an important part of my life," said one woman, "I find myself wishing his penis could reach clear up to my neck, that he would just crawl inside of me. He can't seem to get deep enough or close enough." Another woman said: "If it's really good, I feel an intense wanting to suck his penis into me, inside my vagina deeper and deeper."[22]

The pleasures of sex are certainly contingent on getting absorbed in it. Genital stimulation is necessary but in itself is not sufficient. Stimulation without attentional involvement leads to what is often called "mechanical sex," an unsatisfying experience where the pleasure is minimal. In order to experience sex fully, a total attentional state must develop, dependent, as Ellis stated, on what the person "thinks and imagines." As in all absorbed experience, the person must be able to suspend self-consciousness. According to Dr. Money, the more absorbed the sexual partners, the greater the pleasure and enjoyment.

> Whatever the antecedents to an orgasm that is better than others, the final common pathway is the same. The two lovers are able to experience a feeling of unrestrained and untamed abandonment to one another. It is not necessary for them to pay attention either to what the self is doing or what the partner is doing. All the movements take care of themselves, as if reflexively. . . . The two bodies writhe, unheedingly. The two minds drift into the oblivion of attending only to their own feeling. . . . Two minds, mindlessly lost in one another. This is the perfect orgasmic experience.[23]

It seems that total attention is especially important when arousal is uncertain, or so reported the women in the Hite survey:

> Full concentration like hypnosis is needed to attain orgasm — your whole mind and body is focusing on it.

"Yes, I have to *want* to come and think about only that. Forget everything
except what I am doing and what is being done to me. I close my eyes and
picture it in my mind."

"Yes, I definitely have to concentrate to orgasm. If I think about anything
other than the sensation, or any unsexual thoughts, I immediately lose the
excitement."[24]

Nothing so well illustrates the importance of total attention as its loss.
In general, distraction is fatal to the absorbed spell, and when it occurs during
sex, it deflates arousal. In their lab observations, Masters and Johnson found
that distracted males usually could not maintain potency.

Penile erection may be impaired easily by the introduction of asexual stimuli,
even though sexual stimulation is continued simultaneously. Despite constantly maintained somatogenic penile stimulation, a sudden loud noise,
vocalization on an extraneous subject, or an obvious change in lighting,
temperature, or attendant personnel may result in partial or even complete
loss of penile erection.[25]

Women may be more distractible than men in the sexual situation, which
would help explain the greater difficulty they have had with arousal and
orgasm.

Once aroused, the male is less easily distracted than the female. Any discon-
tinuance of physical stimulation interrupts her response. The crying of a
baby, the creaking of the bed, the thought of ironing to be done — such things
as these divert women from the sexual act. This is true of other mammals,
too; food placed before a copulating pair will distract the female.[26]

Impotence and frigidity are the most common sexual problems. Today,
authorities agree that most of the time these problems are psychological
and due to distraction. The kind of distraction that usually cripples sexual
arousal, however, comes not from the outside, but from within. The most injurious distraction to sex is self — self-consciousness, self-preoccupation.
Masters and Johnson wrote that "preoccupation remains a major deterrent
to male as well as female sexuality."[27] Anxiety keeps self in the foreground
of attention, making it impossible to lose oneself in sexual stimuli. Ironically,
modern sex manuals tend to encourage self-awareness and thus make absorption difficult. Although attitudes are favorable toward sex, they view it as a
workaday task, involving techniques and goals. Such an evaluative process
fosters self-preoccupation and anxiety. In a discussion of frigidity, Ellis noted
that the sexually unresponsive woman, instead of losing herself and focusing
on *what* she is experiencing, is anxiously evaluating *how* she is doing.[28] Nat
Lehrman wrote that "fear makes a person overly conscious of what he or she
is doing; in sex (as in some other physical activities), the more self-conscious

we become about our physiological function, the less likely is it that the function will perform as expected."[29]

The natural habitat of sex is privacy — usually the darkened bedroom. The fact that sex almost always occurs in such a setting confirms that the integrity of erotic arousal depends on undisturbed attention. A recent book on the fundamentals of human sexuality observed that there "is a general human preference for privacy during coitus. Why is not clear."[30] Despite that author's uncertainty, it is very clear why privacy is not only desirable but mandatory: Almost every absorbed state requires a private or sheltered setting.

The epitome of a private sexual situation is masturbation. With no partner to consider, the person who masturbates is more likely to give all attention to sexual images and fantasies. As might be expected, this attention apparently leads to more intense arousal, according to numerous reports.[31] Just as total attention on the novel makes the story seem real, so total attention on sexual images makes them vivid and arousing. Under the procreational ethic, masturbation was viewed as an inferior outlet that men resorted to when sex was not available from women. But now, ironically, it is recognized as the opportunity for pure sexual experience, for men and women alike.

There is another reason why a sheltered setting is important for sex: It offers the feeling of something non-everyday. The fascination in sex is greatly dependent on the sense of entering a forbidden domain. One of the ancient associations to sex was the notion of "obscenity," which literally means "off the scene," or separated from public view.[32] Sex is exciting and absorbing because it has nudity, forbidden fantasy, and acts that are never seen and seldom talked about in everyday life. It is a violation of personal space and the separateness that people normally maintain. To a great extent, therefore, sex is fascinating because it involves the violation of taboos. "The idea of the forbidden is essential in sex," wrote Colin Wilson. "Without the sense of the violation of an alien being, sexual excitement would be weakened, or perhaps completely dissipated."[33] Expressing the same idea, De Rougemont wrote, "No passion is conceivable or in fact declared in a world where everything is permitted."[34] For example, in Polynesia, where women do not cover their breasts, this part of the female anatomy has no sexual significance and is not arousing to the males.[35]

When sex has become boring, it can usually be made more exciting by violating more and more taboos, which makes it increasingly distanced from everyday life. Oral and anal sex violate more taboos than intercourse: "Cunnilingus, fellatio, and sodomy," wrote Wilson, "can be regarded as attempts to restore the strangeness and intensity to sexual contact."[36] And just as masturbation is flight from a sexual partner, promiscuity is a denial of the personality of the partner. "Male and female promiscuity have one thing in common: the impersonality of the sexual object."[37] Wilson pointed out that perverted and degenerate sex is not the result of excessive libido or sex drive,

but just the opposite; such acts are extreme measures to excite individuals who
are sexually bored, satiated, or deficient in arousal. "All sexual perversions,
from mere adultery to necrophily, can be seen as attempts to increase the alien-
ness of the act by increasing the number of taboos involved."[38]

Another way of adding diversion value to sex is to visit a prostitute.
Especially in a highly procreational culture, prostitution offers novelty, adventure into sexual fantasy, and the violation of many taboos.[39] Prostitution at-
tracts primarily married men looking for something different.[40] Winick and
Kinsie wrote that most men who seek out prostitutes want a woman "who is
the exact opposite of their wives."[41] According to a study by Martha Stein,
there seems to be an increasing tendency for men to ask for deviant kinds of
sex from prostitutes, preferring especially fellatio. Stein also observed that going to a prostitute today often involves other erotic stimulants like pornographic movies, sexual devices, drugs, and talk about perversions.[42] In his
book on sexual fantasies, Dally summed all of this up:

> The main reason why prostitutes continue to flourish today is that they pro-
> vide facilities for those aspects of childhood sexuality that men crave through
> their fantasies, and that they cannot or dare not experience at home except
> through masturbation.[43]

Sexual fantasy is probably the most common way of increasing the diversion value of sex. In their book on the fundamentals of sexuality, Katchadourian and Lunde declared that "erotic fantasies must be the most ubiquitous
of all sexual phenomena."[44] Fantasy is to the psychology of sex what the
genitalia are to the physiology. It is a mechanism for keeping attention on sexual matters, fostering the development of an absorbed spell. Sexy images in
the mind can mobilize attention and arousal when the reality stimulus is weak.
For example, in one study of well-adjusted married women, it was found that
a typical fantasy during intercourse was that the partner was a handsome
imaginary lover, not the husband.[45] Fantasy is the most convenient way of
making sex more fascinating and diverting.

It is important to note that sexual fantasy is not idle daydreaming that
might change from day to day. Rather, the fantasy stays basically the same,
allowing only minor variations on a theme. The fantasy is imprinted into the
organism early in life, and it consists of a set of signals and patterned reactions,
highly effective in producing sexual arousal. Dally wrote that "sexual fantasies
take shape in early childhood, become fixed in adolescence or early adulthood,
and remain with us until the end of our lives."[46] Images from current life are
often incorporated into sexual fantasies, but they are selected and given meaning by codes programmed years before. Sexual fantasy probably exists outside
the master code system, and comes to the fore only when the latter has been
suspended. Also, one might guess that to the extent the sexual fantasies were

programmed prior to the development of the master code system, they are likely to be autonomous, irrational, and compulsively forceful.

Sexual fantasy represents the attentional aspect of sex, just as important as the realistic and physical aspects. A wise quip passed on by John Money states that in sex "what goes on between the legs is equalled in importance by what goes on between the ears." In other words, genital sex should be accompanied by sexy thought. "The component that unites and directs the human sexual impulses," wrote Colin Wilson, "is purely mental or imaginative, although it is usually strongly tied to sensual impressions."[47] The same idea was expressed by Joseph Slade:

> And, lest we champion the supremacy of real sex over fantasy too quickly, we should remember as well that whatever else sex may involve, and this is considerable, it includes fantasy. This should be so obvious as not to need stating. Sex is in part mental . . . and not just gonadal. The gonads provide a necessary force, but emotional and intellectual energy carry it forward. When one makes love to someone else . . . one really makes love to a matrix of complex experiences, a continuum, as it were, of past sexual feelings and associations, present sensations and momentary anticipations, perhaps centered around the partner, perhaps not. The obvious analogy is that we have a kind of sexual movie reel inside our consciousness. . . . This personal projector may play back impressions of someone seen on the street. . . . Or the projector can draw on fantasy from whatever source it can, and that includes pornography. The sex in [commercial] films may be impersonal, for all the miserable plots, the beauty of the women and the romantic music, but it does not stay that way for the patron. The viewer's mind uses the scenes as grist for his own imagination. To fantasize sexually is not to be crippled psychologically. On the contrary, accumulated fantasies contribute to a richer sex life. One could go further. Fantasy is the rock on which a stable marriage stands, since it permits mental adultery while preserving monogamy.[48]

There have been two opposing views about sexual fantasy. The older one, usually voiced by psychoanalysts, claims that fantasy involvement during sex is the exception, not the rule; most people do not engage in it, and those who do are sexually inhibited, withdrawn from reality, or suffering from neurotic disorder. The other view asserts that most people have sexual fantasies, and that this is a normal and useful way to enhance sexual experience. Surveys tend to support the latter view. It has generally been accepted that men indulge in sexual fantasies, and it is becoming increasingly clear that women do too. For example, after a careful empirical study of this matter, Hariton and Singer concluded: "Perhaps the major outcome of this investigation is the evidence that in a sample of reasonably normal married women the occurrence of daydreams during sexual relations is quite common and not generally related to interpersonal disturbances, adjustment problems, or lack of fulfillment in the sexual area." According to these authors, sexual fantasies are directed at the "enhancement of desire and pleasure."[49]

Naturally, if fantasies are to enhance the fascination level of sex, they cannot be mundane; they must violate taboos. Thus they are usually about imaginary lovers, role reversals, rape, and oral and anal activity. In Nancy Friday's book on men's sexual fantasies, the table of contents runs as follows: "Oral Sex," "Semen," "Anal Sex," "Fetishism," "Water Sports," "Voyeurs and Exhibitionists," "Women with Women," "Animals," and so on for another ten pornographic chapters.[50]

Pornography is sexual fantasy made visible. The images in the mind are turned into pictures in a magazine or erotic scenes in a story. This is the literature of lust, as Ortega y Gasset called it, and like other kinds of literature its function is to enhance experience. Pornography, of course, has a long history, and is not just some deviant development of modern times. The fact that pornography is so offensive to so many people only illustrates to what extent sex is diversion; it is truly outside the bounds of everyday life.

The purpose of pornography, and sexual fantasy in general, is to focus total attention on the fascinating aspects of sex, and therefore bring about arousal. This is done primarily through exaggeration and distortion, according to the Kronhausens, who made an extensive study of pornographic literature. Basically, pornography tries to hypnotize by focusing in a very explicit and visual way on the physical aspects of sex — a kind of Hypno-Fiction of sex. Genital organs and sexual functions are described with a lot of "dirty" language which is much more stimulating than technical terms. Sex is distanced and divorced from reality. As the Kronhausens note, "All disturbing reality elements are carefully avoided, so that one rarely hears of unwanted pregnancy, abortion, venereal disease, and other similar undesirable side-effects that occasionally accompany sexual relations."[51] But more to the point, sex is presented as something that is above and beyond everyday reality, something stronger than the social restrictions meant to control it. Sex is presented as an all-powerful urge; both men and women in pornographic stories are supersexed. Male sexual functioning is typically depicted in concrete terms with an emphasis "upon the exaggerated size of the male organ and of the testicles, and the copious amounts of seminal fluid ejaculated" (p. 852). The women in these stories are sensuous, fiercely passionate, and aggressive; even though defloration and rape are favorite themes, the women are usually willing victims. Finally, it is a standard device in pornography to magnify sexual significance by describing a forbidden world where taboos are violated. Sex occurs where it is least likely to be found in everyday life — between parents and children, with animals, or in sacred settings. "Many pornographic books include, among their central figures, persons connected with the clergy and religion, such as nuns, priests, and monks" (p. 851).

Sexual fantasy and pornography have no place in everyday life, and should not be judged by everyday standards. They belong to the world of adult play. Thus there is nothing to be gained from acting out sexual fantasies. They are fine where they are—in the head, serving to mobilize attention and arousal. There are good reasons for sexual fantasies to be immature and unrealistic; they develop in childhood, and their function is to capture attention. As we have seen, they almost have to be deviant in order to be arousing. But the immaturity and distortion found in sexual fantasy have no relationship to everyday personality.

> Many excitingly imagined activities would be much less exciting and much less pleasant if they actually occurred. Perhaps a prime example is rape. Females may report rape fantasies as arousing and pleasurable, but actual rape, in contrast, involves fear, pain and humiliation. Similarly, many individuals who are turned on by sadomasochistic themes in fantasy would be repelled by the stark reality of administering or receiving pain. Sexual imagery can sometimes be preferable to its real-life counterparts.[52]

A good example of the separation between sex and everyday personality is evident in the most common kind of erotic fantasy, namely, masochistic themes. In such fantasies the person is subject to domination or humiliation, and finds this sexually arousing. Apparently, both men and women often use such fantasies to enhance erotic experience. In her survey of sexual fantasies among men, Nancy Friday reported that the majority were of the masochistic type.[53] Likewise, in the study discussed earlier regarding women's fantasies during marital intercourse, one of the most frequently reported themes was that of rape and submission ("I imagine I am being overpowered or forced to surrender").[54] In his book *The Fantasy Game*, British psychiatrist Peter Dally classified fantasies as being either masochistic or sadistic, and he agrees with other investigators that the former are more common.[55]

What does this mass masochism mean? Does it mean that deep down most people crave to be hurt, humiliated and punished? Some psychotherapists would so claim, even though it goes against common sense.

It seems that a better understanding of such fantasies is achieved when they are seen as diversions rather than reflections of everyday personality. First of all, sexual fantasy is encoded in the early years when the child is weak and helpless. Thus it is highly probable that sexual arousal would be conditioned to stimuli regarding obedience, punishment, and control by powerful (parental) figures. Furthermore, masochistic fantasy is relatively high on taboo violation; it permits the normally active, responsible adult to indulge in the forbidden experience of being submissive. Thus, if anything, masochistic fantasy represents a striking reversal of everyday behavior, and therefore is exciting and makes a good arousal device. Nancy Friday pointed out that masochistic fantasy is a denial of self-responsibility and so encourages full play of sexual arousal.

There is an interesting parallel between women's rape fantasies and male S&M scenarios. Not one woman I have ever met actually wanted to be raped in reality; what she wanted from a fantasy of being forced was release from responsibility. "I'm a good girl, but he made me do it. It's not my fault." The men who invent these fantasies don't want to be blamed either.[56]

In addition to all of this, masochistic fantasies may be common simply because they fit in so well with absorbed experience. In other words, it is easier to give in and get absorbed in pleasure when one's mind is on images of self-surrender and loss of control. Erich Fromm has commented on the fact that a masochistic orientation is involved in various kinds of absorbing experiences: "There can be masochistic submission to . . . rhythmic music, to the orgiastic state produced by drugs or under hypnotic trance — in all these instances the person renounces his integrity, makes himself the instrument of somebody or something outside of himself."[57] At the level of sexual fantasy, it seems that masochism is not so much finding pleasure in pain, but being sexually aroused by the idea of being controlled by someone stronger. For example, in discussing the masochistic treatment that men requested from prostitutes, Martha Stein wrote that "it was clearly the loss of control and submission to someone who was mentally stronger, that excited these men, not pain of itself."[58]

There is a profound paradox about the modern sexual scene. With the sexual revolution and the recreational ethic, society has become very permissive about people having sex. Why, then, does prostitution continue to thrive, and why has pornography become a major industry, so much so that it has aroused national concern? In the 1980s, the annual profits from pornography exceed those of the movie and record businesses, combined; one proprietor was quoted in the newspapers as saying that it is now impossible to lose money in the porno trade.[59] This increase in pornography cannot be due to a few perverted individuals, but must reflect something about the modern sexual condition. However, one is not likely to be enlightened on this matter by the traditional psychology of sex with its notions of procreational love-bonding, interpersonal intimacy, tension-outlets, pleasuring techniques, and the belief that the partner should be a sufficient stimulus for sexual arousal.

Prostitution and pornography reflect the importance of diversion in sex — the need to make it distanced from reality. Like all absorbed experience, sex requires an object of fascination. Can it be that today's sexual permissiveness has made sex "everyday," so that the attentional boosters provided by pornography are needed to distance it and make it exciting again?

Chapter 9

Motion and Emotion
in Music

Wherein lies the peculiar power and charm of music? What is
its innermost nature and meaning? What enables it to lift us out
of the prosaic atmosphere of everyday life and carry us
into purer, ideal realms of being? — *Albert Gehring*

Wine . . . love . . . and now song. This chapter completes the great triad
of adult diversion — intoxication, love-and-sex, and music.

Except for speech, the sounds of everyday life are drab — machine noises,
traffic, doors slamming, sirens. Much of the time our auditory experience is
likely to consist of droning background noises which we tend to tune out after
a while.

The most significant sound we hear is human speech, which is processed
primarily for its informational content, not its sound quality. As sound, con-
versational speech is limited in pitch and loudness. It has a frequency range
from about 300 to 3,000 cycles per second; the loudness level averages 50 to
60 decibels. Yet the human ear can handle a range of 20 to 20,000 frequencies,
and can comfortably tolerate loudness levels up to about 90 decibels. Thus,
in everyday life hearing is almost deprived, especially compared to vision,
which is constantly stimulated by ever-changing input. As an old journal article put it, "We are, when awake, always seeing, but by no means always
hearing."[1]

Music, however, does justice to the human ear. With its rhythm, melody,
harmony, and tempo changes, music so far exceeds everyday sound in
richness and variety that it amounts to a qualitatively different domain of experience. This gap between everyday sound and music makes the latter all
the more attention-getting.

Music as Relaxed Arousal

> The suggestion of motion is one of the most powerful effects of music.
> It simply compels our attention and absorbs all of our motor activities.
> It pulls us into line and determines the direction of our forces. We must move,
> and move with the music. — *Kate Hevner*

Somehow music comes to us with self and reality already suspended. After hearing it we may imbue it with personal meanings, but inherently music is a nonself object, belonging solely to the domain of experience. Because there is no business in music, it by-passes the master codes, and seems to take us "by surprise." Unless often repeated, it is experienced as fresh and intense. There does not seem to be much psychological mediation when experiencing music — an observation made long ago by German philosopher Eduard Hanslick:

> Music operates on our emotional faculty with greater intensity and rapidity than the product of any other art. A few chords may give rise to a frame of mind which a poem can induce only by a lengthy exposition, or a picture by prolonged contemplation, despite the fact that the arts to which the latter belong boast the advantage over music of having at their service the whole range of ideas on which we know our feelings of joy or sorrow to depend. The action of sound is not only more sudden, but also more powerful and direct. The other arts persuade us, but music takes us by surprise.[2]

While everybody agrees that music makes us emotional, careful scholars have pointed out that these are not the emotions of normal life. The emotional experiences induced by music are somehow felt as pure, without connections to self or reality. "What music expresses," wrote composer Richard Wagner, "is eternal, infinite and ideal; it does not express the passion, love, or longing of such-and-such an individual on such-and-such an occasion, but passion, love or longing in itself."[3] In a similar vein the distinguished psychologist Carroll Pratt wrote: "The sadness of music is not the sadness produced by a particular event, but universal sadness, without accessories or motives or consequences." He pointed out that music lovers "insist that in listening to music they do not themselves experience real emotion. The music in some elusive manner has an emotional significance, but the experience is said to be in no way comparable to the real emotions of everyday life."[4] In other words, music produces relaxed arousal — experience without processing or self-reference.

Actually, the emotions that we experience while listening to music come directly from the motions inherent in the musical sounds. It is as though we mimic the motions in music with reflex reactions that we experience as emotion. When the music stops, the sense of motion stops, and we cease to have the emotions.

There is always a sense of movement in our emotions. For example, excitement is felt as fast and up, while sadness is slow and down. Thus music that is fast in tempo and ascending in pitch tends to produce excitement. Because music is capable of endless variety of motion, both in pattern and quality, it has an unlimited ability to arouse the entire range of human feeling. This intriguing theory of musical experience was formulated by Carroll Pratt, who coined the phrase, "Music sounds the way emotions feel."

> The rise and fall of a melodic line seems to correspond to the rise and fall of feeling itself; the movement of a melody from its beginning to its conclusion gives a sense of how feelings move from a start to an end.
>
> A description of what it feels like to be restless might include references to such things as increased rate of breathing and heartbeat, unsteady organics in the region of the diaphragm, tapping of the feet or fingers, inability to keep still, etc. It requires no great knowledge of music to appreciate the fact that much the same kind of movements may easily be produced in musical phrases. Staccato passages, trills, strong accents, quavers, rapid accelerandos and crescendos, shakes, wide jumps in pitch — all such devices conduce to the creation of an auditory structure which is appropriately described as restless.[5]

If music aroused everyday emotions, it would represent a handy device for therapeutic intervention — for arousing and releasing pent-up emotions, or making up for emotional deficiencies. Apparently, however, music has no therapeutic effect. Colbert reviewed the literature on this topic and concluded that there is no basis for stating that music can alter a person's everyday emotional status. What music does is to produce a "narrowing of the focus of attention . . . on a reduced segment of the over-all range of available stimulation."[6] In other words, at most music temporarily diverts attention from everyday stimuli and problems. When the music is over, problems return. Likewise, there is no evidence that similar psychiatric patients prefer the same kind of music. In a recent study that compared the musical preferences of neurotics, psychotics, and character disorders, no pattern of musical preference was found in these three major categories of psychiatric disorder.[7]

Music then, cannot be used to flush out the complexes that are bottled up by the pressure of self and everyday problems. Rather, it goes in another direction — it enlivens, it makes things more significant. It stimulates the experience factor, negating self-conscious attitudes so that we can experience certain moods in an almost "luminous" way. Music is right hemisphere and deep brain; it evokes the undercurrents, the intuitive meanings, the sense of significance about things.

If sex is body, music is spirit. It gives us a feeling of the important things that cannot be seen or verbalized. How devoid of spirit would religious ritual, holiday parades, and high civic occasions be without music, which has a way of making any situation more meaningful. Imagine, for instance, the playing

of taps at a Veterans Day service or military funeral. For the short time it takes
to play them, the simple notes of taps can induce an indefinable sense of loss,
sadness, and passing away. The music conveys these feelings much better than
words or even the real objects related to death. It evokes the mood of the occasion as something universal—an effect comparable to that described by
George Du Maurier in one of his short stories:

> He had never heard such music as this. . . . He was conscious, while it lasted,
> that he saw deeper into the beauty, the sadness of things, the very heart of
> them, and their pathetic evanescence, as with a new inner eye—even into
> eternity itself, beyond the veil, a vague cosmic vision that faded when the
> music was over.[8]

The relaxed arousal that characterizes musical experience is greatly
bolstered by rhythm. Many scholars have pointed out that rhythm seems to
have opposing effects simultaneously; Carl Seashore, a psychologist who
wrote extensively about music, stated that rhythm "stimulates and lulls, contradictory as this may seem."[9] In a way it is contradictory—unless regarded
as an experience of relaxed arousal, combining emotional stimulation with
a relaxed cognitive condition. In rhythm, the continuous accenting of a beat
leads to a buildup that energizes experiencing, while the repetition lulls attention into a hypnotized spell.

Surrender to rhythm and it ceases to be a stimulus perceived "out there,"
instead taking control of attention. At one time, rhythmic devices were standard equipment for hypnotists, who would get control of the subject's attention
by means of a swinging pendulum, metronome, or flickering candle. Probably
one of the most dramatic instances of rhythmic power is the temporary cure
it can effect in stuttering.[10] Stutterers may suddenly become fluent when singing, speaking rhythmically, or speaking with a metronome. Presumably,
rhythm lulls the self-consciousness of the stutterer, helping him to flow with
speech rather than struggle with it.

Rhythm is such a unifying and pleasing quality that it is sought after not
just in music, but in most other arts, particularly poetry. William Butler Yeats
probably made the definitive statement about rhythm when he said that its
function is to "lull the mind into a waking trance," thus making us more susceptible to the images and ideas presented.

> The purpose of rhythm it has always seemed to me, is to prolong the moment
> of contemplation, the moment when we are both asleep and awake, which
> is the one moment of creation, by hushing us with an alluring monotony,
> while it holds us waking by variety, to keep us in that state of perhaps real
> trance in which the mind liberated from the pressure of the will is unfolded
> in symbols.[11]

This is an intriguing explanation of rhythm because, as we shall see in later chapters, most of the meaningful effects of meditation, inspiration, and dreaming also occur when we are "both asleep and awake," i.e., in an absorbed or hypnogogic state. In such a condition it seems that we have greater access to the deep brain, which is probably the source of intense spiritual and mystical experience.

It is believed that music originated as a device for making the other-worldly come alive, starting with rhythmic beating and drumming used to evoke spirits and induce religious experience. In his book *Battle for the Mind,* William Sargant discussed how in many tribal societies rhythmic drumming, chanting, and dancing are used to put group members in a highly emotional and suggestible state in order to bring about healing or spiritual rebirth.[12] The high point of this trance state is a feeling of being possessed by (being one-with) a god or nature spirit. To some extent, the hypnotic impact of these rhythmic rituals can be explained by cultural conditioning, but Sargant believed that the effects transcend culture. He told of a sociologist who went to Haiti on a Guggenheim Fellowship to study the local tribal customs. She later admitted that she herself had succumbed to the religious frenzies. She described how, in the course of the ritual, the rhythmic drumming induced uncontrollable bodily movements and then the feeling of being possessed. Other Westerners who have observed these phenomena firsthand also attest to their power. Aldous Huxley wrote:

> No man, however highly civilized, can listen for very long to African drum-ming, or Indian chanting, or Welsh hymn-singing, and retain intact his critical and self-conscious personality. . . . If exposed long enough to the tom-toms and the singing, every one of our philosophers would end by capering and howling with the savages.[13]

A physician at Oxford tested the hypothesis that intense rhythmic ex-perience leads to reduction of critical thinking.[14] His subjects listened to highly rhythmic jazz music while EEG recordings measured cerebral processing. The subjects fell in with the mood of the music, reported "being sent" by it, and responded with hand-clapping and rhythmic body movements. Even dur-ing the loudest and most violent parts of the music, EEG recordings revealed low frequency waves, indicating reduced cerebral vigilance. In fact, the EEG waves were reduced to the extent that they could be called incipient sleep signs. In other words, the EEG record indicated that the subjects were "both asleep and awake," mentally lulled yet emotionally activated by the jazz—the epitome of relaxed arousal.

From "Stardust" to Rock: Mild to Extreme Diversion

Music is like story entertainment in that it is almost universally enjoyed. Most adults enjoy what has been called "popular music," especially ballads and folk songs. These are short tunes with lyrics and expressive melodies that are easy to sing and dance to. Popular songs are usually about the "soft underbelly" of human existence — sentiment, nostalgia, and especially romantic love. While many songs are about the joys of being in love, many others express the ache of a broken heart. Songs about loss, loneliness, and vagabond yearnings abound. If we verbalized these sentiments in everyday life as they are expressed in songs, they would seem silly; but, as Santayana wrote, music "can make persuasive and obvious sentiments which, if not set to music, might seem absurd, as often in love songs and in psalmody."[15]

Early in the twentieth century, the invention of the radio and the phonograph stimulated widespread interest in popular music. New songs were continually being released, and keeping up with the latest songs was a national pastime. The songwriters came primarily from show business, and although they had little formal training, they did have a kind of "street" talent for music, and were adept at catering to popular taste.[16] People spent freely on sheet music and 78 rpm records. "Everybody's singing it" was the standard way of describing a popular tune.

Since the 1950s, however, there have been radical changes in popular music. As many have observed, "They don't write songs like they used to." Instead, we have cool jazz, rock 'n' roll, and hard rock. All of these new musical forms emphasize the attentional factors of music like fast tempo, loudness, and rhythm; thus, they are designed to induce absorbed experience. This development was probably abetted by stereo and the new listening devices that give wraparound sound, fostering a totally involving experience. However, it should be noted that this new kind of music is also consistent with the recreational trend of our time. As in the case of story entertainment, drugs, and sex, so also popular music has become more extremely diverting.

The first indication that popular music was changing came in the late 1940s with the advent of progressive jazz, music played by a small group of performers who improvised on the jazz idiom in complex and abstract ways. Rublowsky wrote that progressive jazz "resembled nothing so much as a sound version of what the abstract expressionists were doing in painting."[17] This music was created on the spot in a free-flowing way. It had no set melody or lyrics. People did not dance to this music; a few intellectuals just sat and listened to it, much like a spectator diversion.

The next development in popular music was rock 'n' roll, which seemed to be a reaction to progressive jazz. While the latter was cool, abstract, intellectual, and quiet, the former was hot, earthy, emotional, and loud. Rock 'n' roll was also absorbing, but in a different way. Based on the psychology of rhythm, it epitomized relaxed arousal — energized dancing combined with a lulled mental condition.

There is a general need for rock 'n' roll, a need rooted in strong feelings, a need fulfilled only by the one standard ingredient of all rock 'n' roll: its steady, heavy, simple beat.

When the listener submits himself to the beat, he loosens his mind from its moorings in space and time; no longer does he feel a separation between himself and his surroundings. The difficult world of external objects is blurred and unreal; only the inner pulse is real, the beat its outer projection. Earthly worries are submerged in a tide of rising exaltation. Dream and dreamer merge, object and feeling jell: the whole universe is compressed into the medium of the beat, where all things unite and pound forward, rhythmic, regular, not to be denied.

. . . . Rock 'n' roll dulls the capacity for attention; the steady beat creates instead a kind of hypnotic monotony. Seen in this light, RnR is only the latest in a series of rituals which have existed in many societies for the purpose of inducing mystic ecstasy, usually in connection with religion. One might think not only of African or American Indian drumbeating frenzies but also of the cults of frenzied dancing and shaking which periodically rose up from the main body of European Christianity. In the United States, Negro "gospel music" often creates ecstasy through repeated phrases of enormous energy, and has been more than casually influential in the formation of rock 'n' roll. Through gospel music, RnR draws directly on both Christian and African cults of rhythmic ecstasy. . . .

But one should not take RnR lyrics too literally, for it is the rhythm of rock 'n' roll that carries its psychic message. "Positive" lyrics are mostly a sop to minds that do not want to know what they are thinking.[18]

Gradually, rock 'n' roll gave way to a driving, thrusting kind of music, full of raw emotion. While rock 'n' roll had some semblance of melody, sentiment, and lyrics, all of this was gradually abandoned in the new rock music. The lyrics in this new "rock" were usually oversimplified and repetitious; often they were unintelligible. In his book on rock music, Richard Bobbitt wrote: "Nonsense syllables and meaningless word sequences have been deliberately employed as a rejection of conventional communication procedures. The late Jim Morrison of the Doors stated, 'I am interested in anything about disorder, chaos, especially activity which seems to have no meaning.'"[19] Surveys of young people who listen to rock indicated that most did not understand the lyrics or were indifferent to them. Seventy percent said that they liked the music more for the beat than for the message.[20]

Rock was anti-meaning, anti-sentiment, and anti-establishment; it was in fact, the antithesis of conventional music and everyday reality. It emphasized the most elemental aspects of music — rhythm and loudness. In conventional music, melody stands out and rhythm is in the background. Rock reversed this relationship. Bobbit wrote that "in the music of the rock idiom the beat came to the fore and dominated the entire ensemble texture." Thus, rock constitutes a figure-ground reversal of conventional music, something that is clearly evident in the performing and staging of rock; "the rhythm section, which had consistently played an accompanimental role in jazz bands, moved to the front of the stage and became a free force."[21]

Similarly distanced from everyday life are the other aspects of rock such as the theatrical way in which the music is performed, the exaggerated actions and costumes of the musicians, the metallic-sounding instruments, and the disembodied, frenzied vocals. Rublowsky wrote that rock exploits the human voice "in totally novel and unexpected ways, raising the glissando, speech, and falsetto to new levels of expressiveness."[22]

Every style of music has its own kind of dancing, and for rock 'n' roll this was the "twist." Just as these new forms of music were weak on melody and lyrics, the twist was weak on formal pattern and social interaction. Conventional dancing has always been a sociable affair with the partners holding each other and moving around the floor in patterned steps. But the rock dancer more or less stood in one place, and in a solitary spell surrendered himself to the pounding beat of the music with frenzied, gyrating movements. As Rublowsky noted about the twist, "its execution demanded nothing more than an uninhibited abandon to the rhythm of the music. There was nothing to learn, nothing to do. There were no partners and no recognizable steps. All that the dancer needed to do was twist in time to the music."[23] A survey made by Csikszentmihalyi found that "a clear, consistent beat was frequently cited as the most important aspect of 'good' rock dance music."[24]

What almost forces the rock dancer to abandon himself to the beat is its extreme loudness. At a rock dance or concert, the music is literally forced into the center of consciousness by electronic amplification. Csikszentmihalyi wrote: "The high volume of musical sound in a rock-dance situation serves to eliminate distractions and focus attention. Loudness also furthers the loss of self and a 'merging with the music' which many subjects report." This observation was based on reports that individuals had made about their experience of dancing to rock music; for example:

> When you feel [the music] resonating through you, it really helps. 'Cause when it's loud, like when you're dancing to a rock group, you can really feel yourself vibrate almost. And also, the louder it is, the more it blocks out other noises, so it's more of a total immersion in the music, which is also a very good sensation and is also conducive to just dancing and being part of the music — almost incorporating it.[25]

Absorption in amplified sound is an inherent aspect of rock. The practice of listening to music with stereophonic headphones became widespread in the rock era; with this device, one immediately passes into another domain, being inside the music. At a live concert, absorption is encouraged by crowd psychology and drugs. The audience at a rock concert is usually made up of young, like-minded people who are intensely enthusiastic about the music and react as one to it; the norms of this subculture encourage abandonment of everyday standards in the process of getting totally immersed in the music. The use of drugs also helps to amplify the musical experience.

Flight from the conventional was also evident in another development from the rock tradition: disco dancing. For the brief life of this fad in the United States, the disco was a fantasy place, highly distanced from ordinary life. It had psychedelic decor, unusual lighting, rock music, drugs, high style, and beautiful people who danced the way that Fred Astaire and Ginger Rogers used to in the movies. Disco diversion not only transported one to a new reality, it actually aimed to alter identity through a change in role and behavior. As depicted in the movie *Saturday Night Fever,* the typical disco patron was someone who at night achieved a dramatic reversal in his life, from mundane existence to something like stardom. The *Washington Post* documented one such case:

> To the residents of Arlington's Adams House apartments, Tom Davidson, a 27-year-old maintenance man with green work clothes and a grease smudge on his face, is the one to call when the sink's stopped up.
> But they see him only by day. When the sun sets, Davidson springs forth, transformed, in a two-piece form-fitting vest suit, silk shirt and black platform shoes. By night he is "T.T.," the self-proclaimed king of the disco dance floor.
> Twirling his way through the mirrored strobe-lit world of Washington's pulsing night life, he lives out a glittering fantasy far removed from the reality of radiators and wrenches.
> "A disco has a totally different atmosphere," Davidson explains. "You go there and do what you feel. . . . You can have style . . . you can be a star."
> Out on the dance floor, Davidson and his girlfriend, Laura Luby, are doing the freak. "FREAK OUT," the song screams, and the strobe lights flash, freezing his moves as he bobs and shakes from point to point to point.[26]

What made disco such a popular diversion? Salesmen, mechanics, secretaries, and other blue- and white-collar workers gave answers like the following:

> "To get away from the hum-drum of everyday life."
> "Dancing makes me high and even without booze, but booze makes it even better. It makes me feel alive."
> "I work all day, five days a week, typing and filing and answering the phone. It's not bad — I mean, you have to work to eat — but its boring. But when I come to a disco, I can be exciting . . . mysterious. When I'm here I'm one of the beautiful people."
> "You can be anyone you want. It's a good change from the real world. There are no hassles."[27]

There is no question that since the 1950s there has been a radical change in music, moving it toward absorbed experience. Unlike popular songs which exist as objects "out there" and have a mild effect of relaxing or inducing a mood, this new rock music is meant to engulf us, transforming experience and sense of reality. Rublowsky stated that today popular music is becoming like spectator sports. In the past people used to say that "everybody's singing it"; today they say that "everybody's listening to it"—apparently with absorbed attention.

Listening to Classical Music

It seems that most of the time we experience music as a recreational influence rather than as a recreation per se. Music can coexist with most other activities, and, as we have seen, it is often used to enhance and support other experiences—to enliven sociable get-togethers, to make possible singing and dancing. It gives added dimension to our entertainments and brings out the spirit of many other occasions. At such times, music is supportive and secondary, and so we hear it but do not listen attentively to it.

Only in classical or aesthetic works do we have music for its own sake—music at its best. Aesthetic music constitutes one of the great arts—some say the greatest—and it is appropriately embodied in a distinguished tradition of composers, scholars, critics, wealthy and aristocratic patrons, magnificent concert halls, and works of genius that range from grand opera to the delicate minuet. Classical music is truly one of the peaks of civilization.

Despite these impressive credentials, many people do not care for classical music. Perhaps its fascinations are not always readily apparent. A sensibility for its subtleties has to be cultivated through study and training. This is usually referred to as "music appreciation," which means listening to music in an analytical frame of mind. It is a common belief that while we can enjoy other kinds of music, classical music is just for "appreciation."

However, as we shall see in the following chapters on cultivated diversions, intellectual appreciation is but a preliminary stage. In the end, classical music is meant to be enjoyed like any other entertainment. And there is ample evidence that it is, indeed, enjoyed in that state of absorbed attention. For example, in an early study by music scholar Max Schoen, prominent musical artists were asked to describe their own personal experience of music. After analyzing their responses, Schoen concluded that musical experience is characterized by a "unique attitude" that seems to be the equivalent of absorbed attention.

> In the truly musical experience ... everything that is not of the sum and substance of the music itself is ruled out of consciousness, and nothing is present in the mind of the listener but an awareness of "the thing itself." Attention is completely focused upon and absorbed by the music itself to an extent that the subject and object become merged one with the other.[28]

While classical music is listened to attentively, most other kinds of music are simply heard on the periphery of consciousness. This was demonstrated in a survey which asked subjects to indicate how much time they spent listening to music, how intently, and what type was preferred.[29] It was found that "high listeners," those who listened to music for four or more hours per week, preferred chamber music and symphonies. "Low listeners," on the other hand, preferred popular music. In addition, the high listeners rated their involvement with classical music as "deeply or very deeply absorbed" and stated that they were very strongly annoyed by interruptions. The low listeners rated their absorption with popular music as "moderate," and they were not particularly annoyed by interruptions.

A current college text on music points out how listening to aesthetic music is different from listening to popular music. The difference is in the degree of attentional involvement.

> In order to share the impact of [aesthetic] music, you must be willing to throw yourself into the experience with all your powers of concentration and all your capacity for feeling. The music we are concerned with *demands* your involvement; it was not created to soothe you or to calm you or to tickle your ears without intruding into your brain but was created to absorb you . . . to add *more* awareness rather than less. It cannot do these things without your help. So when you listen to music *musically,* you must put aside letter writing, knitting, chatting, reading a magazine, or doing homework.[30]

The authors go on to point out that the person should not daydream to the music, or dwell on fantasies, scenes, or stories stimulated by the music. It is likely that most people do some of this "imaginative" listening, but to the extent that it occurs, attention is focused on mental content rather than on the external object which should control attention totally. By attending to our thoughts and associations, we tune out the music. As these authors state, we must instead "focus on the sounds and what they are doing" (p. 51). The aesthetic experience of music requires that we attend to the sensuous qualities of the sounds, as well as the developing process of the composition. Music is motion, and in the aesthetic response we let ourselves be carried along by its flow. The music-lover

> anticipates tendencies; he is absorbed in deviations from patterns; he is surprised by improbable events, is delighted by the fulfillment of an expectation, is challenged by delays in the unfolding ideas, is puzzled by an unusual situation, wonders how it will be resolved, watches and waits and follows and jumps ahead, totally absorbed in the world of structured sound that is presented to his mind and feelings.
>
> At this level of response it is truly possible to say that the listener becomes one with the music. He emerges from such an experience exhausted and wrung out but also rejuvenated, excited, and exalted. A new and deeper level of experience has enriched his life. People who cherish music have shared

some of this excitement; they know how special such experience is and how
fulfilling it can be. It is little wonder that they seek it out at every
opportunity.[31]

As noted earlier, rock music is absorbing—but in a way very different
from aesthetic music. Rock absorbs by virtue of its powerful beat and it
loudness; these elements are so strong that they almost force a hypnotic
takeover of attention. Aesthetic music, on the other hand, absorbs by virtue
of its rich patterns; the hypnotic involvement is based on the suggestibility
and sensibility of the listener. In one case it is a matter of succumbing to the
effects of loudness and rhythm; in the other case it is a matter of contemplating
hidden beauty. Josephine Hilgard addressed this issue in her book which
relates hypnotic experience to various kinds of entertainment.

> We have had the good fortune of having a musical expert, a musician and
> conductor, as one of our research collaborators (John Lenox). He happens
> also to be highly hypnotizable and readily relates the hypnotic experience to
> music listening. When listening to a symphony, he points out, one has almost
> an [hypnotic] "induction" experience in the slow, brief, monotonous in-
> troduction, in which attention is captured while other processes are inhibited.
> Examples are Mozart's Thirty-ninth and Forty-first symphonies, about half
> of Beethoven's symphonies, of which the Ninth would be a prime example,
> and many of Haydn's works. The listener sits quietly and tends to inhibit
> voluntary movement. This is in contrast with the violent motor respon-
> siveness of the jazz listener, or the rhythmic responses to martial music. The
> responsive mood is created, and as the symphony moves on the listener is
> "transported." The response does not die immediately when the last note is
> heard but continues during the silence that follows a really good performance.
> It is as though a partial dissociation has been created which persists for a time.
> Something along these lines appears to relate listening to classical music to
> the experience of hypnosis.[32]

It should be noted that the view presented here runs counter to the traditional doctrines of music appreciation. It is commonly believed that listening
to classical music is basically a cognitive exercise of evaluating the music. Such
a process, emphasizing intellectual activity, is just the opposite of absorption,
which entails suggestibility, total involvement, and experiencing.

A recent study tested the validity of these two approaches — cognitive appreciation versus absorbed experience — by attempting to determine which
cerebral hemisphere is primarily involved in listening to music. The left
hemisphere of the brain specializes in intellectual analysis and verbal, sequential processing; the right, in wholistic perception and the recognition of overall
relationships.[33] In a general way, the two hemispheric functions correspond
to the two possible ways of reacting to music. This study tested the two approaches by comparing people who had been trained in music appreciation
with those who had no such training. It was assumed that people who had at

least seven years of musical training would tend to process music primarily by way of the left hemisphere, by analyzing it. On the other hand, people untrained in music should process it by means of the right hemisphere, with global, uncritical perception. Musical discrimination and recognition tasks were presented to the right and left ears separately. Since auditory (and all other) nerves cross over in the brain, it was assumed that superior performance with the right ear would indicate utilization of the left hemisphere, and vice versa. The results showed that *all* subjects, musicians as well as nonmusicians, performed better with the left ear, suggesting that the music was processed primarily in the right hemisphere.[34] Even people who were trained to be analytical about music apparently experienced it primarily in a global way that would be consistent with absorption.

Another study casts similar doubt on the usual "appreciation" doctrine. Panzarella was interested in trying to determine in an empirical way the meaning of that nebulous term "aesthetic experience." Believing it to be something more than just making judgments about art, he sought to identify the basic components of what musicians would consider good musical experience. Panzarella told his subjects, music professionals, that he was not interested in their average or routine reactions in listening to classical music, but wanted them to describe an occasion when their experience of music was excellent. This request brought responses depicting intensely absorbing involvements, usually known as peak experiences. In his conclusions, Panzarella wrote that these "accounts seldom followed the norms of aesthetics or psychological models of aesthetics appreciation."[35] Here is a sample of what musicians considered excellent musical experience. (If these descriptions seem a little disjointed, it is because each is a composite of answers written to specific questions, the first of which requested the name of the particular musical work that evoked the excellent response.)

"Rhapsody in Blue by George Gershwin. I began to have difficulty keeping my place in the music. I began to feel high. As I became more absorbed into the music, I lost my place. My body felt electrified. I felt like moving with the music, so I did. I forgot about the audience and the other musicians around me. I felt as if there was only me and the music. I felt like I was going to explode. A tremendous chill ran through my body. I felt very alone and I wished I were."

"Act II of *Tristan and Isolde.* I was lying on a bed with my eyes closed, anticipating what I have known in the past to be a great experience. This time the whole piece made more sense than ever and I began to "understand" the reason for every note in the piece. I gradually began to lose the intellectual cognizance of what was happening in the music—the side ended and I put the next record on. The love duet began and I felt no longer any sense of time or place and a complete and intense relationship with the music began to develop. The hearing of the music began to leave the area of my ears and I felt like I was hearing with my entire body. With this came an awareness of waves, seemed to be going through my limbs and the total feeling could only be said to what one wishes in orgasm. . . . I felt exhilarated (no longer lazy) and thought about the piece. I felt like crying for the realization of the drama of the opera was so complete and indeed quite overwhelming."

"I became aware of a feeling of elevation, as though my mind were not part of my body, but floating above it, in complete freedom. The music seemed to be a force that could be felt moving through my body. My thoughts were very free floating, although the sounds and vibrations of the music held my attention. I was completely free."

"Transported for a few moments. A feeling of great good will—troubles and cares were gone—everything seemed right and wonderful—a feeling of having been in touch with something great and beautiful, yet not quite understanding it. There was a great feeling of being uplifted, ennobled—joy in having stumbled onto the concert by accident, the richness of the experience, marvel at how differently I could feel so suddenly."[36]

In these examples there is nothing to indicate that the person was standing back and critically analyzing the music. Nor is there any sense of the supposedly desirable "half in the world and half out of it" arrangement. Rather, what is most evident in these reports is enjoyment and a total surrender to the music—being carried along by it. This is absorption, an external stimulus taking complete control of attention and organismic experience. It is reflected in phrases like "the music seemed to be a force," "awareness of waves," "felt electrified," "going to explode," "hearing with my entire body." Similar "hallucinatory" effects have been reported in other states of extreme absorption such as psychedelic, sexual, and meditational experiences.

Santayana wrote that music is, "like mathematics, very nearly a world by itself."[37] To be absorbed in that world, therefore, is to feel elevated out of the mundane. Of course, some music scholars have been saying this for a long time. Charles Myers wrote: "Nowhere in art or nature as in music do we more keenly feel this 'uplifting of the soul.'"[38] Paul Elmer More wrote that "when we listen to the harmonies of instrumental music or the melody of the human voice, there arises a strange emotion within us which seems to magnify us out of ourselves into some expanse of illimitable experiences, to lift us above the present cares of petty life into some vast concern."[39]

Maslow's research showed that ecstasy and peak experience are often aroused by aesthetic music.

So far, I have found that these peak experiences are reported from what we might call "classical music." I have not found a peak experience from John Cage or from an Andy Warhol movie. . . . The peak experience that has reported the great joy, the ecstasy, the visions of another world, or another level of living, have come from classical music—the great classics.[40]

The absorbed qualities so prominent in listening to classical music are also evident in other aesthetic experiences, as we shall see in the next chapter.

Chapter 10

Cultivated Diversions: Art

The hours when the mind is absorbed by beauty
are the only hours when we really live. — *Richard Jefferies*

Most of the diversions we have discussed so far can be enjoyed by any adult. They require no special training. They are simple and direct so that the ability to enjoy them is easily learned.

Many other diversions, however, require special training and sometimes talent. These take the form of hobbies but can also be considered *cultivated diversions;* they are enjoyed only after the person has acquired a particular system of skills and codes. One kind of cultivated diversion is art, which consists of excellent *perceptual* experience as provided by looking at paintings, listening to classical music, watching ballet, etc. Enjoying art is a spectator diversion par excellence.

Another kind of cultivated diversion, to be discussed in the next chapter, consists of creative activities, crafts, games and sports. All of these provide diversion through excellent *performance;* they are mental or physical activities enjoyed for their own sake. The category would include a wide range of hobbies, such as stamp collecting, making art objects, playing chess, creative writing, mountain climbing, or playing a musical instrument.

A final category of cultivated diversion centers around meditational practices. Meditation is diversion because it provides mental relaxation and withdrawal from everyday reality. It is excellent *awareness* — cleansed of everyday distractions.

These are the elite diversions, meant for only a dedicated few. Most people do not have the inclination or resources to pursue a cultivated diversion, and fail to understand what can be so enjoyable about them. In fact, some of these hobbies — like stamp collecting, meditating, or watching ballet — might seem downright boring. Others appear to have similar disadvantages; chess might be too brainy, mountain climbing could be hazardous to one's health, and most of the others seem to be too worklike to be recreational.

Evidently, however, it is not so important what is done, but *how* — the experiencing of it, the degree and quality of involvement. The content becomes secondary. It is not just a matter of acquiring a skill, as we do all the time in everyday life, but the absorbed experiences that the skill makes possible. Cultivated diversions can seem strange, uninteresting, or difficult, but there is little doubt that these pastimes are sustained by the relaxed fascinations of absorbed experience.

Cultivated diversions are not diverting at first. When they are initially undertaken, which is often in childhood, they are usually more work than play. Acquiring whatever skill is involved demands study, practice, concentration, effort, and frustration. It may take years of such effortful application before spending time with the hobby starts to become recreational and enjoyable. As the person becomes more proficient, matching his skill to the challenge presented by the hobby becomes a source of fascination and absorbed experience. Gradually, the hobby becomes a genuine diversion.

For example, playing the piano is a typical cultivated hobby, and the experience of it changes over time as the skill is mastered. Learning to play the piano always starts out as an effortful task. However, if the person becomes an accomplished pianist, his experience of playing music will change considerably. While work and practice are still needed, more and more these alternate with periods of absorbed experience where the pianist feels one-with the music. At these times, he might feel that he is not playing the musical score, but that the *it* is playing *him* — controlling what we might call his "skill-codes" so completely that he is simply carried along by the whole experience. The more developed his system of skill-codes, the more he can venture into very demanding music, on the one hand being one-with it in an almost slavish way, but also taking chances with it by following his own intuitions. Getting such enjoyable experiences time and again tend to make him deeply attached to his playing. To the extent that his life is centered around playing the piano, the hobby would be like another master code system, a "second nature."

Appreciation vs. Enjoyment

Is art work? Or is it play? Are we supposed to be studious about art, or are we supposed to enjoy it? Is it a special kind of mental exercise, or a special kind of entertainment?

Nobody has been able to give satisfactory answers to these longstanding questions. The learned ones have merely taken sides on this issue, with the result that two different philosophies about art have evolved. The older and more established school has taken the position that art is work; the view that it is play is a more recent development. The former represents the conservative-traditional position, while the latter is the purist-extremist position. Aesthetics scholar Melvin Rader described these two contrasting views in terms of a *critical-contemplative* dimension.[1] In other words, if art is work it is processed by critical thinking. If it is play it is enjoyed in a contemplative mood.

The conservative position states that our response to art should be evaluative, cognitive, realistic. This view originated with the Greek philosophers, who believed that art has an instructional function since it embodies the highest values of beauty and goodness. The discernment of these values is of utmost importance, hence the term "art appreciation" — appraising the values in art. Making this appraisal requires critical thinking, thus art is serious and high-minded business. In this view, art is associated with other values such as truth and love, and it should be expressive of man's relationship with himself and his community. This position leads to a whole philosophy about art: that it should be integrated with everyday life, that it should reflect reality, that it should make a statement about life, and that it is best understood when viewed in the context of its time and place, the artist's intentions, and other social and ethical issues.

The contemplative-purist position is best expressed by the dictum "art for art's sake." Art needs no justification in terms of meeting practical needs; it is not defined by its connections with reality. Rather, according to this view art exists as a domain in its own right, and its worth is determined by what it does for our experience. This approach emphasizes immediacy of experiencing rather than acuity of critical judgment. Aesthetic experience should start in contemplation and end in ecstasy. Art is inherently distanced from everyday life, according to Clive Bell, one of the high priests of this school. "The recognition of a correspondence between the forms of a work of art and the familiar forms of life," he wrote, "cannot possibly provoke aesthetic emotion." Bell enunciated a view of art as extreme diversion.

> The representative element in a work of art may or may not be harmful; always it is irrelevant. For, to appreciate a work of art we need to bring with us nothing from life, no knowledge of its ideas and affairs, no familiarity with its emotions. Art transports us from the world of man's activity to a world of aesthetic exaltation. For a moment we are shut off from human interests; our anticipations and memories are arrested; we are lifted above the stream of life.[2]

Neither of these approaches to art, the conservative or the contemplative-purist, seems complete in itself. And what a paradox! Art — presumably one of the highest achievements of the human race, and still we have no entirely satisfactory way to deal with it.

Can it be that both approaches are correct? Although they are directly opposite, can they be synthesized in some way? The resolution to this problem may be found in the concept of cultivated diversion, which implies an alternation of work and play. In other words, art is what these opposed views say it is — appreciation *and* enjoyment — but at different times. Initially, like all cultivated diversions, art is study, work, and critical thinking in order to acquire the necessary perceptual codes. Once these are programmed in, however, art should become more and more a diversion. In the first stage (appreciation), a person learns how art works. In the second stage (enjoyment), he lets art work on him, or more precisely, he lets it play with his perceptual codes, his acquired sensibility.

It seems to be generally agreed that an aesthetic experience is possible only to the educated eye and ear. Simply looking at a great painting does not automatically lead to an aesthetic response, no matter how much we like it; if we do not have the necessary perceptual codes, it is just a pretty picture. Training in art appreciation is the initial skill-acquisition stage when the person is programmed with codes and sensitivities, learning to perceive aesthetically. This is the time to consult with the critics, and to have at our side teachers to guide perception and tell us what to look for. "Even in poetry and the arts," wrote William James, "someone has to come and tell us what aspects we may single out, and what effects we may admire, before our aesthetic nature can 'dilate' to its full extent and never 'with the wrong emotion.'"[3] The beauty found in art is not as immediately apparent as the beauty in nature. One must be sensitized to it and know how to find it. Since most people do not have this kind of training, they "see" nothing in art. Even Clive Bell made it clear that "without sensibility a man can have no aesthetic experience."[4] In general, the more extensive the study, the greater will be the eventual enjoyment. Thus, completely new art objects or our first exposure to an artistic style may lead to weak or uncertain enjoyment because the necessary codes are not available to be played upon. At their best, the fine arts consist of a body of classics and masterpieces that we return to again and again for even richer enjoyment.

The second stage of a cultivated diversion is enjoyment, total involvement, and being carried away with the thing. For this to happen in art, the aesthetic codes must be ready to be played upon. Kate Hevner wrote that the person just starting out in art appreciation

> will be utterly and indescribably bored with the picture, completely impatient and exasperated with the music. He will resent them as bitterly as the child resents his piano scales and his problems in long division. But we must remember that the objective was not ... the enjoyment of the picture, but the building up of habits of observation, the awakening of the senses and the training of the perception so that the apprehension of the details will be ready and nimble. For if the skill in perception is slow and awkward, if the mere task of comprehending the form demands all the attention, there will be no time or energy left for the enjoyment of it. The pleasure of the total effect would be lost, just as the smack of a French epigram is lost to a beginner whose French is so poor that he must decipher each syllable with painstaking care. To achieve any pleasure in art, as in language, the facility must be so ready that as the sentence proceeds (or as the music proceeds) one is aware

of the trend of the ideas and approaches the end with a certain foresight. Then the conclusion will be important as a fulfillment and it will be rich with satisfaction because it was wanted and needed. The moment for its enjoyment, however, must always be free. For the inexpert, the effort and confusion and uncertainty will crowd out the pleasure, and the experience can not be crowned with success.[5]

Thus, the enjoyment itself does not come from a self-conscious application of aesthetic principles. To dissect the art object in an intellectual way is to prevent involvement and experience. Evaluating art in terms of standards "too often acts as an effective and all but insuperable obstacle, which must be somehow hurdled or evaded before genuine aesthetic (as distinct from practical or critical) perception can get under way."[6]

As in the case of all absorbed experience, the person must let art happen, rather than try to force it to happen. Aesthetic enjoyment grows out of a contemplative approach that is leisurely, patient, and unself-conscious. Bernard Berenson, who spent most of his life in the study of visual art, believed that when it came time for enjoyment one should "muse and ruminate." He wrote: "I deplore the 'machine-age' mentality which urges one to inquire instead of enjoying almost passively and being fed by that enjoyment." He felt that the typical person attacks art "with scalpel and microscope. . . . instead of letting it soak into him as he gazes and looks." Berenson wrote: "You must look, and look, and look, until you are blind with looking, and out of the blindness will come illumination."[7] In other words, the old ways of looking must adapt out; they must be negated by the contemplative approach. And out of this "blindness" and passivity will come an "awakening of the senses," as Hevner called it. This is aesthetic experience at its best — as extreme diversion and as figure-ground reversal of everyday life. It is art making possible "a new vision," allowing us to see more deeply. "Anything can make us look;" wrote Archibald MacLeish, "only art makes us see." Paul Klee voiced a similar notion: "Art does not reproduce the visible but makes visible." And Marshall McLuhan wrote that "art is a means of giving us new awareness through an intensification of our sensory life."[8]

Just as physical exercise can enhance the functioning of the muscles, so the study of art appreciation can enhance perceptual functioning, extending our ability to see and hear. It does not improve our actual eyesight or hearing, of course, but exercise in art appreciation can greatly enhance certain perceptual capacities and codes that are a part of the organism. Aesthetics training sensitizes these latent codes, the art object is designed to stimulate them, and together the result is perfect, i.e. aesthetic, experience.

Gestalt psychology, which specializes in the study of perception, has made us aware of a variety of organismic codes that structure perception. The role of these codes in aesthetic experience was examined by Rudolf Arnheim in his book *Art and Visual Perception*. With specific illustrations, he showed how

a painting's structure arouses these perceptual effects, which carry the principal meaning of art. For example, he analyzed Cezanne's portrait of his wife
sitting in a yellow chair, a painting noted for conveying a sense of tranquility
as well as potential strength and activity. These effects are felt if one is sensitive
to the two directional forces that play against each other in the perceptual field
of the painting, which create a unique experience of a complex and somewhat
enigmatic personality. According to Arnheim, there are "more things in the
field of vision than those that strike the retinas of the eyes."[9]

Aesthetic enjoyment consists of just such an enrichment of perceptual and
intuitive experience. The art lover does not care about whether the painting
looks like the real thing or not, or what message is being communicated. In
the painting *The Last Supper,* Leonardo da Vinci's representation of Jesus and
the apostles is a necessary but only a minor consideration. It is the radiating
composition that induces the sense of wholeness that gives the picture its
spiritual quality. Obviously the content and the meanings that the picture conveys are important, but these must be integrated with the composition and
the perceptual forces of the painting. In fact, the meanings come alive only
by virtue of these forces. For example, the painting of *The Bellelli Family* by
Edgar Degas seems to be a straightforward portrait of a young family whose
members look a little strained. But if one can look at the painting in terms
of its perceptual dynamics, then it takes on a dark and disturbing intuitive
charge that is almost palpable. Perceptual dynamics become family dynamics;
to experience one is to experience the other.

A similar situation exists in the fine art of poetry, only here the aesthetic
experience is based on language rather than perceptual codes. Normally,
language is a means to an end; in poetry it is an end in itself. In everyday
life, language serves the business of living, being the tool with which we think
and communicate. But in the poetic situation, language does not have to work.
It is played upon for its intrinsic characteristics of rhythm, imagery, sensuous
sounds, symbols. As McMullen noted, poetry pushes "discursive language
toward non-discursive." This switch in the language function was the central
idea in Santayana's definition of poetry.

> A tolerable definition of poetry, on its formal side, might be found in this:
> that poetry is speech in which the instrument counts as well as the meaning —
> poetry is speech for its own sake and for its own sweetness. . . . so, while the
> purest prose is a mere vehicle of thought, verse, like stained glass, arrests
> attention in its own intricacies, confuses it in its own glories, and is even at
> times allowed to darken and puzzle in the hope of casting over us a super-
> natural spell.
>   . . . . The reader gathers, probably, no definite meaning, but is conscious
> of a poetic medium, of speech euphonious and measured, and redolent of
> a kind of objectless passion which is little more than the sensation of the move-
> ment and sensuous richness of the lines.[10]

The fine arts have become very complex and erudite institutions; however, it is well to remember that each is based on a certain kind of experience that is a reversal of everyday life. In a manner of speaking, each art celebrates experiencing and organismic function. In everyday life, these functions act to process the environment. But in the aesthetic situation, workaday interactions cease, and the organism is presented with an art object designed to bring out the fullest possibilities of experience. Music serves the ear, eliciting rich aural experience that is never possible in everyday life. Visual art is designed to fit in with various perceptual codes, making for pleasing, harmonious, and natural experience. Poetry plays with speech sounds, rhythm, and meaning. In this sense, art is organismic and experiential, not cognitive — as Walter Pater pointed out: "Art, then, is thus always striving to be independent of the mere intelligence, to become a matter of pure perception, to get rid of its responsibilities to its subject or material. . . . so that the meaning reaches us through ways not distinctly traceable by the understanding." This emphasis on experience is why art makes us come alive; as various scholars have noted, it provides a "quickened sense of life," "multiplied consciousness," and "life-enhancement."[11]

Art has never flourished among the masses because it requires intense cultivation in terms of time, study, and availability of art objects. Most working people do not have the resources to pursue such a demanding entertainment. Thus, throughout history, it was primarily the privileged, upper classes who enjoyed cultivated diversions. Apparently, this continues to be true, according to sociologists who study the consumption patterns of art or "high culture." For example, surveys reveal that the majority of individuals who cultivate the arts have attended college and even graduate school, generally in the liberal arts programs of the better universities. In addition to formal education, it appears that art cultivation requires an early start, usually when the individual is a young child. After reviewing the pertinent literature, Kando concluded that the true art consumers "come from families in which high culture has been a way of life for generations."[12] Wilensky suggested that it may take close "supervision over more than a generation to inculcate a taste for high culture."[13] Any society can have story, song, and alcohol, but only those groups who have leisure and affluence can afford to take up cultivated diversions like art.

Absorption as Psychic Distance and Empathy

> The effect of a work of art upon the person who enjoys it is an experience different in kind from any experience not of art. — *T.S. Eliot*

In 1912, British psychologist Edward Bullough made a singular contribution to the field of aesthetics. He introduced the concept of *psychic distance* to help explain how aesthetic feeling is different from everyday experience. Up to this time, there was only a vague notion about this difference. Scholars recognized that aesthetic experience was somehow objective and "disinterested," yet also intensely interesting and involving. Bullough resolved this paradox with his concept of psychic distance, pointing out that in aesthetic experience the person is not psychologically distant from the art object — but from himself! This distance from self allows him to be more involved with the art object and therefore to experience it more intensely. What Bullough was conceptualizing for aesthetics was exactly what Samuel Taylor Coleridge had done for literature about a hundred years earlier with his principle of "the willing suspension of disbelief." The latter talked about *suspending* self, while the former talked about *distancing* the self.

> Distance is produced . . . by putting the phenomenon, so to speak, out of gear with our practical, actual self; by allowing it to stand outside the context of our personal needs and ends. . . . It has a *negative,* inhibitory aspect — the cutting-out of the practical sides of things and of our practical attitude to them — and a *positive* side — the elaboration of the experience on the new basis created by the inhibitory action of Distance.[14]

The "negative, inhibitory" side of psychic distance is mental relaxation, the shutting out of everyday self-referent concerns. The "positive" side is the enhancement of experiencing. So again we find scholars attempting to deal with the paradoxical aspects of what appears to be another example of relaxed arousal.

Bullough realized that psychological distance can be induced by simply adopting a different "outlook" and looking at art in a contemplative mood. However, he was also interested in showing how cues in the art object help trigger psychic distance. Drama, for example, contains numerous signals that the play is not reality, and so permits a relaxation of self and evaluative thinking. The artificial lighting, costumes, makeup, and the fact that the play is limited to the stage area all create the feeling of a world separate from everyday reality. Similarly, sculpture is often set apart by its placement on pedestals. Painting is framed and depicts an imaginary space usually with a perspective different from that of everyday life. The content of an art object — depending on how unrealistic it is — can also neutralize and distance self. If the object is too idealistic, absurd, or abstract, then the result is extreme distance; paradoxically, over-distanced art tends to cause anxiety, which brings back the self in order to cope with what might seem strange and threatening. On the other hand, if the art object is under-distanced by being too realistic, this too keeps the self engaged. Aesthetic experience is possible only when there is optimal distancing from self and reality. Bullough wrote that "'artistic' is synonymous with 'anti-realistic.'" He asserted that "beauty in the widest sense of aesthetic value is impossible without the insertion of Distance."[15]

Bullough apparently was a conservative in art; he believed that aesthetic experience is best served when there "is the *utmost decrease of Distance without its disappearance.*"[16] In other words, he preferred art to be mild diversion — as little distanced as possible. One wonders what he thought of abstract painting. Ironically, the first abstract paintings were done in the very year that Bullough's article was published. Since then, visual art has been revolutionized by abstractionism, which today is synonymous with modern art. Because abstract art is nonrepresentational and unrealistic, it may be considered to be highly distanced, and an attempt at extreme diversion. Although it violates Bullough's canon for minimal distance, abstract art is best understood in terms of his ideas about distance. Thus two events of 1912 — the conceptualization of psychic distance, and the appearance of abstract painting — were a forecast of things to come at mid-century, when numerous other entertainments would move in the direction of extreme diversion.

Abstract painting was created in order to force visual art into a more aesthetic direction. Artists and scholars had long known that most people were attracted to visual art simply becuase it depicted interesting objects and scenes from life. Apparently people tended to like pretty pictures that were colorful, expressed ideas, or induced sentiment. Such values are anti-aesthetic, however, and they put art at the level of popular music. Painting needed more distance from reality. Modern art, therefore, purified itself of all reminders of the everyday and became nonrepresentational. Human figures were eliminated so that the viewer would not be distracted by reminders of himself or other people. There is no reality to relate to, no meanings to process, no likenesses to judge. In other words, abstract art makes irrelevant the master codes; it creates the conditions for their suspension, so that we can look at the object for its own sake. We can only let the painting hit us, and let it have what effects it does. With nothing to attend to but form and color, we are almost forced to experience the perceptual dynamics. Presumably, for the true art lover this should suffice; in this sense abstract art may be the acid test for aesthetic sensibility. Abstract art, of course, epitomizes the purist-contemplative approach to art where, as Clive Bell said, to enjoy it "we need to bring with us nothing from life." Clement Greenberg made it clear that abstract art strives to be extreme diversion, and it is meant to be enjoyed with absorbed attention.

> Ideally the whole of a picture should be taken in at a glance; its unity should be immediately evident and the supreme quality of a picture, the highest measure of its power to move and control the visual imagination, should reside in its unity. And this is something to be grasped only in an indivisible instant of time. . . . It's all there at once, like a sudden revelation. This "at-onceness" an abstract picture usually drives home to us with greater singleness and clarity than a representational painting does. And to apprehend this "at-onceness" demands a freedom of mind and untrammeled-

ness of eye that constitute "at-onceness" in their own right. Those who have grown capable of experiencing this know what I mean. You are summoned and gathered into one point in the continuum of duration. . . . You become all attention, which means that you become, for the moment, selfless and in a sense entirely identified with the object of your attention. . . .

The special, unique value of abstract art, I repeat, lies in the high degree of detached contemplativeness that its appreciation requires. Contemplativeness is demanded in greater or lesser degree for the appreciation of every kind of art, but abstract art tends to present this requirement in quintessential form, at its purest, least diluted, most immediate. . . .

How many people I know who have hung abstract pictures on their walls and found themselves gazing at them endlessly, and then exclaiming, "I don't know what there is in that painting, but I can't take my eyes off it." This kind of bewilderment is salutary. It does us good not to be able to explain, either to ourselves or to others, what we enjoy or love; it expands our capacity for experience.[17]

A second concept, *empathy*, has traditionally been linked with psychic distance to describe reactions to art. This term was mentioned earlier in our discussion of being one-with, which is its technical meaning. "Empathy" has acquired numerous other meanings in psychotherapy, but in aesthetics it refers to an intense involvement of oneness with the art object. Theodor Lipps was the person who, several years before Bullough's article, formulated the concept of empathy: "Empathy is the fact here established, that the object is myself and by the very same token this self of mine is the object. Empathy is the fact that the antithesis between myself and the object disappears."[18]

Melvin Rader has called psychic distance and empathy the "complementary moments in the systole-diastole of aesthetic experience."[19] In other words, they are two aspects of the altered attentional state that makes possible aesthetic experience. Distance refers to what is lost (self) while empathy refers to what is gained (enhanced involvement). More recent definitions of aesthetic experience formulate this directly in terms of attention, as in this statement by aesthetics scholar Eliseo Vivas:

Attention is esthetic when it is so controlled by the object that it does not fly away from it to meanings not present immanently in the object; or in other words that attention is so controlled that the object specifies concretely and immediately through reflexive cross-references its meanings and objective characters. And thus we may contrast esthetic with all other modes of attention by noting that other modes of attention discover in objects not immanent but referential meanings, which is to say, meanings which carry us beyond the object to other objects or meaning not present upon it. . . .

Rapt attention on an object excludes self-consciousness. . . .

The autonomy of the esthetic experience follows from the fact that to the degree to which it is controlled fully and adequately by the object, to that degree does it seem after its enjoyment to have been thoroughly disengaged from the rest of our experience and to possess a *sui generis* character. It also throws light on a phenomenon which has been the spring board for a great deal of mysticism, namely, the deep conviction of the superior reality of the object in which the experience often leaves us. This conviction springs from the intransitive nature of our attention, since during the experience the object remains in complete monopolistic possession of consciousness. [20]

All this suggests that there is nothing mysterious about aesthetic experience, as we are sometimes led to believe. It involves the same kind of attentional orientation found in other absorbing diversions. What Vivas says about the control of attention in aesthetic experience could just as well be said about story entertainment or sexual passion. While the content of art may be more profound, and as a diversion it requires some cultivation, the kind of involvement we have with it is on a continuum with other entertainments. It seems that the great scholars, like Henry James, have always recognized this:

> The *effect* of . . . any work of art — is to entertain. . . . The success of a work of art, to my mind, may be measured by the degree to which it produces a certain illusion; that illusion makes it appear to us for the time that we have lived another life — that we have had a miraculous enlargement of experience. The greater the art the greater the miracle, and the more certain also the fact that we have been entertained — in the best meaning of that word. [21]

In his book *The Sacred Wood,* T.S. Eliot voiced similar opinions about the experience of poetry. "The end of the enjoyment of poetry is a pure contemplation from which all the accidents of personal emotion are removed," he wrote. "Poetry is not a turning loose of emotion, but an escape from emotion; it is not the expression of personality, but an escape from personality. . . . Poetry is a superior amusement." [22]

Peak Experience through Aesthetic Absorption

> A good work of visual art carries a person who is capable of appreciating it out of life into ecstasy; to use art as a means to the emotions of life is to use a telescope for reading the news. — *Clive Bell*

George Steiner, distinguished literary scholar and critic, appeared on the WNET television program "Bill Moyers' Journal." In the course of the interview, Moyers asked, "What is there in literature that has been worth the great investment of your life in it?" Steiner replied:

> Oh, unquestionably, something which one can't paraphrase, and which is very dangerous. That the page in front of you, or the poem you learn by heart, or the play you've seen comes to possess you more than any other order of experience. That living things seem unreal compared to the intensity of the

imaginative experience. I think that's the most exciting thing that can happen. Why do I say it's dangerous? Because like many other people too addicted to literature, I've often noticed in myself that the cry in the street [is] mysteriously less powerful, less important, than the cry in the book, in the story. And that the tears that come over the great tragic scene have a bitter despair which after all should be elicited by what is happening in the city around us. So there is a danger. An imagintion too utterly absorbed and fascinated by great art and literature can become autistic and whirl within its own very closed world. On the other hand, great art is probably our one . . . constant window on something much larger than ourselves.[23]

This is cultivated diversion speaking. Undoubtedly, Dr. Steiner spent untold hours in the study of literature, and at some point this study became the basis for a most rewarding enjoyment. His remarks show how powerful and captivating aesthetic experience can be when cultivated to the fullest.

Yet nothing in the formal doctrines of aesthetics even hints that such intensity and passion is possible with art. There are no concepts to suggest that art can be so involving, no warnings that it can be addictive and even dangerous to one's reality orientation. In the traditional approach to art there is only an anemic and intellectualistic conception of aesthetic enjoyment, indicating that it is merely a mild diversion, a matter of minimal distance, a half-and-half involvement.

More and more, however, there is increasing recognition that art and other cultivated diversions are capable of yielding intensely absorbing enjoyments. Whereas in the past cautious scholars only sniffed at the notion of aesthetic enjoyment and talked of "appreciating" art, today there is a readiness to explore the upper limits of aesthetic experience, the excellent response. Such investigations have lead to the notion of peak experience, where, as Maslow wrote, individuals "report having had something like mystic experiences, moments of great awe, moments of the most intense happiness or even rapture, ecstasy or bliss."[24]

Clive Bell frequently described his reactions to visual art in terms of "ecstasy." Bernard Berenson felt that his grasp of art matured only after he had what apparently was a peak experience. Earlier in his career, Berenson studied for years but had only an uncertain, intellectual knowledge of art. After the peak experience, however, art came alive for him to the extent that he had complete confidence in his feel for it. He described the experience as a "direct contact with an otherness," which was "in essence a mystical experience." It must have been this episode that inspired Berenson's famous definition of aesthetic experience.

In visual art the aesthetic moment is that flitting instant, so brief as to be almost timeless, when the spectator is at one with the work of art he is looking at, or with actuality of any kind that the spectator himself sees in terms of art, as form and colour. He ceases to be his ordinary self, and the picture or building, statue, landscape, or aesthetic actuality is no longer outside himself. The two become one entity; time and space are abolished and the spectator is possessed by one awareness. When he recovers workaday consciousness it is as if he had been initiated into illuminating, exalting, formative mysteries. In short, the aesthetic moment is a moment of mystic vision.[25]

Berenson seems to be saying that aesthetic enjoyment does not stop with the art object, but can catapult human experience to a new level. The experience, then, can be something much more than the stimulus would seem to warrant; it can be a rich expansion of consciousness that puts us in touch with something universal.

Abraham Maslow came to the same conclusion after extensive research on this topic. According to him, not only art but numerous other diversions can lead to enjoyments so intense that they culminate in an altered state of consciousness that he referred to as a "peak experience."[26] At advanced levels of enjoyment, art, music, sex, meditation and other diversions lose their distinctive flavor and elevate the organism to this level. Maslow based his ideas on a survey wherein subjects were asked to describe "ecstatic moments, moments of rapture, perhaps from being in love, or from listening to music or suddenly 'being hit' by a book or painting." In addition to these data, he researched the "immense literatures of mysticism, religion, art, creativeness, love, etc." From all this information, he culled a list of eighteen criteria for peak experience. Some of these characteristics are the basis of absorbed experience — total attention, egoless perception, feeling detached from everyday life, sense of wholeness and unity, etc.

The term "peak experience" refers to any kind of ecstatic-mystical experience. Surveys that attempt to determine whether a person has had a peak experience usually ask, "Have you ever had the feeling of being close to a powerful spiritual force that seemed to lift you outside of yourself?"[27] The sensing of a "spiritual force" does not just have a religious connotation but can refer to the awareness of any external, invisible influence that seems to take control of the person.

Peak experience is equivalent to what in the past was referred to as ecstasy or mystical trance, a phenomenon so unusual that society has never been able to deal with it in a level-headed way. In ancient times when religion was the dominant cultural institution, peak experiences were thought to be visitations from divine beings. With the coming of secular, more scientific society, this belief gave way to the view that such occurrences represented mental aberrations. However, a recent study reported in the *British Journal of Psychiatry* found no evidence for such a view. The study showed that people who reported having mystical experiences did not exhibit deviant traits such as pathological lying, hysterical personality, or psychotic disorder.[28] Nevertheless, psychological science has always looked on this phenomenon with suspicion.

Even the great William James, who discussed these states in his classic *The Varieties of Religious Experience,* was unable to make them the subject of legitimate scientific inquiry. Finally, with the coming of humanistic psychology, Maslow took a major step in revamping this long-abused concept. He brought it respectability by giving it a more objective name, de-emphasizing religion and mysticism, and broadening the concept to include the high points of aesthetic, sexual, and creative experience.

Maslow's work, which was published in the early 1960s, suited perfectly the zeitgeist of extreme diversion that had started to develop at mid-century. Interestingly, another major investigation along similar lines appeared at this time: Marghanita Laski's book *Ecstasy.* [29] By means of a questionnaire, Laski elicited descriptive information about ecstasy experiences from people who admitted having had one or more of them. When the results were analyzed, Laski found that most of the descriptive statements could be classified as representing some kind of loss and gain. In other words, as everyday consciousness changes and is reorganized into an ecstasy experience, certain psychological factors are lost while new ones are gained. In effect, these changes seem to represent a state of relaxed arousal. The "loss" statements reflected mental relaxation as subjects reported loss of words, thoughts, memories, self, the senses, worldly and conventional things, time and place, desires, sorrow, and personal limitations. On the other hand, the "gain" statements reflected an enhancement of experiencing; subjects reported receiving joy, a new life, a sense of being in another world, a feeling of contact or union or identification, and deep understanding and certainty.

One of the surprising findings of Laski's study was that ecstatic episodes apparently are not as random and spontaneous as had always been thought. In fact, they are triggered by specific stimuli. The two "triggers" for ecstasy most frequently mentioned were art and nature; these beauty-related categories accounted for about half of the ecstasies reported. By far, the most common art form noted was music, usually classical music. The other art forms mentioned were music- or rhythm-related, such as poetry, and the stage arts, such as opera, ballet, and drama. Under the nature category were listed landscapes, city scenes, and seasonal characteristics.

Information provided by the studies of Maslow and Laski suggests that the ecstatic-mystical experience is not so mysterious as is generally believed. Although it is usually viewed as a condition that the person suddenly pops in and out of, actually the experience seems to occur in the context of absorbed attention and is continuous with it. Maslow's term "peak experience" is apropos because the state seems to represent a high point of absorption. The more intensely absorbed a person becomes, the more he experiences a figure-ground reversal and, therefore, is likely to feel that he had suddenly been transported.

Peak experiences are not predictable, but their probabilities can be stated in terms of absorption and cultivated diversion. First, peak experiences always occur during diversion. People do not have peak experiences on the job, when they are task-oriented and meeting responsibilities, or when they are interacting in social situations. Further, if the person has an abiding interest or hobby, like listening to classical music, then the peak experience is more likely to occur during such a pastime than during milder diversions such as a party or volleyball game. Finally, the probability of a peak experience occurring is increased if the person is of a type that is easily absorbed — not intellectualizing, over-abstract, or compulsive. In general, the more absorbed the person can get in his cultivated diversion, the greater the likelihood of peak experience.

These high points of enjoyment do not occur to the man on the street who has no cultivated diversions. They do not occur to the dabbler or the dilettante, but to the enthusiast, the lover, and the devotee.

All in all, then, aesthetic experience seems to be a function of three factors: the excellence of the art object, the ease with which a person gets absorbed, and the long-term cultivation of an aesthetic sensibility through study and appreciation.

Chapter 11

Cultivated Diversions of Body and Mind

True happiness, we are told, consists in getting out of one's self,
but the point is not only to get out — you must stay out;
and to stay out you must have some absorbing errand. — *Henry James*

Throughout this book, it has been emphasized that a person is inactive when in the absorbed state. He has usually stopped moving, talking, thinking; he simply sits and looks and listens and *experiences.*

However, as we shall see in this chapter, there are exceptions to this rule. Under some conditions, it is possible to be physically or mentally active and at the same time absorbed. This is most evident in what is referred to as hobby activity. Except for the person immersed in a story, there is no better example of someone being in "another world" than the individual absorbed in a hobby — the craftsman carving wood, the collector classifying his specimens, the ham radio operator beaming in faraway messages.

Most hobbies have intrinsic diversion value because they are out of the ordinary, sometimes even exotic. They are derived from other times and places, as is evident in hobbies like building and flying kites or model rockets, exploring caves, old-time fiddling, growing Alpine plants — or becoming an expert on Victorian cooking, Dracula, Great Lakes steamboats or Texas outlaws.[1] Hobbies sometimes consist of collecting useless objects: postcards, old airline schedules, license plates, beer cans, etc. The nature of the objects guarantees that the activity will be nonbusiness and experienced for its own sake.

Hobbies are most likely to become absorbing recreations when they develop out of an individual's curiosities or talents, and are started early in life. The hobby that will yield the most recreational enjoyment is the one that is seriously pursued over a long period of time, not the one that is picked up casually when there is nothing better to do. Hobbies operate on the principle of cultivated diversion: They are most rewarding as long-term ventures. The enjoyment comes after a skill has been perfected and absorbed experience is possible. The best hobbies come from endeavors that are rich in complexity and conceptual development, making possible continuing challenge — sports, crafts, artwork, scientific pursuits, playing or composing music, games of strategy like bridge or chess.

Hobbies taken up for extrinsic reasons have a poor recreational prognosis. When the anxious psychiatric patient needs a source of relaxation, when the smoker who is trying to kick the habit needs some distraction from his craving, or when the retired worker needs to fill the void in his life — all are told to take up a hobby. This is poor advice because it assumes that recreational enjoyment will automatically come from doing something called a hobby. This is not so; in fact, if some skill is involved, as is usually the case, then learning it could be frustrating. Learning always involves study, memorizing instructions, trial and error, mistakes, and failures — all of which is work, not play. It would probably take a lot of such work before the hobby became a significant source of relaxation and recreational enjoyment.

This chapter will focus on two major kinds of hobbies: sport and creative activity. The one epitomizes the cultivation of physical action; the other, cognitive action. Normally, both kinds of action are geared to conducting the business of living. However, as hobbies, physical and cognitive action can be cultivated for their own sake, and so become the source of intensely absorbing experience.

When Action Is Absorbing

It is likely that in sport, as in art, the one who dabbles has the lesser enjoyment. This statement runs contrary to the general assumption that it is the occasional player, the layman who plays some sport "for fun," who gets the pleasure out of participating in sports. It might be noted, however, that adults who play sports infrequently will usually tire easily, feel awkward with their rusty skills, and be self-conscious if others are present and watching. While the occasional playing of sports can provide a lot of sociable gratifications, it hardly amounts to activity for its own sake.

On the other hand, the individual who cultivates a sport over a long period of time is likely to approach the recreational ideal of total involvement. As skills are perfected, actions become effortless and unself-conscious so that total attention can be given to the sport. As in the case of art, the cultivation of sport starts out as work, but with increased mastery, there is a greater capacity to move harmoniously with the sport. This makes it intensely absorbing and enjoyable.

The extensive cultivation of a sport, with its continual honing of skills, confers on the athlete a physical sensibility somewhat comparable to the aesthetic one. Just as the art lover can see what others cannot, so the athlete can do what others cannot. His feats of strength, coordination, and speed seem almost superhuman to someone of only normal physical condition, as George Plimpton showed.[2]

With this highly developed physical sensibility comes experience to match. In the folklore of sport, it is recognized that athletes sometimes get a high when their actions are completely in tune with the rapidly changing demands of a sport. This is known as "the greatest moment" or "the perfect moment." In his book *Beyond Boredom and Anxiety,* Csikszentmihalyi referred to this experience as "flow," and called it a special kind of enjoyment "that is not accessible in 'everyday life.'" The phenomenon of flow seems to be an example of absorbed action; it is a feeling of being harmoniously "carried along":

> In the flow state, action follows upon action according to an internal logic that seems to need no conscious intervention by the actor. He experiences it as a unified flowing from one moment to the next, in which . . . there is little distinction between self and environment, between stimulus and response, or between past, present, and future.[3]

Some sports, like skiing or swimming, would seem to naturally lend themselves to flow experiences. However, Csikszentmihalyi's studies revealed that such experiences occur even to participants in arduous sports — for example, rock climbing. Apparently individuals do not engage in this sport just to get to the top of the mountain; what is reflected in the following accounts is not work, but adult play and altered consciousness.

> "One tends to get immersed in what is going on around him, in the rock, in the moves that are involved . . . search for handholds . . . proper position of body — so involved he might lose the consciousness of his own identity and melt into the rock. . . ."
>
> "It's like when I was talking about things becoming 'automatic' . . . almost like an egoless thing in a way — somehow the right thing is done without . . . thinking about it or doing anything at all. . . . It just happens . . . and yet you're more concentrated. It might be like meditation, like Zen is a concentration. . . ."
>
> "It's a pleasant feeling of total involvement. You become like a robot . . . no, more like an animal . . . getting lost in kinesthetic sensation . . . a panther powering up the rock. . . ."
>
> "When things are going poorly, you start thinking about yourself. When things go well, you do things automatically without thinking. You pick the right holds, equipment, and it is right. . . ."
>
> "The right decisions are made, but not rationally. Your mind is shut down and your body just goes. It's one of the extremes of human experience."[4]

In these descriptions one would have expected a sense of struggle and fear about ever-present dangers. Instead, there is a feeling of effortless, harmonious action, totally involved in the here-and-now. Apparently, when one is accomplished in an activity and absorbed in it, normal relations are turned around; one's orientation changes, allowing the external object to take complete control, without mediation by the self-referent master code system. Just as the musical score seems to play the pianist, so also in this hobby the rock plays directly upon the skill codes of the climbers.

Although Csikszentmihalyi stated that the rock climbers in this study represented a wide range of experience, there is little doubt that the sport was highly cultivated in this group. For example, it was reported that the "mean length of experience was five years of technical rock climbing and eight years of general mountaineering." Furthermore, based on an international rating system for climbing skills, those "interviewed in the course of this study ranged in ability . . . from moderate skill to the limit of human potential, as it is currently estimated. Mean ratings indicate a slight skew toward the upper reaches of the spectrum." In terms of time devoted to the sport, most of these individuals climbed once every two weeks, "though some get out as often as four times a week and others as infrequently as once a month."[5] This was the level of summertime involvement; in the winter, it was half as much.

Individuals who cultivate sport to this extent will usually take every opportunity to engage in it. It becomes a pervasive influence in their lives. When not actively engaged in the sport, they are talking about it, thinking about it, or preparing for it. The sport may function like a master code in their lives, determining not only leisure activities but also choice of friends, group affiliations, career, and possibly even marital partner. Professional athletes, Olympic champions, and performing stars all come from the ranks of individuals who cultivate sport to this extent. An example of such cultivation-addiction can be found in the biography of Casey Stengel.

> Baseball absorbed Stengel. It was his life, and if that sounds like a cliche it is still true. He was born in Kansas City, Missouri, in 1890 and died in Glendale, California, in 1975, and for most of the 85 years in between baseball mattered more to him than almost anything else. During his life he grew famous and came to know and talk with kings, presidents, actors, writers. That was important to him—he *liked* being famous—but it was secondary to baseball. Baseball was the thread his life hung on. "He doesn't talk about anything else," his wife said. "He doesn't think about anything else. He has only one life, and that's baseball. That way he's happy, and I'm happy for him."[6]

Flow experience apparently can occur when the athlete is participating in competitive sports, according to a study by Kenneth Ravizza. In this study the subjects were asked to describe their "greatest moment" in sports, and it is noteworthy that they tended to pick episodes, not from recreational playing, but from competitive activities such as intercollegiate or international contests. Over half of the subjects in the study participated on university teams, some at the Olympic level, indicating a high level of sport cultivation. Many different kinds of athletes (e.g. skier, lacrosse player, cyclist) were interviewed, and their descriptions of the "greatest moment" always indicated that it was an absorbed experience, similar to the accounts of flow and peak experience.

> Subjects reported that they were not aware of their normal selves, but instead were completely absorbed in the activity. The experience appears similar to what some psychologists have referred to as an "ego-transcending experience" into a union with the phenomenon. . . .
> The athletes' reports contained many similarities to Maslow's description of peak experience. Athletes gave their experiences total attention, resulting in temporary ego loss, union with the experience as a whole, and disorientation in time and space. . . . The experience is reported as being perfect; consequently, the athlete is "passive" in the experience since it is effortless. The usual fears associated with the activity are nonexistent. Another parallel to Maslow's description is the awe and wonder that accompanies the experience and the sense that it is an involuntary and ecstatic phenomenon.[7]

The sense of flow and physical perfection can be greatly enhanced by the rhythmic quality of much sport activity. The word "rhythm" comes from the ancient Greek term meaning "to flow." Rhythm has absorbing effects, as we have seen, because of its tendency to stimulate physically while lulling mentally. This can be a great advantage in endurance sports like swimming and running. Track athletes and joggers sometimes report a high that seems to come from the rhythmic sensations of their activity. Runner George Sheehan stated that he relied on the carrying power of rhythm and was aware of its absorbing effects. He lost it only in the agony of running up hills. Otherwise, the "ecstasy of distance running is felt in those periods of rhythm and grace when everything is easy and flowing and natural."[8]

In recent years, jogging has become popular among some adults, most of whom have taken up the sport for health reasons. Dr. Sheehan, however, recommended it for diversion, as a source of many recreational, spiritual, and creative experiences not to be found in everyday life. Sheehan enunciated a whole new perspective: sports as extreme diversion. His prescription for breaking out of the everyday rut is to run out of it, literally and figuratively. At its best, according to Sheehan, running makes possible the feeling of being outside of everyday life, with a different sense of self and in another reality. "My ten years of almost daily running," wrote Sheehan, "had brought me to an area of consciousness, a level of being, that I never knew existed." He recognized, however, that not just running, but any activity could provide absorbing diversion if it were sufficiently cultivated.

> I cannot bring visions of immortality to a nonrunner by dragging him along on my afternoon runs. What you do must absorb you utterly and intensely; and to do that it must be your game, your sport, your play. . . .

For the dancer, the dance brings this feeling for life, this intimation of immortality. ("When a jump works," says Jacques d'Amboise, "it feels like forever. I'm riding on top of time.") Others get the same sort of experience from skiing, surfing, karate, golf, football or what have you.

How long it will take is another story. One must go through discipline to get to freedom. Be assured it does not occur to beginners. Only when how you do a thing surpasses the thing you are doing can you break through the barriers to these levels of consciousness, your own inner depths.[9]

Zen Sport: Letting the Body Take Over

I've always been able to lose myself in the games, to concentrate on the play.... If you're worried about the crowd, if you hear what the fans yell, if you're thinking about how you look or what you're going to do after the game, it's bound to take a lot away from your performance. —*Jerry West*

If if occurs at all, the flow experience develops after the athlete has reached a peak of coordinated movement, and feels carried along by the rhythm, tempo, and challenge of the sport. It is only then, on the crest of harmonious action, that he might coast into an absorbed spell. Thus absorption is not a prerequisite for sport activity as it is for story enjoyment or aesthetic experience. Absorption is a by-product; it is the cream of sport.

Since absorption is found at the ultimate levels of sport activity, could not such an attentional orientation be routinely utilized to improve sport performance? One school of thought says this is possible. It asserts that sport should *begin* with absorbed attention. It was developed ages ago by Zen Buddhists, whose meditational approach to life is close to absorption.

The Zen approach to sport contains three main points: eliminate distraction and thought, attend wholistically to the situation, and react intuitively and naturally. As we shall see in the next chapter, Zen is "no-mind"; it rejects thoughts, words, and abstractions, all of which make artificial distinctions. Instead, it strives for unification of experience through spontaneous, intuitive action that is in tune with the external world. Such a philosophy is highly congenial to sport, which glorifies the reacting body, not the thinking mind. The best sport performance relies on instinct and the well-practiced reaction; there is little room for intellectualizing.

Westerners were given a firsthand account of Zen sport in Eugen Herrigel's now classic *Zen in the Art of Archery.* Herrigel was a German professor who taught at the University of Tokyo between the World Wars; his book describes his six years of study under a Japanese master, learning archery the Zen way. Most of this training was aimed at unlearning willfulness and self-consciousness, while letting the innocent and instinctive side of human nature come forth. This probably turned out to be a more profound task than

Professor Herrigel bargained for, because after four years of training he had
not yet shot at any targets but was still learning to release the arrow in a natural
way. At one point, Herrigel complained to the Zen master about the tension
of not knowing when to let the arrow go. The master replied:

> "You only feel it because you haven't really let go of yourself. It is all so
> simple. You can learn from an ordinary bamboo leaf what ought to happen.
> It bends lower and lower under the weight of snow. Suddenly the snow slips
> to the ground without the leaf having stirred. Stay like that at the point of
> highest tension until the shot falls from you. So, indeed, it is: when the tension
> is fulfilled, the shot *must* fall, it must fall from the archer like snow from a
> bamboo leaf, before he even thinks of it."
>
> One day I asked the Master: "How can the shot be loosed if 'I' do not do it?"
> "'It' shoots," he replied.
> "I have heard you say that several times before, so let me put it another
> way: How can I wait self-obliviously for the shot if 'I' am no longer
> there?"
> "'It' waits at the highest tension."
> "And who or what is this 'It?'"
> "Once you have understood that, you will have no further need of me."
>
> During these weeks and months I passed through the hardest schooling
> of my life, and though the discipline was not always easy for me to accept,
> I gradually came to see how much I was indebted to it. It destroyed the last
> traces of any preoccupation with myself and the fluctuations of my mood.
> "Do you now understand," the Master asked me one day after a particularly
> good shot, "what I mean by 'It shoots,' 'It hits?'"
> "I'm afraid I don't understand anything more at all," I answered, "even
> the simplest things have got in a muddle. Is it 'I' who draw the bow, or is
> it the bow that draws me into the state of highest tension? Do 'I' hit the goal,
> or does the goal hit me? Is 'It' spiritual when seen by the eyes of the body,
> and corporeal when seen by the eyes of the spirit—or both or neither? Bow,
> arrow, goal and ego, all melt into one another, so that I can no longer separate
> them. And even the need to separate has gone. For as soon as I take the bow
> and shoot, everything becomes so clear and straightforward and so
> ridiculously simple...."
> "Now at last," the Master broke in, "the bowstring has cut right through
> you."[10]

This is the Zen reversal: the bowstring controls the person; the object
comes to the fore while self fades to the background. In the traditional way
that most people would learn to shoot the bow and arrow, or play any sport
for that matter, the self-referent master codes would be controlling the action.
There would be concern about the performance, self-reminders about following instructions, etc. All of this mental activity is nothing but distraction, according to the Zen approach; it prevents us from experiencing the sport purely
for its own sake. Better to let body relate directly and naively to the bow and
arrow, so that "it" shoots in the same way that the body breathes. To bring
archery to the level of breathing obviously is basically an unlearning process,

a scuttling of ego-habits and verbal information to the point where "the bow-string has cut right through you."

Although Zen requires a long and arduous cultivation, it has a tradition of producing master athletes, especially in swordsmanship and the martial arts. For this reason, Westerners have recently become interested in these oriental techniques. As sport assumes an ever larger role in our leisure society, there is a great effort to develop physical capability to its utmost, and it seems that Zen has much to teach us, especially about the attentional orientation of the athlete. As a result, more and more emphasis is placed on the Zen orientation, which today is referred to as "relaxed concentration" or "passive concentration." These terms are similar to the concept of "relaxed arousal"— intense noncognitive experiencing. In his book *The Inner Athlete,* sports psychologist Robert Nideffer assigns a central role to this kind of attentional orientation, and examines it in depth through chapters on hypnosis, self-induced relaxation, and Transcendental Meditation (TM).

> Because of their emphasis on passive concentration, TM procedures may help you perform in those situations where you are not concentrating on the act but are simply *being* the act. For example, complicated gymnastics routines or dives are often practiced to the point where they are almost reflex-ive.... Even some of the sports which demand that we react to the moves of opponents can be developed to the point where little if any thought is required on our part. A certain punch by an opponent always leads to our making the same block and counterpunch.
>   It would be absurd to say that you should never think during competition. However, the major downfall for many of us is that we think too much. When this happens, it is because we are so eager to anticipate what our opponent will do that we lose awareness of what is actually going on. This type of mistake is responsible for an end dropping the pass because he is thinking of running for the goal line before he catches the ball, or a tennis player who misjudges a lob because she's thinking about where she will place her return.[11]

Another modern version of Zen sport was introduced by Timothy Gallwey in his book *The Inner Game of Tennis.* Gallwey's approach to the game is based on two Zen ideas: quieting the mind, and letting it happen. As a tennis pro and seasoned instructor, Gallwey came to distrust the value of verbal instruction, which usually becomes distracting to the pupil and results in over-controlled body movements. Better to let the body take over and discover its own rhythm and style. "The first skill to learn" wrote Gallwey, "is the art of letting go the human inclination to judge ourselves and our performance as either good or bad.... When we *un*learn how to be judgmental, it is possible to achieve spontaneous, concentrated play."[12] Gallwey recommended that the tennis player maintain total attention on the concrete aspects of the game, focusing, on the very seams of the ball so as to avoid distractions.

It might seem incongruous that some sports can be played more effectively in the absorbed state. Absorption somehow seems to be a "soft" orientation, associated with sedentary spectator entertainment, and not at all consistent with the muscular action, maximum effort, daring, and fight that are needed in sport activity. However, in some sports the issue is not effort or combativeness, but to what extent the body can be liberated for excellent action. For this purpose, absorption may be the method of choice, especially for such feats as are performed by acrobats and aerialists. In fact, it seems that those sports, where performance depends on split-second decisions, cannot even be performed in everyday consciousness. Roger Caillois pointed out that everyday attentional processing would never work in the death-defying acts performed on the high wire or the trapeze.

> An ascetic existence is necessary to obtain this supreme skill. It involves a regime of severe privation and strict continence, ceaseless exercise, continuous repetition of the same movements, and the acquisition of impeccable reflexes and faultless responses. Somersaults are performed in a state bordering on hypnosis. Supple and strong muscles and imperturbable self-control are necessary conditions. To be sure, the acrobat must calculate the effort, time, distance, and trajectory of the trapeze. But he lives in terror of thinking of it at the decisive moment, when it nearly always has fatal consequences. It paralyzes instead of aiding, at a moment when the least hesitation is disastrous. Consciousness is the killer. It is disturbing to his somnambulistic infallibility and compromises the functioning of a mechanism whose extreme precision cannot tolerate doubts or regrets. The tightrope walker only succeeds if he is hypnotized by the rope.[13]

Inspiration and the Play of Ideas

> Ideas often flash across our minds more complete than we could make them after much labor. — *François de La Rochefoucauld*

It is possible to have absorbed *cognitive* activity comparable to the absorbed *physical* activity we have just examined. It consists of thought that flows just as action does in the "perfect moment" of sport. It is the state of mind known as "being inspired."

From our standpoint, all actions of the organism are equivalent. Physical and cognitive activity are simply two aspects of the organism's processing system. The organism uses physical action to move itself in the external environment. It uses cognitive activity to move in the psychological environment — from problem to solution, from "felt difficulty" to adjustment. Cognitive activity is usually geared to conducting the business of living, and it is as effortful, interactive, and self-referent as bodily action.

This equivalence makes absorption of mind comparable to that of the body. However, when one is mentally absorbed or inspired, there is fluency of ideas rather than actions. There is an experience that "it" thinks, much as the Zen archer feels that "it" shoots. And finally, just as flow experience occurs only in athletes who are physically endowed and have cultivated the sport for a long time, inspired thinking occurs primarily in gifted individuals who have spent much time in intellectual pursuits.

Feeling inspired is a cognitive high; it consists of a burst of excellent ideas that propel one along effortlessly in some intellectual endeavor. This experience is one of the intrinsic enjoyments of creative activity. William James referred to such moments as "fevered states" when "ideas are shooting together," and when one "can think of no finite things." Logan Pearsall Smith referred to being inspired as "a rush of thought" which to him was "the only true happiness." French mathematician Henri Poincaré said that "ideas rose in crowds." Bernard Berenson talked about "flights of lawless speculation" and "shooting stars of cerebration, some lighting dazzlingly a vast horizon." All of these descriptions suggest a type of cognitive entertainment — mental fireworks, an intellectual display that is not only enlightening but also enjoyable. "It would be vain to try to put into words," wrote Tchaikovsky, "that immeasurable sense of bliss which comes over me directly a new idea awakens in me and begins to assume a definite form. I forget everything and behave like a madman. Everything within me starts pulsing and quivering."[14]

A good example of the difference between everyday mental functioning and inspired cognitive activity can be found in Sigmund Koch's conception of "States A and B." Koch is a distinguished psychologist who has directed numerous projects for the American Psychological Association and the National Science Foundation. By his account the experience of cognitive activity can vary greatly. Often it is unpleasant, effortful, and worklike — or what he called "State A." According to Koch, it is in "State B" that a person is likely to feel inspired and be creative. His description of State B makes it sound very much like absorbed experience.

> In State B, you do not merely "work at" or "on" the task; you have *committed yourself* to the task, and in some sense you *are* the task, or vice versa.
>
> Perhaps one of the most remarkable properties of B is that thoughts relevant to the problem context seem to well up with no apparent effort. They merely present themselves. The spontaneity and fluency of ideation and the freedom from customary blockages seem similar to certain characteristics of the dream or certain states of near dissociation. As in these latter conditions, it is often difficult to "fix," hold in mind, the thoughts which occur. In fact, in State B, most of the "effortfulness" or "strain" encountered has to do not with the generation of ideas relevant to the problem context but with their decoding, fixing, or verbalization, and their selection and assemblage with respect to socially standardized requirements of communication. . . .
>
> Curiously enough, there seem to be two occasions in the B sequence of

a given day when the spontaneous emergence of ideas (the "it thinks" phenomenon) is at a maximum. One is shortly after awakening—even from a sleep produced by strong sedation. (In A, on the other hand, not an engram begins to twitch until late in the afternoon.) The other occasion is towards the very end of the work sequence, either during its terminal phase, or while preparing for, or falling, asleep. I might add that the ideas which present themselves on these occasions tend to be, in some sense, the most organized, the most relevant to the problem context, of any in the entire pedestrian array of a given day.[15]

Cognitive absorption is not mere daydreaming, which is usually self-centered and self-directed. In most daydreams we are simply conducting business in an unrealistic and wish-fulfilling way, but it is still business. In the inspired state, on the other hand, ideas emerge suddenly and effortlessly, capturing total attention. While the ideas may help solve a problem, the excitement that they engender comes from an almost aesthetic enjoyment of their fit and perfection.

Throughout history, the phenomenon of inspiration has most often been associated with poetry—the art form that plays with language and cognition. Poets have always placed high value on the inspired state. In ancient times it was thought to represent a visitation from the gods; since the ideas were so excellent and did not seem to be brought on by conscious effort, they were thought to be caused by the Muse. Literary scholar C.M. Bowra believed that the phenomenon of inspiration is a genuine one and that it has an important role in the composing of poetry.

> The all-absorbing activity which comes with inspiration means that the poet not only forgets anything outside the immediate object of his vision but loses his sense of time. Past and future no longer exist for him, and he enjoys a timeless condition. Nor is this condition negative, a mere state of omissions and absences. It is strikingly positive. In it the poet feels that his whole being is enlarged and that he is able to enjoy in an unprecedented completeness what in his ordinary life he enjoys only in fragments with after-thoughts and misgivings and distractions. This experience receives its fullest treatment from the Romantics, who use for it the word "eternity" and through this seek to convey its absolute, all-absorbing character.[16]

Scholars and critics claim that they can tell when a work of art was created in an inspired state. Presumably, an inspired work is somehow more vital, harmonious, and unified. In some manner the qualities of absorption get imbued in the work, making it superior to something that was merely "intellectually contrived." Bowra believed this true of poetry. "There is no doubt of the fact: what the poets have conceived through inspiration is also what we feel to be their most essential and most authentic poetry, and we are justified in calling it inspired."[17] Bowra cited instances where poetry contained inspired qualities, and indeed was written in an absorbed state. For example, Milton was so moved in the writing of *Paradise Lost* that he believed he was prompted by the Holy Spirit; Blake's rapturous songs were written in visionary exaltation; Pushkin could not write unless he felt possessed; Blok's most powerful poems were born in a condition of ecstasy.

Feeling inspired does not always lead to inspiration. Being absorbed by a burst of exciting ideas is an enjoyable and intoxicating state, but it does not always lead to something worthwhile. Ideas that flash and sparkle at one moment can quickly fizzle out when tested against reality. Nevertheless, it seems that much of what is truly creative does indeed occur in the inspired state. The insights, breakthroughs, and innovative solutions of art and science have generally occurred when the individual was absorbed, mentally relaxed, or at least somehow distanced from everyday life.

Research conducted by Patricia Bowers has shown that creativity is significantly related to measures of hypnotizability, absorption, and effortless experiencing.[18] This supports Rollo May's assertion regarding the absorbing nature of creative experience: "The words 'absorption,' 'being caught up in,' 'wholly involved,' and so on are used commonly to describe the state of the artist or scientist when creating." Furthermore, May pointed out that "genuine creativity is characterized by an intensity of awareness, a heightened consciousness," but at the same time "the heightened awareness we are speaking of does not all mean increased self-consciousness. It is rather correlated more with abandon, absorption."[19] This conclusion was also drawn by Rosamond Harding, who collected an enormous amount of historical data regarding the "mind in creation." Her book *An Anatomy of Inspiration* offers convincing proof that when the moment of inspiration came for well-known creative individuals, it was totally unrelated to everyday self and reality, and it had all the marks of absorbed experience. Harding found that statements made by famous innovators showed their moments of inspiration usually occurred in a trancelike state. "Many are the stories told of the absorption and absence of mind of men and women of genius when 'compelled' by an idea."[20] In the creative moment, highly insightful ideas simply take possession of the mind, as psychologist Gardner Murphy pointed out.

> One regularly recurring feature of creative thought . . . is its tendency to get out of hand, its habit of rushing uninvited upon the scientist or inventor or composer or dramatist. . . . Indeed, not content with knocking at the door, such material may suddenly fall like a landslide into the very center of the mind. Many of Blake's finest integrations, for example, took shape as wholes hurled at him by forces which seemed to him to stand beyond the limits of his own selfhood.[21]

In the previous chapter it was noted that peak experiences occur in the context of diversion, not work. Much the same is true of inspiration, which is a kind of peak experience. Inspiration does not occur in the heat of mental effort or in the hustle and bustle of everyday living when the person is actively processing realistic business.[22] Rather, this absorbed event occurs when the business computer is down, i.e., during sleep, drowsiness, diversion, relaxed arousal, and in the breaks from daily routine when one is alone and unpreoccupied. Creative insights have been reported to occur in dreams, which, as we shall see in the last chapter, are a form of absorbed experience. Like Sigmund Koch, many individuals have reported getting their inspirations in the twilight state of half-sleep before falling off, or in the middle of the night, or before getting out of bed in the morning. Daytime inspirations typically have been found to occur when everyday business is at a low level—for example, when a person is bathing or dressing, riding on a bus or train, loafing or hiking alone.[23] Helmholz wrote that his insights and inspirations often occurred "in the morning when I awoke. . . . But they liked specially to make their appearance while I was taking an easy walk over wooded hills in sunny weather."[24] Henry Poincaré noted that while on an excursion, the "changes of travel made me forget my mathematical work," and it was at this time that he made his most brilliant mathematical conceptualization.[25] In much the same way Arnold Toynbee got the inspiration for his momentous undertaking of the *Study of History*. In an article on Toynbee and his works, the *New York Times* reported: "The 3.5-million word, twelve-volume story of mankind, which took forty years to complete, was begun on Saturday, September 17, 1921, when the author was traveling west from Istanbul in the fabled Orient Express. He had spent the day watching the awesome Thracian countryside slip by and pondering the region's glorious and gory past." Toynbee described the moment of inspiration as follows:

> That evening I was still standing at the window, overwhelmed by the beauty of the Bela Palanka Gorge in the light of the full moon, as our train bore down the Nish. If I had been cross-examined on my activities during that day, I should have sworn that my attention had been wholly absorbed by the entrancing scenes that were passing continually before my outward eye. Yet, before I went to sleep that night, I found that I had put down on half a sheet of notepaper a list of topics which in its contents and their order, was substantially identical with the plan of this book as it now stands.[26]

Psychologists have long recognized that when one is faced with a problem that cannot be solved with the usual intellectual approach, it is helpful to turn one's mind to other things. Getting away from the problem weakens unproductive mental sets and loosens associations so that new and useful ideas can come forth. Experimental psychologists emphasize the importance of "the overcoming of a particular set." In his review of the literature, Wilbert Ray concluded that original thinking is most likely to occur only after there has been a decrease in task anxiety, self-criticism, and achievement pressure.[27] That is, attention must be diverted.

Apparently, so-called creative personalities can, within limits, attain this diversion without leaving the task. Such individuals seem to be capable of switching to a more relaxed mode which investigators have described in terms of "effortless experiencing," "divergent thinking," "remote associations," and the utilization of primitive levels of thought.[28] This was demonstrated in one study which found that creative and noncreative subjects have different EEG patterns when working on tasks that require innovative solutions.[29] The noncreative subjects apparently attacked the tasks intellectually, with intense and discriminating mental activity; their EEG records showed high cortical arousal and focused attention. The creative subjects, on the other hand, approached the tasks in a more leisurely fashion. Their EEG records were indicative of low cortical arousal and diffuse attention; they contained a significant amount of alpha rhythm, which reflects relaxed and nonpurposeful thinking. In other words, while the noncreative subjects worked at the tasks, the creative ones toyed with them.

Arthur Koestler pointed out that creative insight is not a matter of making something from nothing, but rather of combining ideas that rationally do not belong together.[30] In his book *Act of Creation,* he reconstructed some of the famous breakthroughs in history, such as the invention of the printing press and the discovery of the mechanism for evolution. The idea for the printing press came from the wine press. According to Koestler, this connection would never have been made on logical grounds because the two ideas have such different associations. The wine press has a "context of the mushy pulp, the flowing red liquid, the jolly revelry," all of which are opposite of the clean, neat printing process. Gutenberg had been searching for a way to stamp letters onto paper but could not come up with a workable method. The inspiration that equated wine pressing with print pressing occurred when he had left his work and was attending a wine harvest, presumably in a relaxed and leisurely mood.

Koestler referred to the making of such connections as *bisociation,* i.e., the association of two different ideas. Most significant is that bisociation is most likely to occur when ideas are stripped of their everyday connotations: for example, the idea of *pressing* perceived independently of the business matrix of making wine. It is not surprising, therefore, that inspiration tends to occur when the person is mentally relaxed, absorbed, or half-asleep, since at such times thinking would be relatively free of perceptual habits.

The importance of mental relaxation and distance is seen even more clearly in Darwin's insight regarding the mechanism for evolution. This famous bisociation brought together the ideas of the struggle for existence and evolution. Both ideas were well known in Darwin's time and even much earlier, but they existed in two different domains of discourse — one in economics, the other in biology. In a well-known treatise on economics, Thomas Malthus had expounded on the evils of overpopulation, which, he said, would lead to an increased struggle for limited resources, resulting eventually in famine, war, and disease. Forty years after its publication, Darwin read this treatise "for amusement," and in a flash connected the idea of struggle for survival with the idea of evolutionary change, and came up with the insight about survival of the fittest. Once again, the original notion had to be taken out of its habitual business matrix, which is related to overpopulation as an evil and a danger to the human race. For Darwin, it became the mechanism by which species evolve.

Koestler's concept of bisociation makes obsolete the old notion of "incubation." Traditional views of the creative process make much of the fact that the flash of inspiration is always delayed, occurring at some random time often long after the solution was sought. It is thought that this period of time is needed by the unconscious to digest the problem and come up with a solution. Hence the term "incubation," meaning that, like an egg, the solution grows in the unconscious, and then hatches at some appropriate time, producing a flash of insight. The concept of incubation states that the creative work is magically done by unconscious processing, but what this processing involves has never been specified. Likewise, it has never been explained why some inspirations occur after only a short period of incubation, while others might require years of unconscious gestation. Nor has it been shown that incubation in itself is beneficial, i.e., the longer the incubating, the better the result. Although the notion of incubation seems untenable, this term is still widely used in the literature. Actually, what is important is not a mandatory incubation period, but rather certain conditions that favor inspiration—namely, mental relaxation and diversion, which make the person more suggestible to intuitive and outside cues that might get combined into productive bisociations.

Creative inspiration does not just happen to anyone. It occurs only in cultivated diversions, after a hobby has been extensively developed through study and practice—so much so that the person can lose himself in it. Rollo May wrote that "creative impulses may indeed come in times of relaxation or in reverie or in other times when we alternate play with work; but what is entirely clear is that they come in those areas in which the person has worked laboriously and with dedication."[31] The importance of long-term cultivation was also emphasized by Maslow. Attempting to distinguish "primary creativity" from mere everyday resourcefulness and imaginativeness, he wrote that the former has "not only the flash, the inspiration, the peak-experience, it also needs hard work, long training, unrelenting criticism, perfectionistic standards."[32]

Creative inspiration is such a supreme occurrence that it could never be just a matter of personality traits. It is a coming together of antithetical factors from the domains of work and play. This kind of synthesis can emerge only from a long-term cultivated diversion with its alternations of work and play—

involving critical thinking as well as intuition, skill as well as spirit, automatism as well as abandon. The work sequence provides the benefits of training and disciplined thought. The play sequence provides the benefits of absorbed attention: "spontaneous intuitions . . . sudden leaps of imagination . . . and unconscious guidance by quasi-religious or by aesthetic sensibilities."[33] The hunches obtained in the absorbed phase are tested in the work phase. Work and play influence each other and develop into something greater than both. Inspired creativity is a consummate human achievement because it utilizes the organism's entire psychology—the work modes and the play modes. It is this double-barreled approach which makes inspiration so different from, and so much more than, everyday cognition. It is a way of having one's head in the clouds and feet on the ground at the same time.

To be truly creative a person must live for the cultivated diversion. All else becomes secondary, including normal self-related activities like social relationships, personal comforts, and sometimes even eating and sleeping. What one reviewer said about Irish author Frank O'Connor applies in all creative lives: "He lived by the savage rule that an artist has to put his writing first, ahead of everything else including family and friends."[34] A person must be able to abandon himself; or as Jerome Brunner defined the basic condition for creativity, there must be the "freedom to be dominated by the object."[35] T.S. Eliot wrote that "the progress of an artist is a continual self-sacrifice, a continual extinction of personality. What happens is a continual surrender of himself as he is at the moment to something which is more valuable."[36] American novelist Joyce Carol Oates showed how widespread the psychological effects of cultivated diversion can be when she described her involvement with literature. "I am always reading or thinking about reading, or I am writing, or thinking about it. . . . My consciousness is almost entirely given up to literature; in a sense, I belong to literature and have no permanent identity apart from it."[37] Likewise, in this quote from Neil Simon, one detects an alter ego—a master code for writing plays—that vies with the business of living, and is a major aspect of the playwright's psychological existence.

I've always felt, and I think this is very true of most writers that I know, we are observers rather than participants. Even though I do participate in life, I don't consider myself participating. I'm always sort of on the outside, watching it all, noting it, not necessarily with an eye to putting it down as an experience in writing, but just as a human being, because I find it harder to relate to life personally—much easier to go upstairs, put a piece of paper in, and live my life there. Although, that too, is a fantasy in a way, because I do participate in life. I have friends. I have problems. I have a marriage. I have children. And I'm involved in all of these things. Still, I consider myself on the outside of it. When I am sitting and having a conversation with a friend, I hear the conversation. I become the third person at the table listening to the two of us. And I think that is what gives me my ability as a writer, really. To observe this objectively.[38]

Undoubtedly the worst thing that can happen to a writer, poet, or com-poser is loss of inspiration. Apparently, creative people can function at the inspired level for only a limited period of time, and then they drop from these heights. The heady feeling, the ideas "shooting together," the breathtaking in-sights and connections—all of it stops. Sometimes inspiration simply fades with age, but there are many perplexing cases where it dies shortly after blooming. Something like this evidently happened to the American writer Sherwood Anderson, who later in life lamented: "I had a world and it slipped away from me."

It seems that creative individuals have always been concerned about the waning of their inspiration. In the nineteenth century, absinthe was a popular drink among French artists because it was thought to kindle inspiration; later it was found that this substance produced neurological impairment, and it was banned.[39] In ancient times poets called upon the Muses to sustain inspiration, and as Emerson observed, "this is the reason why bards love wine, mead, nar-cotics, coffee, tea, opium, fumes of sandal-wood and tobacco, or whatever other species of animal exhilaration."[40] Stories are legion of attempts to rejuvenate lost creative powers by means of various intoxicants. The disappearance of in-spiration takes a heavy toll on creative individuals; the psychological losses are probably greater than the financial ones. It is likely that these problems have much to do with the high rate of alcoholism and suicide found among writers and artists. Having once tasted the nectar of inspiration, these individuals must find life unbearably flat without such delights.

Loss of inspiration is not simply a fizzling out of talents, if we think of talents as skills programmed into the organism; such codes do not simply fizzle out. Loss of inspiration, then, must be related to the other factor in creative experience—the ability to get absorbed. Ironically, creativity may often have the seeds of its own destruction. The more successful the creative person is, the more serious and evaluative he is likely to become about his cultivated diversion, and this in turn precludes absorbed involvement in it. What was once a diversion ends up becoming all business. For example, when a longstanding hobby is turned into a professional career, making it the source of money, ego gratifications, and social recognition, then the person becomes dependent on these extrinsic rewards and is likely to become evaluative and self-conscious. He is less likely to see the adventure that once absorbed him in the hobby; it no longer transports him to another reality, and he is less likely to be inspired by it. Something similar must happen with the successful writer or artist. Success brings special treatment, critical reviews, and professional responsibilities—in other words, all of the things that are likely to increase preoccupation with one's position. If such concerns are allowed to become up-permost, it is impossible to abandon oneself to the cultivated diversion. "When people become successful," said Elia Kazan, "a certain defensiveness comes into them and they start protecting an image."[41]

If creativity were simply a matter of skill or personality traits, one would expect it to increase with age. Actually, it seems that individuals are most creative in their mid-life years, and become less so the older they get.[42] Age, like success, seems to affect creativity adversely. As people get older, they become increasingly concerned about security and creature comforts — factors that work against self-abandonment. In his book on creativity, Frank Barron related the observations of one of his subjects, an older man who had settled down to a secure and conventional life after a turbulent and creative youth.[43] The man doubted that he would be able to write anything new or creative again because he could no longer "throw himself away" and "die unto himself" — a graphic way of describing his inability to suspend and subordinate the normal business of living and its gratifications in order to attain total involvement in his writing. A recent biography of Alfred, Lord Tennyson, the eminent Victorian poet, offers a melancholy example of inspiration lost.[44] Tennyson's literary career consisted of two phases. The first was one of much psychological turmoil and, as one reviewer described it, there were many experiences of "'trances' into which composition threw him, those states of 'lost identity' in which he was absorbed into his vision."[45] These experiences were so intense that Tennyson thought he had epilepsy. Yet it was at this very time that he produced his greatest works. Later in life came the second phase, much more settled and comfortable, and marked by cessation of the trances. But as the reviewer noted, "the success story makes sad reading" because there also occurred a significant decline in his creativity. Although Tennyson continued to write poems during this time, they seldom matched the Olympian achievements of his earlier, inspired period.

Diversion and distance are at the very heart of the creative process. As we have seen, the hobby activity is cultivated as a solitary and often passionate endeavor, usually outside the bounds of everyday routines, and often at the expense of social relationships. Diversion is also evident in the conditions most likely to precipitate inspiration, i.e., mental relaxation, leisure, hypnogogic state. And finally, inspiration is always experienced as an absorbed spell and so is highly distanced from everyday life. There is probably nothing so fatal to creativity as the involvements and entanglements of the everyday.

Chapter 12

Meditation: The Cleansing of Awareness

> I teach only two things, O disciples, the fact of suffering
> and the possibility of escape from suffering. — *Buddha*

Historically, meditation has been a religious practice. Today, it is touted as a relaxation device and an antidote to stress.

Actually, meditation might best be viewed as something broader: a genuine diversion. The rationale for meditation has always been escapist; it has always been associated with rejection of the everyday world. And although it is a quiet diversion, it is capable of vitalizing experience and transporting a person to other psychological realities. A number of studies have shown that meditation consists of an attentional orientation closely related to absorption and the hypnotic state.[1] *Time* magazine was on the mark when it called meditation "the turn-on of the '70s — a drugless high."[2]

Because it entails a complete break with everyday life, meditation can be classified as an extreme diversion — the newest of the four such diversions that appeared in the twentieth century. The traditional culture gave us movies and television; counterculture gave us psychedelic drugs and meditation. Compared to the others, meditation is probably the least popular. While the other diversions act quickly, meditation needs to be cultivated, and its effects are slow and uncertain.

The Limits of Lulling

Contrary to the dictionary definition, meditation is not the act of reflecting on something. Technically, it is just the opposite: stopping thought. According to the *Encyclopaedia Britannica,* it is the "progressive nullifying of every psychic activity and emotional or mental faculty."[3] Although there are many brands of meditation, most strive for this basic goal of making null the psychological functions, especially the cognitive ones.

Why this goal? Meditation originated as a religious purification rite, a

170

spiritual practice for escaping the defilements of the world. Historically, the practice of meditation evolved from Hindu doctrine, which held that the external world is false and corrupting. It was believed that only by blacking out the external and emptying the mind of all worldly content would it be possible for a person to be liberated and restored to his natural being. The Hindus developed the extreme techniques of Yoga, including meditation, as a way of purifying body and mind.

Everyone has heard about the feats of yogis who can stop breathing or prevent the heart from beating for unbelievably long periods of time. In addition to control of breath and heartbeat, many other bodily functions were stopped, and even reversed, in the ancient discipline of Hatha Yoga. In his book *The Lotus and the Robot,* Arthur Koestler gave an eye-opening account of these practices.[4] For example, the yogi not only stopped eating for long periods of time, but also learned to reverse peristalsis and eject liquids from the stomach through the mouth or nose. Koestler took note of the many contortions, spine twists, "airlocks," and bowel gymnastics that made up yogic exercises, the purposes of which were to conserve energy, cleanse the body, and seal off all of its orifices from contamination. In one advanced technique, the tongue was stretched and even cut so that it could be used to block the nasal passages in the back of the mouth.

Meditation comes to us from this tradition. What these exercises did for the body, meditation was supposed to do for the mind. Attention is like a body orifice, bringing input into the psychological system. The purpose of meditation was to block off this particular opening and empty the mind of all content.

In everyday life, attention thrives on variety, and it is in constant motion. Yogic technique checks attention with the one thing it cannot tolerate: monotony. The yogi attempted to fixate on one point or stimulus, repeated over and over again. The purpose was to starve attention, emptying it of all content related to inner thought or external stimulation. Research has tended to support the yogic claim that this meditational technique completely blocks the attentional channel. For example, EEG recordings taken from expert yogis during meditation failed to show any cerebral reaction to repeated noises.[5]

Is it possible to empty the mind absolutely, as the yogis claim? Their meditational literature often refers to such an end state, described in nihilistic terms like "nothingness," "the void," "the blanking out of consciousness," and of course "nirvana." The implication is that an emptying-out process is possible, so that all that is left is the container—pure consciousness, pure mind.

According to modern psychology, however, it is not possible to have consciousness without some content. There is no pure mind, just as there is no pure vision or hearing. Mind, consciousness, sensation, and attention are not entities. They are psychophysical functions that come into existence as the organism interacts with the environment. As John Welwood wrote: "Psychological events must be understood as forms of interaction, rather than as separate mental phenomena."[6] Consciousness and awareness exist only to the extent that the organism attends to something. Thus, the stopping of thought in meditation is always relative. It is not possible to empty the mind in an absolute sense. To do so would have the effect of extinguishing consciousness and inducing sleep. It is interesting to note that in studying the ancient Hindu writings and discussing this question with modern gurus, Koestler found that again and again meditation was described as "deep sleep."

This obscure and impossible yogic goal of emptying the mind gave way in time to a new way of meditating that developed out of Zen Buddhism. Instead of trying to block and extinguish attention, the Zen approach did nearly the opposite. It allowed attention to flourish but reduced its personal significance. In other words, it put attention out of gear with the self, just as psychic distance does for art. In Zen, thoughts are permitted to occur, but instead of being personally involved with them one merely observes them in a detached and minimal way known as "Bare Attention" or "Mindfulness." Such attention is devoid of the usual codes that bias, select, and "rubricize" perception; presumably it is a way of suspending the master code system. "It is called 'bare' because it attends to the bare facts of a perception without reacting to them by deed, speech, or mental comment."[7] Ornstein has pointed out that in various religions this kind of attention is referred to by the metaphor of a mirror.[8] A mirror simply reflects all objects equally; it does not filter or distort. The mirror's reflection is not affected by past or repeated reflections. Attention should be like that in Zen meditation.

However, since there is no fascination object in meditation, attention inevitably tends to revert to the self-referent trivia that continually worry the human mind in its everyday orientation. Here is how a Zen master might handle this problem. (These instructions were taken from a meditational manual by Alan Watts, an Englishman who was probably one of the foremost exponents of Zen in the West.)

> Now that you are sitting . . . the easiest way to get into the meditative state is to begin listening. Simply close your eyes and allow yourself to hear all the sounds that are going on around you, listen to the general hum and buzz of the world as if you were listening to music. Don't try to identify the sounds you are hearing, don't put names on them, simply allow them to play with your eardrums. Let them go. In other words, let your ears hear whatever they want to hear. Don't judge the sounds — there are no proper sounds nor improper sounds, and it doesn't matter if somebody coughs or sneezes or drops something — it's all just sound. . . .
>
> As you pursue that experiment you will very naturally find that you can't help naming sounds, identifying them, and go on thinking, talking to yourself inside your head, automatically. But it's important that you don't try to repress

those thoughts by forcing them out of your mind because that will have precisely the same effect as if you were trying to smooth rough water with a flatiron — you're just going to disturb it all the more. What you do is this: As you hear sounds coming into your head, thoughts, you simply listen to them as part of the general noise going on just as you would be listening to cars going by, or to birds chattering outside the window. So look at your own thoughts as just noises. And soon you will find that the outside world and the inside world come together. They are a happening. Your thoughts are a happening just like the sounds going on outside, and everything is simply a happening and all you are doing is watching it.

Don't hurry anything, don't worry about the future, don't worry about what progress you're making. Be entirely content to be aware of what is. Don't be selective — "I should think of this not that." Just watch whatever is happening.[9]

This kind of "looking inward" should not be confused with introspection. Actually, it is not so much "looking inward" as "watching inward." Zen meditation is simply watching experience develop, "as if you are observing it from outside, without any subjective reaction, as a scientist observes some object. Here, too, you should not look at it as 'my feeling' or 'my sensation' subjectively, but only look at it as 'a feeling' or 'a sensation' objectively." Zen meditation should proceed like an internal spectator sport wherein we are lost in experiencing.

Mindfulness, or awareness, does not mean that you should think and be conscious "I am doing this" or "I am doing that." No. Just the contrary. The moment you think "I am doing this," you become self-conscious, and then you do not live in the action, but you live in the idea "I am," and consequently your work too is spoilt. You should forget yourself completely, and lose yourself in what you do. The moment a speaker becomes self-conscious and thinks "I am addressing an audience," his speech is disturbed and his trend of thought broken. But when he forgets himself in his speech, in his subject, then he is at his best, he speaks well and explains things clearly. All great work — artistic, poetic, intellectual or spiritual — is produced at those moments when its creators are lost completely in their actions, when they forget themselves altogether, and are free from self-consciousness.[10]

The sharp difference between Yoga and Zen was dramatically illustrated by two EEG studies. As noted earlier, EEG recordings from meditating yogis showed no cerebral reaction to repeated noises. On the other hand, EEG recordings from meditating Zen masters revealed a mild cortical reaction that remained the same no matter how often the stimuli were presented. Normally, repeated presentations of a stimulus adapt out and lead to weaker and weaker reactions. This effect did not occur in the Zen meditators, suggesting that their attentional orientation remained fresh and intense for all presentations of the stimulus.[11] This is what would be expected from mirrorlike, code-free attention. Koestler summed up the difference between the two meditational approaches: "While both Yoga and Zazen aim at penetrating beyond the captive mind, the 'beyond' means in one case trance-sleep and death, in the other case a more intense awareness of the Now and Here."[12]

While Yoga and Zen are, strictly speaking, two separate systems, in a broader sense they can be viewed as two aspects of the meditational experience. After making a review of the many meditational techniques, Ornstein concluded that most contain two basic processes.[13] The first is a "turning off of awareness" of everyday reality; all meditational systems emphasize the importance of blocking out external stimuli and weakening everyday thought patterns. Yoga carries this aspect to the extreme with its goal of emptying the mind absolutely. The other characteristic that seems to be universally present in all meditational systems is "an opening up" of awareness, best exemplified by the Zen ideal. These two aspects are comparable to the two elements that characterize all absorbed states, and which have been described here in various ways: mental lulling and enhancement of experience; mental relaxation and total attention; psychic distance and empathy.

Meditation, however, is different from other diversions in one important way: It is a subtractive process rather than an additive one. All other diversions bring on the absorbed state by presenting a fascination stimulus—a story, music, exciting sport action, etc. The stimulus takes complete control of attention so that it is relatively easy to block out surrounding distractions and suspend everyday thought patterns. Meditation, on the other hand, has no external fascination stimulus. In fact, the very heart of the meditation process is an attempt to remove all stimuli and nullify the props of psychological functioning. Instead of exciting us, it simplifies, allowing the person to feel clear, calm, serene. It is a way of distilling existence down to an elemental experience of being. While other diversions give us new identities, meditation purifies the one we have. What it lacks in excitement, it makes up for with a sense of wholeness. In the end, for someone who has cultivated this diversion, the mental relaxation can be so complete and purifying that the new psychological reality attained can be—yes, fascinating.

In ancient and modern discussions of meditation, the practice is described as a return to a natural state. According to both Yoga and Zen, meditation is liberation; it frees us from false and fragmenting verbal conceptions, and allows us to function at a more intuitive, unified level. Erich Fromm described it as a benign and healing regression.[14] Reading the literature, then, one would expect meditation to be an easy, appealing practice.

However, nothing could be further from the truth. Meditation is difficult and often discouraging. Like all cultivated diversions, it requires effort, patience, and practice. Before the absorbing enjoyments can occur, there must be a long training period wherein the person learns to concentrate and fix attention. However, performance is not easily evaluated or corrected since this is an invisible process. It is important, therefore, that the beginner have the guidance of an expert. Furthermore, the person learning to meditate must put himself in conditions that are usually seen as unpleasant or even punishing — silence, darkness, immobility, and isolation. Meditation requires that we go against deeply ingrained habits. It is nothing less than a program to de-program ourselves for a brief period of time, nullifying long-standing habits of self-referent thinking and attention. Meditation is certainly not a naturally developing state; in fact, even in ancient times it was recognized that a harsh kind of discipline was required to master it. In Yoga, meditation was associated with unnatural exercises and body contortions. Zen lore tells us that the master often had to make an assault about the head and shoulders of hapless monks whose attention happened to wander.

Most meditational techniques allow the use of some gentler device to help control the ever-roving attention. The most common ones make use of repetition and rhythm in order to lull attention. Examples of such devices are chanting a mantra, attending to one's breathing, or counting to ten over and over again. Although some systems make a fetish of the mantra and assign magical properties to it, actually it is to meditation what counting sheep is to falling asleep; it is not the content that matters, but the repetition. To hear and feel one's breathing in the quiet of meditation returns us to something vital and organismic. Breathing is sometimes made more salient during meditation by the inhalation of some scent, such as the odor of burnt incense. It is well known that aromas, like rhythm, somehow entrace us perceptually. Sometimes the meditator uses a visual aid, as when he fixes attention on a religious symbol. All of these attentional devices, as Ornstein pointed out, are basically equivalent.[15]

The rhythmic repetition of a mantra, the quietness and the closing of one's eyes, the letting go of everyday concerns — all of these lulling factors can lead but to one thing. It seems that in both beginners and experts, meditation is at risk for going over the line into sleep. As an example, *Time* magazine quoted one man who had attempted to learn Transcendental Meditation and then quit. "Look, I really tried," he said. "I paid my $125, attended all the sessions ... and do you know what happened? I fell asleep every time."[16]

EEG studies of advanced meditators show that cortical processing is slowed down to such an extent that sleep is often the outcome. In one such study, meditators spent as much as 41 percent of their meditation time in sleep stages 1 and 2.[17] In another study that used five individuals who had at least two and a half years experience with TM, it was found that significant parts of meditation sessions were spent in sleep stages 2, 3, and 4. In addition to five meditation sessions, the subjects in this study had five nap sessions when they were to lie down on a bed and actually sleep. By and large, there were no statistical EEG differences between the two kinds of sessions.[18]

Such findings are an embarrassment to those who claim that meditation leads to a special level of consciousness. These and similar EEG studies show

that meditation is not a qualitatively unique state, but rather is on the continuum between wakefulness and sleep, part of the normal sleep-inducing process.[19] Apparently, whatever unique experiences occur in meditation come
from that in-between, twilight condition known as the hypnogogic state. It
is well known that interesting and vivid experiences often occur in this state,
which takes place as we start to drop off into sleep — a time when attention
and experience are no longer controlled by everyday codes. On the EEG, hypnogogic state is represented by lower-frequency alpha waves and the theta
wave range, which is the level of cortical functioning often found in
meditators.[20] It would seem, then, that the cultivation of meditation is the
cultivation and enhancement of the hypnogogic state — a view that more and
more investigators are endorsing:

> The findings of this study add to the evidence that stage 1 "sleep" is a transi-
> tional phase, unlike full wakefulness and unlike unambiguous sleep. With
> appropriate training one can apparently learn to "hold on" to this stage, a
> feat which has not been demonstrated for any other "sleep" stage. . . . If the
> normal process of falling asleep involves a sequential series of
> neurophysiological events . . . then meditation might be seen as stimulating
> earlier events, while inhibiting the occurrence of later ones. In this very
> limited sense, regular meditaiton might be described as a program involving
> repeated practice in "freezing" the hypnogogic process at later and later stages
> (first in predominantly alpha wave stage, later in the predominantly theta
> wave ranges).[21]

Meditation hovers precariously close to sleep, at the very edge of consciousness. The person learning to meditate has to define and redefine this
in-between point continually by practice and consultation with the guru.
Meditational enjoyments are unreliable and hard to come by just because they
spring from the unstable hypnogogic condition. In the end, meditation
amounts to a near-impossible balancing act: The meditator should not fall
asleep, but he must not stay awake (at least not with everyday consciousness).
All of this makes meditation a very elusive and unnatural state, one that requires extensive cultivation to master.

The difficulty of meditational experience was amply demonstrated in an
experiment conducted at the University of Michigan.[22] In order to recruit
male subjects for a study of meditation, an advertisement in the campus
newspaper offered instructions in Zen meditation. Thirty-nine men
responded and showed up for the initial interview. Eleven of these dropped
out either before the meditation sessions began or before enough sessions were
completed to provide a sample of their responses. Thus, only twenty-eight participated, completing at least nine meditation sessions. After each session,
subjects filled out a report on the effects they experienced. When these were
scored according to certain criteria, it was found that 65 percent of the sessions

showed no meditation effect. In many other cases, however, the scorers were uncertain; in fact, there was complete agreement that a meditation effect occurred in only 16 percent of the sessions. Finally, of the twenty-eight men who participated, only six experienced the highest meditation effect at least once during the ten sessions. These results give new meaning to the old scripture that "many are called but few are chosen."

Spiritual Effects through the Suspension of Perceptual Codes

What is worship? It is not love. To worship is
to be put in a trance by an image. — *V.S. Pritchett*

Any procedure that takes us to the limits of lulling should be unsurpassed as a means of relaxation. Researchers have wondered whether meditation is more relaxing than just sitting quietly and resting; apparently, the answer is yes. As most adults have discovered for themselves, resting does not guarantee mental relaxation; anxious thoughts do not disappear just because the body is inactive. Meditation, on the other hand, weakens the mental sets most responsible for cueing anxiety and maintaining tension in the body. There already exists a large body of research which demonstrates the relaxation effects of meditation.[23]

But meditation is more than just a relaxation technique. It is a different "modality of being," as Naranjo described it.[24] In meditating we become serene; there is a feeling of being on another level of existence, above and beyond the mundane. Such detachment is the first stage of spiritual experience.

At times meditation leads to vivid experiences which are perceived as breakthroughs or flashes of insight. In the literature, these are referred to by such terms as "enlightenment," "illumination," or "awakening." These terms, however, are not to be taken literally. Enlightenment is not a cognitive kind of knowledge; illumination does not refer to a visual experience; and awakening does not refer to being aroused. Actually, these meditational high points seem to be comparable to inspiration, the phenomenon discussed in the previous chapter. We have seen that inspiration occurs only when the master code system is suspended, often developing out of the hypnogogic state. While normally this state is just a brief transition on the way to sleep, during meditation it is prolonged and enhanced. And since everyday codes are in abeyance, meditation becomes fertile ground for the development of intuitive connections, peak experiences, bisociations, and the feeling of opening up to something broader — apparently what meditators mean by terms like "enlightenment" and "awakening."

Furthermore, the immobility and sensory-social isolation that characterize meditation can also lead to changes in how basic aspects of life, like space and time, are experienced.[25] Immobility and isolation weaken the psychophysical codes that keep us oriented to the world — codes related to body position, sense of time, and sense of self — with the result that unique qualities of experience come into being. For example, as the codes that mediate adjustments to surrounding reality are neutralized, there is likely to be a feeling of being in a void or a cosmic dimension. With the fading away of the codes that keep track of time, there is likely to be a sense of timelessness, even eternity. Just as the cues in a story convey a sense of another time and place, making us feel we are in that reality, so also the complete absence of cues as is characteristic of meditation can give the feeling of being in no particular place or time. The weakening of these codes does not reduce or halt experience, but reorganizes it. Perceptual experience becomes more generalized; we become more aware of background and the broader meanings underlying human existence. As John Welwood put it, one experiences "a larger sense of one's life, apart from the struggle to 'be somebody.'"[26]

Earlier (page 47) we referred to a study (by psychiatrist Arthur Deikman) in which subjects had nothing to do but contemplate a blue vase that was placed before them.[27] The extent to which meditation can destabilize perceptual experience was dramatically demonstrated by this study. Subjects were placed in a quiet, comfortable room, where they were told to discontinue everyday modes of thought and give undivided attention to the vase for half an hour. There were some ten to thirty weekly sessions such as this, after each of which the subjects gave a report of their perceptual experiences.

This experiment had all of the makings of a very boring time for the subjects — staring at the same object for long periods of time, restricted movement, no social interaction, no thinking. One would expect that after a short time they would tire of this pointless task and would find their minds wandering. It would also be reasonable to expect that the experience of looking at the vase would become weak and minimal on the basis of the adaptation principle, which states that the organism becomes insensitive to a repeated stimulus.

Nothing of the kind occurred. It might have if the subjects had processed the vase in an everyday frame of mind. However, their attentional orientation was different, and so was their experience. They meditated on the vase, presumably allocating all attention to it, and instead of becoming weakly perceived, the vase was vividly experienced, as Deikman reported.

> Common to all [subjects] was the reported alteration of their perception of the vase. Sooner or later they experienced a shift to a deeper and more intense blue. "More vivid" was a phrase they used frequently. [Subjects] experienced the base as becoming brighter while everything in their visual field became quite dark and indistinct. The adjective "luminous" was often applied to the vase, as if it were a source of light.[28]

The perception of the vase was changed in other ways too. For example, the subjects reported that it seemed to move, change in size and shape, and lose its boundaries. Some perceived that the vase was exuding a force, or a magnetic attraction, or that it was pulsating rhythmically. All of these effects, together with the increased intensity and luminosity, gave the vase a come-alive quality. One of the principal effects of the meditation experience was the perception of "animation in the vase, which seemed to move with a life of its own."[29]

This study reveals the paradoxical nature of meditation. Psychologically, meditation is a desert—immobility, reduced sensory input, absence of cognitive and social interaction. Given this reduction in psychological input, one would expect reduced experiencing. But Diekman's subjects reported experiences of "luminosity" and "animation," and feelings of oneness. Since there was no obvious stimuli for these experiences, they can be understood only in terms of the suspension of everyday, code-controlled processing that seems to take place in meditational conditions.

The perceptual distortions that occurred in Deikman's study indicate a weakening of the codes and constancies that normally structure attention. We take perceptual experience as something given. But actually it is something "constructed" according to numerous rules built into the organism, which automatically correct for changes in movement, illumination, distance, location, etc. As we go about daily living, these codes are continually firing to maintain consistency and stability in perception.

However, in conditions of immobility and total attention, bodily and cognitive adjustments stop. At such times the organism's code systems are weakened—not only the master codes, but also the sensorimotor and psychophysical ones that mediate perceptual experience. Without the sensorimotor codes, perception becomes "raw," uncorrected, distorted, fluid, unstable, "hallucinatory." In the experiment, perception of the blue vase was uncorrected by the constancy codes, and so it was seen in an unstable and undifferentiated way. Even slight movements made by the meditator must have resulted in apparent movement in the vase; for example, breathing movements would make it appear that the vase was breathing or pulsating. In this fashion, perception of the vase got mixed up with the experiences of the meditator; it was not sufficiently differentiated, not anchored to an external context. Thus the subjects felt merged and one-with the vase, which was in the center of total attention; and it must have seemed very intense since it was unmodified by a context of other objects.

The unique effects reported in this study were attentional in nature—not visual. Thus, Deikman concluded that "the allocation of attention appears to be the principal process involved in meditation."[30] Therefore, the same attentional phenomena of intensity, distortion, and animation also occur when meditating with eyes closed, leading to an unstructured hypnogogic mental condition that could be the basis of unnatural or supernatural experiences.

Sensing the Supernatural

To most, even good people, God is a belief.
To the saints He is an embrace. — *Francis Thompson*

Most of the world's great religions have adopted some form of meditational practice, generally recognizing it as a superior kind of worship, reserved
for those who dedicate their lives to spiritual development. For the general
run of people, religion is mediated by the clergy, weekly rituals, and verbal
prayers that express thoughts and request favors from the deity. Meditation,
however, strives for the ultimate; its goal is nothing less than the direct experience of and communion with the divine being.

In tribal society, experiencing the supernatural usually took the form of
a frenzy of possession, which was incited by Dionysian dancing, whirling,
chanting, and rhythmic drumming. But the major religions have generally
pursued this experience in a muted way through meditation, which has been
the fountainhead of oriental and Western mysticism. In oriental religions,
which are not based on a belief in a personal God, meditation has always been
recognized as the path to the highest spiritual reality. The end states of oriental
meditation — yogic nirvana and Zen satori — represent the ultimate diversions
out of earthly existence. In Western and Christian religions, on the other
hand, supernatural reality was more likely to be experienced in personal
terms, as a sensing of the divine presence. This high point of spiritual experience, of course, was attained only by those mystics who cultivated meditational practice, usually behind the walls of a convent or monastery. Speaking
of these raptures, James Leuba wrote: "The sense of the presence of God is
at times so intense, God is so close, that it becomes a 'spiritual embrace,'
characterized by very ardent delight."[31]

Some of the most striking examples of experiencing the divine presence
are to be found in that religious development known as medieval mysticism.
Most of these mystics were Catholic nuns or monks, participants in the great
monastic tradition that flourished during the Middle Ages. At that time in
Western civilization, when religion was as preeminent in society as commerce
and industry are today, it was not unusual for people to renounce the world
and retreat to a convent or monastery, there to dedicate their lives to spiritual
development, mostly in the form of meditation. Monastic existence itself was
modeled after meditation. Monasteries and convents were always set apart
from the world, and were meant to shut it out. The monks and nuns lived
in obedience to a strict regimen so that there was little need for mental or social
business. Not only was there much silence and solitude, but an attempt was
made to implement meditation in a living way. For example, a sense
of selflessness became a permanent condition; when the monk donned
the religious habit, he became a nonperson, giving up his worldly name,

possessions, and ties to family and friends. The monastery provided no excitements or opportunities for independent action or achievement. Rather, it was designed to lull by much chanting, praying, meditating, and living a daily rhythm of ritual. This is not to say that the monastic ideal was always realized, or that conflict and competitiveness did not occur as they almost always do when people live together. What is significant is that a way of life evolved that was based on the elemental aspects of absorbed experience: nullifying self and the surrounding reality.

Monastic individuals who experienced divine visitations were considered to be mystics. Most of us have heard of only a few, like St. Teresa of Avila or St. John of the Cross. However, according to a review by Herbert Moller, there were many more, and their literary output was impressive.[32] Hundreds left published accounts of their experiences. In addition, the writings of two or three thousand others lie unpublished in European archives. The experience of divine visitation was highly valued by these individuals, and it usually became the basis for an intense emotional and even romantic relationship with Jesus. In their writings, the mystics often referred to the divine presence in glowing terms such as "my beloved," "my spouse," "my one love," and "sweetness of my heart." Moller referred to this as "affective mysticism" because its central feature was a "striving for union with the divine, which was accompanied with deep emotional satisfaction."

> The most striking element of this type of mysticism was a decidedly personal relationship to God. Its highest avowed aim was the attainment of unity with the divinity in a flow of feeling (*unio mystica*): and the divinity was expected to respond as a person to the amorous longings of the mystic.[33]

Mystical experience does not refer to something imagined or to religious thoughts. Rather, it is an intense experience felt with force and conviction, as though it were being stimulated through the sensory channels like a reality event. However, there is no obvious stimulus for the experience, either in the external environment or in the inner, psychological one. The experience is not under the control of the mystic and cannot be voluntarily induced. When it occurs, therefore, the mystic has the startling feeling of being acted on by some unseen presence. Because nothing about the occurrence conforms to the laws of physical reality, there is the haunting and extraordinary feeling of being in touch with something not of this world.

Of course, there *is* a stimulus for mystical experience. It is not a specific object, but it is embodied in the same three conditions that predict other peak experiences: long-term cultivation of the diversion, capacity for absorbed attention, and a particular external condition, which in this case consists of social-sensory isolation.

Mystical experience, first of all, occurs primarily to those individuals who have cultivated spiritual development and meditation for a long time, who have made a "career" of seeking the supernatural. It generally does not come to the layperson whose religion is limited to Sunday church service, or to the individual who meditates for only a half an hour a day. Rather, mystic experience is most likely to happen to the person who grew up with intense religious and spiritual training, so that a master code developed that continually directed attention to these matters. Spiritual gratifications are this person's highest priority, as evidenced by his eventual sacrifice of all other gratifications for these. Eventually, he abandons family, friends, worldly pleasures, and creature comforts for a life that is harsh and solitary but has the potential for spiritual development. There is a withdrawal from the world, culminated by spending long periods of time in meditation. These lonely vigils of immobile silence are not spent reciting prayers but in seeking direct communion with God by obliterating all vestiges of self and worldly influence. As in other cultivated diversions, the person must throw himself away, and put himself under complete control of the endeavor. As one stage of mystical development, the person has to go through the agony of purgation, purification, and the dark night of the soul when the conventional self is renounced and broken down.

The second condition necessary for mystical experience is the capacity for absorbed attention, usually realized through meditation. "The first step of the Christian mystical method," wrote Leuba, "is in substance the first step of the hypnotic method; it begins with the fixation of attention upon some thought or external object in order to circumscribe mental activity."[34] As noted earlier, studies show that both meditation and hypnosis are based on an attentional state that is nonanalytic, total, and absorbed. It is just such an attentional orientation that makes possible mystical experience, as also Ortega y Gasset recognized: "Mysticism, too, is a phenomenon of attention.... The mystic, like the lover, attains his abnormal state by 'fixing' his attention upon an object, the function of which is, for the moment, simply to withdraw attention from everything else and permit a vacuum of the mind."[35] Just as total attention on the story can make fictions come alive, so in meditation it can bring animation to images and symbols. It is easy to see how a medieval monk who meditated on the crucifix daily for long periods of time in a barren monastery cell might come to experience the absorbing come-alive effects that Deikman's subjects did, and then be convinced that Christ had appeared before him.

The absorbed state seems to be especially conducive to the impression that something or somebody is *there*. It is interesting to note that whenever humans experience the supernatural, it is always in conditions like meditation, peak experience, psychedelic state, or the frenzied spells of possession — all variations of absorbed experience. Although meditation is an extremely difficult practice, it is probably the only human endeavor that can reliably invoke the otherworldly. Meditation has probably ignited more ecstasy and mystical experience than any other stimulus condition. It is no wonder, therefore, that some type of meditational practice has been incorporated into most major religions. Because religion embodies our beliefs about the supernatural, it has the task of making these beings and forces real. Absorbed meditation, because of its capacity to make images come alive, is an ideal vehicle for giving direct perceptible experience of the supernatural.

The third factor that has a role in producing mystical experience is a certain kind of external stimulus. This is not a fascination object as found in other diversions, but it is, nevertheless, a situation or condition that can have a powerful effect on attention: the condition of social-sensory isolation. Mysticism has always been associated with this condition. Whatever culture or era they lived in, mystics have always cultivated a solitary existence, usually in barren and uninviting conditions. At least in the periods when their divine visitations occurred, they shunned worldly activities and lived away from other people. Such isolation tends to weaken even basic psychophysical codes, making the mystic more suggestible to spiritual images and predisposing the organism to hypnogogic and "hallucinatory" experience. Thus, the stimulus for mystical experience does not capture attention but breaks it down and decodifies it.

The results of sensory deprivation research show how quickly such conditions do break down the structure of everyday attention. (Of course, living in a desert or in the mountains is not as extreme as the social-sensory isolation induced in the experimental lab; nevertheless, the findings are relevant.) In the original study of sensory deprivation, the subjects, after being isolated, spent a lot of time napping, as might be expected. After becoming sleep-satiated, they passed the time thinking and daydreaming. Eventually, however, they reached a point where they could no longer control their thoughts; they were "content to let the mind drift," and some "experienced 'blank periods' when they did not seem to be thinking at all."[36] In fact, ability to concentrate was temporarily impaired, as was revealed by objective testing. While cognitive functioning and control were weakened, it seemed that sheer experiencing was enhanced. Although the subjects wore translucent plastic eye-coverings, many started to see vivid images. Sometimes these were fragmentary and fleeting geometrical forms, while at other times they consisted of organized scenes. The experimenters themselves did not fully appreciate the power and strangeness of these hallucinations until one of them subjected himself to the isolation procedure and experienced them firsthand. They then interpreted these visual phenomena as being similar to the hallucinatory perceptual changes that occur in the psychedelic state.

Also interesting was that sometimes the hallucinations were not visual or auditory but consisted of a sense that someone was present. Even though the subjects were isolated, some "reported that they felt as if another body were lying beside them in the cubicle." The effect was so strong that some "reported that for several days after the experiment they were afraid that they were going to see ghosts."[37] Furthermore, pre- and post-measurement of attitudes revealed that isolation made the subject more likely to believe in the existence of supernatural phenomena. Such findings indicate that sensory deprivation pushes the organism toward the intuitive and suggestible mode, making it more prone to detect hidden meanings and the emotional significance of things. The fact that subjects lost voluntary control of attention and were then bombarded by vivid visual images reflects a weakening of the master codes in the forebrain and strengthening of the deep brain — an upset of the normal relations between these two centers. As discussed in Chapter 6, psychedelic drugs have similar effects, and they too increase spiritual awareness and the sensing of the supernatural.[38]

The greatest fascination experience of all — the experience of God — comes out of nothingness: the empty mind of meditation and a barren, solitary external environment. "The most surprising thing," wrote Ortega y Gasset, "is that once the mind has been cleared of everything, the mystic assures us that he feels God before him, that he is filled with God; that is, God consists of precisely that vacuum. Consequently, Meister Eckhart speaks of the 'silent desert of God.'"[39] Mystic experience, however, does not just come out of nowhere. The nihilistic conditions of mind and environment are necessary in order to nullify the forebrain, allowing the deep brain and its vitalizing images to come into ascendance. Since there is no external stimulus, the pleasure and fascination — the rapture that accompanies the mystic's experience — must originate in the deep brain, as it does in the psychedelic state.

Again and again in our discussion of recreation, we have encountered what amounts to the first principle of diversion, namely, that new and expanded experiencing is possible only when there is a nullifying of self and reality. Mystical experience is the ultimate expression of this principle. It is the supreme diversion. In his book on mysticism, Leuba had a chapter on "The Sense of Invisible Presence" which ended with this observation:

> The development of the mystical technique for the realization of a quasi-physical presence of the Perfect One constitutes the most remarkable achievement of religion. . . . It is one of the outstanding expressions of the creative power working in humanity. It is paralleled in the realm of reason by the development of science. Both lead, if in different ways, to the physical and spiritual realization of man.[40]

Chapter 13

High-Processing Psychological States

I swear to you, gentlemen, that being overly conscious
is a sickness, a real, full-blown sickness. . . . I am, for instance,
terribly self-centered. — *Fyodor Dostoyevsky*

Throughout this book it has been emphasized that absorption is a unique psychological state. In these final two chapters an attempt will be made to show that despite its unique qualities, absorption belongs to a system of psychological states found in the human organism, and that it has a logical relationship to them.

The Four Major Orientations of the Organism

Even if such states of consciousness as the dream are disregarded, the normal man does not always function on the same level of mental activity. . . . His mentality, genetically considered, is not the same when he is utterly distracted as when he is in a state of perfectly organized concentration. It varies as he moves from some sober scientific or·practical work to an emotional surrender to people or things. — *Heinz Werner*

The term "psychological state" refers to the overall attentional orientation of the organism. Apparently, the human organism has the capability of shifting into various orientations, each representing a different relationship to the external world and a different state of being — a major change in consciousness and quality of experiencing. The four psychological states are sleep, absorbed diversion, mental distress, and "everyday life" or what we have referred to as the business of living. Changes from one state into another are brought about by changes in the control of attention.

Attention is controlled by two factors, one external and one internal. One source of control comes from stimuli in the external world; the other is invisible, consisting of internal programs and dispositions, especially the master codes. That attention depends on some combination of these two determinants has long been accepted in psychology.

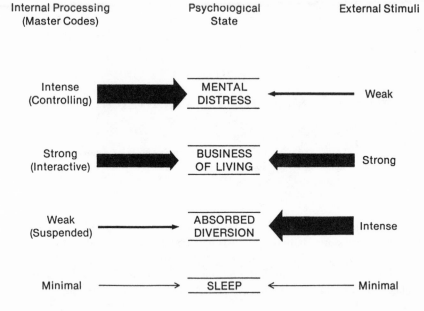

Figure 1. The four psychological states as determined by different combinations of internal and external control of attention.

> Sensory impulses do not act on an empty organism; they interact with certain predispositions and states already there, and immediate experience is the result of that interaction. The nature of experience, then, depends on two interacting sets of contributions: those of the environment, in the form of physical stimulation, and those of the observer himself, which . . . [consist] of selection, organization, and interpretation.[1]

However, the internal and external determinants are not always equal in their interaction. The possible combinations of attentional control can be seen in Figure 1, which presents a framework for the four psychological states. This figure demonstrates how the different orientations of the organism are derived from the same dual control system of attention.

The principal psychological state, here called the *business of living*, is the orientation usually maintained during awake life. In this state, attention is co-controlled by internal and external factors in an interactive way. The next most common psychological state is *sleep*, which is the absence of both factors or at least very minimal control by either. During sleep, the attentional system is nonfunctional, and so consciousness is extinguished. Another psychological state is *mental distress*, in which attention is largely controlled by internal factors. A person who is acutely worried, depressed, or paranoid is being over-controlled by his own mental sets and programs so that he is likely to be highly self-preoccupied, having only a weak interaction with people and the environment. Finally, there is the state of *absorbed diversion*. Here, attention is completely controlled by some external stimulus, usually a play object or an object of fascination. The internal determinant has been suspended and so has no significant role in the control of attention.

Although they are derived from the same system, the psychological states are distinct conditions of the organism; each has its own functions and qualities of experience. Nowhere is this more evident than in the two states which everyone agrees represent radically different orientations: the business of living and sleep. In the former, both determinants of attention are present; in the latter, both are absent. Logically, there should be two other possibilities, created when one or the other determinant has principal control of attention. And indeed, as shown in Figure 1, there is one psychological state where the external determinant has exclusive control of attention (absorbed diversion), and one where the internal determinant has exclusive control (mental distress).

Figure 1 also demonstrates that the psychological states are on a continuum of master code processing. To some degree this is reflected in the appearance and behavior of the organism, especially facial expression, posture, bodily movements, and speech. For example, at the lowest level, sleep, there is no evidence of master code processing; it has been turned off physiologically. There is no animation in the body, no speech, no facial expression, no interaction with the environment. The eyes are closed and the sensory system is relatively unresponsive.

At the next level of processing, which is absorption, the master codes are still not operational, but they are passively present in the background. In this state the person is awake and attentive, but the organism still has no interaction with or orientation toward the broader environment. The person seems to be "in another world." Both sleep and absorption can be considered low-processing psychological states, and will be discussed in the next chapter.

The next level of processing is found in the business of living. Here the master codes are fully operational and interactive with the environment. Thus, while there is an appearance of inner control and purpose, there is at the same time a responsiveness and adaptiveness to external conditions. In other words, in a flexible way the person is alternately controlled by internal and external determinants, and this is reflected in varied, spontaneous facial expressions and body movements. Internal processing can become fairly intense, but it is always directed and corrected by external cues.

Finally, the highest level of processing is seen in acute distress. Spurred on by unmanaged threat, master code processing can become so intense that it over-controls the interaction with the environment, and the person becomes extremely subjective and rigid in his approach to things. With the internal determinant almost exclusively in control, the person often seems to be driven by an inner pressure; eyes peer or dart about, posture and facial expressions are strained, and speech is mostly taken up with worries and self-preoccupations. External cues seem to have little effect on attention and behavior; the person appears distracted and is not easily influenced or reassured.

In the remainder of this chapter we will fully explore the latter two orientations — the high-processing states.

The Everyday Business of Living

There are no special conditions for this psychological state. It is home base for the awake organism. On awakening from sleep, we simply snap into this orientation, set to interact with the physical and social environments, carrying out routines, making plans, thinking about problems, talking to people, fulfilling social obligations. This orientation is reflexive, having been built into the organism by a long socialization process. It is, of course, the orientation in which we spend most of our existence, and the one to which we always return after intervals of sleep or absorption or mental distress. Most people would simply equate the business of living with life itself, not recognizing that is but one of three possible orientations during wakefulness. In fact, in psychology there is no standard term for this particular state. Gradually, certain words are being introduced such as "everyday life," "ordinary consciousness," or "normal reality." Such terms, however, seem bland, and reveal nothing about the quality of this state and how it is actually experienced.

Whatever other characteristics everyday life has, our most basic perception is that it is serious, "for real." What we do here counts for or against us. This is not so in the other psychological states; during sleep, absorption, or mental distress, society tends to recognize that we are not our normal selves. But how we conduct the business of living determines our true worth in the social marketplace. Everyday living is not just a matter of existing, but a matter of earning a living, socially as well as financially. We have to keep up various roles and positions; we have to prove ourselves again and again. The relationships between the organism and the external world is basically an adversarial one, so that we are always being graded as to how well we meet the standards set by society, the physical world, and ourselves. Thus, implicit in this psychological state are qualities of struggle and anxiety.

Ask the man on the street to describe everyday life, and he is likely to use terms like "rat race," "being in a rut," or "one damn thing after another." In the past, they talked about "toil and tribulation," "care and woe." Today, we talk about "stress," "tension," and "frustration." In spite of modern technology and every kind of convenience, people still seem to lead tense, unhappy lives that alternate between anxiety and boredom. The high statistics on suicide, crime, drug abuse, poverty, and mental and physical illness indicate that for millions of people life must be grim and desperate. Many people find everyday life too burdensome to tolerate without medication or professional help.

This gloomy view of human existence has often been reaffirmed by our great scholars and philosophers. The whole philosophy of Existentialism is based on the idea that anxiety and boredom are endemic to life. Thoreau's famous characterization of life has been repeated so often that it must be true: "The mass of men lead lives of quiet desperation." Apparently, Thoreau was referring not just to the era in which he lived — which seems idyllic by today's standards — but rather to a universal human condition. Every age is an age of anxiety. "Life is not a spectacle or a feast," wrote Santayana, "it is a predicament." Walt Whitman envied the contentment that he observed in animals. Schopenhauer declared that *"work, worry, labor and trouble* form the lot of almost all men their whole life long." Schopenhauer, of course, was the world's greatest pessimist, but others, like C.P. Snow, have also viewed human existence with deep philosophical gloom:

> Most of the scientists I have known well have felt — just as deeply as the non-scientists I have known well — that the individual condition of each of us is tragic. Each of us is alone: sometimes we escape from solitariness, through love or affection or perhaps creative moments, but those triumphs of life are pools of light we make for ourselves while the edge of the road is black: each of us dies alone.[2]

No concept in behavioral science recognizes human existence as inherent struggle. Perhaps this is why psychology is sometimes perceived as being incomplete and superficial. There is no conceptualization of the continual testing that goes on in daily existence. According to psychologists, life is simply a matter of making adjustments, of expressing personality, of emitting instrumental responses, or of playing out certain social roles. Such sanitized concepts make for a tidy science but at the price of ignoring the most telling qualities of human life.

To be sure, there has been extensive study of the negative and unpleasant aspects of life, such as fatigue, effort, anxiety, and frustration. These burdens, however, have been studied as deviant conditions. Fatigue and effort have generally been studied as aspects of industrial psychology. Likewise, anxiety and frustration are topics in abnormal psychology, related primarily to mental illness. The very existence of such disciplines as abnormal and clinical psychology conveys the impression that the psychology of normal life is about something other than anxiety, frustration, and conflict. Actually, such troublesome processes are as much a part of everyday life as any other function. Thomas Szasz pointed out that the notion of mental illness evolved as a way of denying "the everyday fact that life for most people is a continuous struggle."[3] According to Szasz, problems in living are the rule, not the exception.

Today, with the growing awareness of stress and its effects, people are beginning to realize that day-to-day life is not a "straight, sunlit path," but "a muddle and struggle," as William James described it. In civilized society, the struggle is due, not to the demands of biological survival or physical danger, but to the pressures of social living. In particular, the testing that starts in school continues through adult life, with all of the fear of failure and ego threat that it entails.

We are put to the test every time we have an obligation to fulfill, a deadline to meet, a question to answer. Nearly every human activity has some standard against which performance can be graded. By virtue of our roles and relationships, certain people have the right to expect things from us and to grade us on how well we fulfill their expectations. When one considers all the commitments the average person has — to spouse, children, parents, fellow workers, friends, various social groups, and society as a whole — it seems just about every aspect of existence is monitored and judged by somebody.

What effect do our "grades" have on our lives? Just as animals develop pecking orders, so humans develop status hierarchies. In a way, it is a matter of survival of the socially fittest — since our grades determine our success in relationships, group memberships, occupation, status, and the other essentials for a full and effective life. There is no escaping this grading process; it is implicitly a part of social living.

The evaluative process is also embedded in everyday consciousness. Thinking is simply a way of talking to ourselves, and this "inner speech" has the same characteristics as public speech. Public speech is always business; whenever people converse, they constantly grade each other — if not overtly, then by tone of voice, innuendo, or nonverbal cue. Inner speech, too, is mostly business, a matter of evaluating the self-environment interaction — making judgments about being right or wrong, good or bad, favored or rejected, lucky or unlucky, winning or losing, passing or failing. As noted in Chapter 2, such mental activity is so pervasive that it has the status of a master code. This evaluative thinking is not necessarily objective or productive; it may be rational or paranoid, but it goes on in an obligatory way. Virtually all thoughts that occur to an awake person are caught in the web of self-environment interaction. Nobody spends a significant amount of time spinning beautiful thoughts devoid of self-interest and evaluation. Thinking — everyday consciousness — is business.

Being tested and graded is a universal fact of social-biological living, and it is a source of continual effort and anxiety. Only when we recognize this can we understand why people might need mental relaxation and diversion — why they might crave self-forgetting experiences.

Mental Distress

There is no doubt that mental distress constitutes a separate psychological state. Anyone who has experienced a bout of it would agree that it certainly makes us feel different from our normal selves. In fact, the prominence of the mental health establishment today indicates that distress is an extreme condition of the organism and one that requires professional help. It is anything but everyday. Mental distress is so seriously different that it requires some form of treatment — counseling, medication, psychiatric hospitalization, sometimes even institutionalization.

Mental distress is not the same as mental illness. Some psychiatric disorders entail little or not distress. But in most of them the central problem is mental distress, often so severe that it overwhelms the person. Mental distress is present whenever there is anxiety, depression, obsessive thinking, paranoid preoccupation, or psychosis. Although these symptoms are generally thought to represent different problems, they can also be viewed as different degrees and varieties of mental distress.

Mental distress is painful, and this is what drives the person to get help, even though he may have no interest in the theories of psychiatry or psychology. The pain of mental distress, of course, is not the same as physical pain. Rather, it is "psychic pain," which is a feeling of acute disharmony, reflecting an unnatural condition of the organism. Specifically, psychic pain is an oppressive feeling of too much self; it is the feeling of being trapped within oneself and blocked from the natural interactions with the environment. Usually, this feeling is due to some unresolved threat to self. This unmanageable threat pushes the master codes to ever more intense levels of functioning, which at some point starts to have maladaptive effects, leading to a painful psychological state.

Just as it is possible to suspend master code processing, so also it is possible to escalate it far above everyday levels. Psychological processing always intensifies when the organism is faced with some task or test. However, if the testing becomes the source of persistent threat to the self, then the master code for self seems to take exclusive control of attention. The person becomes so self-preoccupied that it interferes with his ability to deal with tasks in reality. This principle has been established by extensive research, and it is embodied in the concept of "ego-involvement."[4] The basic idea here is that failure and ego-threat increase self-orientation so much that it impairs task-orientation. Ego-involvement dynamics are at the heart of mental distress, and , as we shall see, they help explain the qualities of experience found in this psychological state.

Mandler and Sarason researched aspects of ego-involvement and discussed the over-attention to self that occurs when people are put on the spot in formal testing conditions.[5] They pointed out that at such times problem-solving is likely to be impaired by self-doubts, self-questioning, loss of self-esteem, fear of punishment, desire to avoid the situation, and heightened awareness of a body that is behaving differently (nervousness, "butterflies in the stomach"). In a review of the numerous studies done on test anxiety, Irwin Sarason concluded that the findings were "consistent with the view that high anxious [subjects] emit personalized, self-oriented interfering responses when threat is perceived in the environment."[6] In another review, Jeri Wine arrived at similar conclusions, finding that evaluative instructions and test conditions do increase anxiety, that anxiety reduces the range of cue utilization, and that highly anxious individuals are self-preoccupied and self-deprecatory.[7]

Ego-involvement research shows that threat and anxiety have a constrictive effect on attention, leading to a narrow range of cue utilization.[8] As a result, relevant information is ignored and performance suffers. When threat and anxiety are present, internal programs (self) become more dominant, so processing is more rigid and subjective. In his review of the effects of anxiety on problem-solving, Wilbert Ray concluded: "Increased stress or motivation will increase the amount or strength of set."[9] Thus, under these conditions there is more evidence of biases and perceptual filtering; the person is relatively more influenced by internal (past) determinants than external (present) ones.[10] This whole process works against a flexible, open-minded task-orientation.

It is often assumed that threat and failure are ego-deflating in the sense that they lower self-esteem and self-confidence. This is true in a narrow sense, in terms of how we feel about ourselves. But in terms of what they do to the organism, threat and failure are ego-inflating because they strengthen internal sets and the master codes. Such conditions make us more self-conscious and perceptually constricted, i.e., overly involved with ego.

Ego-involvement is obviously at work in that ever-bothersome phenomenon of worry. This is a driven kind of thinking that overtakes us whenever we fail, make mistakes, or have our feelings hurt. Although worry seems to be directed at these external threats, basically it is focused on self and the implications of getting poor grades in the business of living. Usually worry is unproductive and has no effect on the external situation; it is rigid and repetitive thinking that consists of recycling old programs. Worry is a speed-up of self-referent processing. When people are acutely worried, they actually come close to talking to themselves — self interacting with self. Even though worry is unpleasant and effortful, we are forced to do it when we feel threatened — which demonstrates the ironclad nature of ego-involvement dynamics.

In addition to worry, ego-involvement helps to explain the more severe psychiatric symptoms resulting from psychological threat. As we shall see shortly, anxiety, depression, paranoia, and psychotic breakdown all have the attentional structure of ego-involvement, i.e., increased self-orientation along with decreased task (reality) orientation. All psychiatric patients are excessively self-preoccupied, and as a result their handling of reality is either impaired or has ceased altogether. The greater the discrepancy between self and reality, the more intense will be the distress and psychic pain, the more the person will feel cut off from the outside world and its benefits.

In carrying on the normal business of living, people are usually able to pass the tests presented to them. They are able to resolve the threats to self-esteem, and so ego-involving worries are but passing annoyances. But sometimes—whether due to poor coping skills, biochemical disorder, or severe or prolonged stresses—the threat is not managed and there is a drastic buildup of worry, ego-involvement, and master code processing. All of this is seen in psychiatric patients, where a more intense and desperate level of business is conducted primarily in their thoughts. Because their reality orientation is weakened, distressed people are likely to be inhibited, apathetic, or withdrawn. Nevertheless, their internal speech always betrays an extremely high level of evaluative processing, which is more in the nature of worry than productive problem-solving. It is for this reason that they look driven and intensely preoccupied; they pace, talk to themselves, are hyper-alert and quick to overreact. They are morbidly preoccupied with failure, guilt, fear, and hostility—all highly self-referent emotions.

In one study which demonstrated this preoccupation, it was found that chronic schizophrenics, although mute and withdrawn in a state hospital, apparently spent their days thinking about such emotional business. By subjecting these patients to sodium amytal interviews, the study revealed the content of their thoughts, which, it turned out, centered around persistent preoccupations with failure and threats to self-esteem.[11] Thus, although distressed people avoid reality, they continue to carry on very intense reality business in their heads.

The common belief about mental illness states the opposite: that in avoiding reality the distressed person gives up and withdraws into an inner shelter.

For example, it is often said that schizophrenia represents a "retreat from sanity," or a withdrawal into a dream world. The implication is that psychiatric patients spend their time engaged in pleasant daydreams. Actually, one study found that these individuals have blocked imagination and are unable to develop enjoyable, image-laden fantasy.[12] The exotic names given to distressed people—like "schizophrenic" and "paranoiac"—reinforce the notion that there is some mysterious or exotic breaking away from reality, when in fact there is only an individual futilely processing everyday business to the point of psychic pain. Mental illness is not a haven or a diversion. It is super business.

While mental distress and absorption both involve a weakening of ties to everyday reality, there is a great difference in how they are weakened. It is the difference between distraction and diversion — between an involuntary interference and a voluntary turning away. In mental distress, reality ties are weakened by ego-involving thoughts which force themselves on attention and impair task-orientation and the ability to conduct the interactive business of everyday living; this is what is referred to as "being driven to distraction." In absorption, on the other hand, we choose to temporarily suspend our ties with reality so that we can more completely enhance our experience and our sense of aliveness.

As seen in Figure 1, the experiences of absorption and mental distress are opposites. Absorption is the voluntary suspension of the business of living; mental distress is the involuntary escalation of it. Absorption is a harmonious and unitary experience; distress is a fragmented condition of being continually distracted by internal preoccupations. Absorption is felt as liberation, as an opening up to new experience; distress is oppressive and closes the mind to anything not related to self. Absorption is enjoyable, even when negative emotions are involved. Mental distress is psychic pain, even though the person is always thinking about himself. The one is play; the other is the worst kind of work.

Absorption and distress represent the positive and negative poles of wakeful existence. Distressed people not only seem unable to play, but they also have a reluctance to try. They generally feel so pressed by important business on their minds that they cannot afford to let go. Distressed individuals usually yearn for mental relaxation, but instead of losing themselves in some diversion they often search vainly for intellectual formulas or magical nostrums that will bring peace of mind.

Severely distressed patients in psychiatric hospitals or institutions usually show no inclination for recreation even though they have plenty of free time. Unable to work or play, they spend their time pacing like caged animals, or, curled up and immobilized in a chair, they ruminate, talk to themselves and objects around them, and carry on interminable inner business. They cannot relax sufficiently even to get involved in spectator diversions. When they watch movies or television, their enjoyment is likely to be spoiled by worrisome self-reminders. Severely distressed individuals might not get involved at all but would merely project their problems and concerns onto the show or perceive ideas of reference in it. In general, they cannot afford to disarm themselves, as one must do in recreation; they retain a compulsive and anxious orientation. As one psychiatric patient reported to her therapist, getting absorbed can be dangerous:

> I forgot myself at the Ice Carnival the other night. I was so absorbed in looking at it that I forgot what time it was and who and where I was. When I suddenly realized I hadn't been thinking about myself I was frightened to death. The unreality feeling came. I must never forget myself for a single minute.[13]

Ego-Involvement as a Basis for Distress and Mental Breakdown

Madness comes from the refusal to develop, to adjust, to dilute one's true
self in the sordid mush of the world. If we want to find the true self
in each of us, we must go to the county lunatic asylum. — *Gerald Brennan*

As noted earlier in the book, the master codes for self and reality usually
function in a closely coordinated way to process the organism's interactions
with the environment. Ego-involvement, however, splits these two master
codes apart, as it weakens task-orientation (reality code) while empowering
self-orientation (self code). Prolonged failure, threat, and unsatisfying interactions with the external world also have the effect of disconfirming the
reality master code so that it is no longer a reliable guide to the external environment. Thus, the basic integrity of the organism's executive function is
severely compromised, as the reality arm of the master code system atrophies
while the self becomes bloated. This unlinking of the two master codes is apparently the basis for the phenomenon of "mental breakdown," so often referred to by individuals who have experienced episodes of psychotic distress,
and have recovered sufficiently to tell about them. Typically they describe
their minds as having been "shattered," "lost," "split," "eclipsed," etc.

It is possible to trace the path to mental breakdown by looking at how
typical psychiatric symptoms reflect increasing degrees of impairment to task-
orientation, and the corresponding over-development of self-orientation.

As noted earlier in the chapter, task orientation at first weakens by
becoming more constricted and rigid, leading to a narrow range of cue utilization and inferior performance. It is interesting to note that "rigid or repetitive
behavior" and "inability to function at capacity" are two of the principal
characteristics of neurotic distress.[14] Loss of flexibility, spontaneity, and
efficiency are generally seen in cases of neurotic-level distress like anxiety,
depression, or compulsiveness. Individuals burdened with neurotic distress
can interact with the external environment but in a faulty way that reflects
impaired task-orientation. They are quick to distort reality according to their
internal sets, so set in their ways that they tend to exasperate people around
them. They do not seem amenable to influence or reassurance; they do not
readily accept advice, and their behavior often remains unmodified by external input. Their processing of the environment becomes so selective and
defensive that self codes seem to recycle themselves and the threat. This tends
to sustain the mental distress, making it an autonomous and self-perpetuating
state.

After the rigidity stage, task-orientation can decline to a state of total collapse. This is seen at severe levels of mental distress such as psychotic and
paranoid experience. These disorders have what psychiatrists call "defective
reality testing." As one psychiatric text notes: "Almost without exception,

schizophrenic patients are characterized by social withdrawal, by the emotional distance one experiences in their presence, and by a lack of capacity for establishing rapport with others."[15] In other words, there is not just the reduced efficiency that is seen in neurotic distress, but an actual cessation of interaction with the external world. There is a loss of social interest and even social ability; the person becomes disabled in terms of carrying on external business. When the psychotic person is supposed to interact with the environment, he seems unprepared, as though the necessary codes were not in place to direct attention. Thus, schizophrenics are slow in processing tasks, they are easily overwhelmed by too much data, and they tend to experience the world in unstable and unreliable ways.[16] Such individuals are usually unable to work, marry, or commit themselves to long-term plans or goals. Their social presentation and interaction tend to be awkward and poorly modulated.

In schizophrenics, task-orientation is so impaired that investigators have considered the possibility of a physiological defect in the attentional mechanism. For example, McGhie and Chapman have suggested a defective filtering mechanism which results in decreased selectivity and inhibitory function, disposing the patient to be overwhelmed by input from the external environment.[17] Recent research, however, has not supported this hypothesis, suggesting instead a broader process wherein attention is reallocated from the external world to internal thoughts.[18] Korboot and Damiani found that when schizophrenics were presented with a processing task their attention tended to be characterized by "periods of de-focusing" and a "tuning-out process" which indicated that it was being withdrawn from the environment.[19] This view was supported by some research reported by Robert Cancro at a symposium on cognitive deficits in mental illness.[20] Using measures of eye movements, eye blinks, and eye fixations to determine how attention is distributed, this researcher tested schizophrenics and controls under a variety of task conditions, and concluded that the former took in significantly less information about the environment. Even during a rest condition the schizophrenics continued to be more involved in their thoughts than in the external world.

Such findings are enlightening, but it should be pointed out that they apparently apply to all forms of mental distress. In other words, the reallocation of attention from external to internal is an inherent characteristic of ego-involvement, which is the basis for all mental distress and psychic suffering. Throughout the entire spectrum of mental distress, as task-orientation declines, self-orientation expands, manifested primarily as over-attention to self.

D.H. Lawrence wrote that "men can suck the heady juice of exalted self-importance from the bitter weed of failure—failures are usually the most conceited of men." Indeed, people distressed by threat or failure inevitably over-attend to themselves. The neurotic is such an individual, and he typically has such traits as "egocentricity" and "hypersensitivity." "The neurotic is constantly self-preoccupied," wrote Coville. "He is more keenly aware of himself than is the normal person and as a consequence is habitually comparing himself and his situation with other persons and their situations. He is frequently demanding and exorbitantly selfish, though he is often driven to express these feelings indirectly."[21] Matters related to self take on a special significance. The subjective side becomes all important: personal biases become as facts, needs become insatiable, whims are experienced as demands. Concerns about self-esteem make the person touchy, and lower the threshold for further injury to self. The distressed person is quick to react with hurt feelings and beliefs that he is being mistreated.

The more one feels at odds with the surrounding world, the more intense will be the sense of self. In mental distress, self becomes an oppressive experience as the organism is cut-off from reality by an impaired task-orientation. Self becomes a burdensome feeling of being exposed, as seen in this description of depressive guilt.

> Everything I saw seemed to be a burden to me; the earth seemed accursed for my sake . . . everything around me seemed to be conspiring my ruin. My sins seemed to be laid open; so that I thought that every one I saw knew them, and sometimes I was almost ready to acknowledge many things, which I thought they knew: sometimes it seemed to me as if every one was pointing me out as the most guilty wretch upon earth.[22]

In the schizophrenic condition, the collapse of a task-reality orientation means that the self is the sole basis of attentional processing. Since the interaction with the environment is weak or nonexistent, self is thrown back on itself, and consists of inactive and immature associations — simple wish-fulfillments, irrational fears, personal memories, and infantile complexes. All of this is experienced with startling intensity. Unopposed by a reality orientation, this domain of self becomes magnified, authoritative, and convincing. It is the virtual supremacy of the self in psychological processing that makes possible delusions and hallucinations. When a person has reached this level of ego-involvement, he generally feels that he is always right, has no need to check things out in reality — and thus he has no insight into the nature of his condition. Although the patient has an intellectual conception of the external world, it is subservient to the grossly exaggerated sense of self. According to Anton Boison, who himself had recovered from a psychotic experience, the schizophrenic may feel that the fate of the world is in his hands.

> Very commonly his eyes are opened to the fact that he is more important than he had ever dreamed. It "comes to him," or "something tells him" that a great responsibility has been resting upon him, and that his failure has brought untold misery to those whom he loves. Perhaps the entire world has been hanging in the balance, its fate dependent upon him.[23]

Such intense egocentricity is the basis for delusions of grandeur, e.g. the belief that one is God or has interactions with God. This is not the brief and rapturous experience of the mystic which results from prolonged meditation and self-deprivation. Rather, it is a driven and highly egocentric belief, unchecked by reason. An example of such a delusion is found in the memoir of Judge Schreber, a famous mental patient whose case was used by Freud to analyze the dynamics of paranoia. Schreber thought he was the center of the universe.

> I can put this point briefly: *everything that happens is in reference to me.* Writing this sentence, I am fully aware that other people may be tempted to think that I am pathologically conceited; I know very well that this tendency to relate everything to oneself, to bring everything that happens into connection with one's own person, is a common phenomenon among mental patients. But in my case the very reverse obtains. Since God entered into nerve-contact with me exclusively, I became in a way for God the only human being, or simply the human being around whom everything turns, to whom everything that happens must be related and who therefore, from his own point of view, must also relate all things to himself.[24]

Earlier in this book it was noted that the normally functioning organism orders all input in terms of self-reference — that is, the more related to self, the more attention it is allocated. But in psychotic-level distress, the self programs are so dominant and over-controlling that self-reference is assigned and detected indiscriminately. This tendency, one of the principal characteristics of schizophrenic behavior, is what is meant by the phrase "ideas of reference." To a pathological degree, the schizophrenic refers everything to himself; for example, he may be convinced that bystanders or even people in a television show are talking about him, laughing at him, or accusing him of immoral practices.

The acutely distressed person can also have ideas of reference regarding objects and events, finding in trivial matters special hidden meanings with much personal significance. One of the earliest and most frequent signs of psychotic distress that is noticed by the patient's family is his tendency to attribute an exaggerated self-reference to the surrounding world. For example, in describing the onset of a psychotic attack that occurred in public, one patient wrote:

> There was a great deal of conversation, noise, and general confusion. But suddenly every noise, every word was aimed at *me.* Everything that was being said, was being said about me. Everything that was being done, was being done because of me. For a short time I did my best to cope with this unusual situation. I tried to answer every remark ... but in a short time it overwhelmed me. I knew something was radically wrong.[25]

Mental health scholars have long recognized the intense self-preoccupation that characterizes schizophrenic psychosis. "It is safe to say," wrote one author, "that much, if not all, of the schizophrenic's bizarre thinking results from the intrusion of subjective, emotionally toned needs into his thinking process, in such a manner that the patient is dominated by these subjective factors and finds it extremely difficult if not totally impossible to deal objectively with reality."[26] In an existential analysis of schizoid-schizophrenic experience, Laing devoted an entire chapter to the trait of self-consciousness, which he felt is strikingly evident in these patients.[27] These and all of the other traditional views, however, do not seem to go far enough in acknowledging the significance of self-preoccupation. It is not just one of the symptoms, but rather seems to be the central organizing process that is at work in all forms of mental distress. What one schizophrenic patient called "my bulging inner life and my timid outer behavior"[28] is the same dilemma evident in all degrees of distress, according to psychiatrist William Freeman.

> Consciousness of the self stands near the top in the hierarchy of attributes of the total personality.... It is one of those forces that underlies accomplishment and adjustment in any society. Without consciousness of the self the human race could not have risen as far as it has in the scale of living beings. On the other hand, we believe there can be too much of a good thing, and if consciousness of the self ... becomes in any way fixed or obsessive, the more useful activities of the personality may be correspondingly diminished. In extreme cases, a disabling psychosis or neurosis may result.
>
> The same mechanism of pathologic egocentricity is seen with slightly different signature in many cases of involutional depression, where feelings of guilt and nihilistic delusions occupy the center of the stage and where the patient is unable to escape from a torturing feeling of inadequacy and failure. In these cases also, the image of the self looms so large in the patient's consciousness that nothing on the outside is able to overcome the preoccupation. Preoccupation of the self with the self is outstanding also in cases of hypochondriasis and many anxiety states....[29]

The exaggerated self-orientation seen in psychotic distress is often interpreted as a return to infantile narcissism, or as an acting out of unconscious impulses, or as the expression of normally private subjective experience. In other words, in the traditional views, psychotic self-preoccupation is seen as a breaking-out of some negative or undesirable part of the personality. Actually, it is the corruption of the best and highest part of personality — which may be why schizophrenia, and to some extent the other distress-filled disorders, are so unyielding and enigmatic. As one ex-patient summed it up: "Madness, like melancholy, *is* self."[30]

Ironically, most of our psychotherapies aim at increasing self-awareness, self-analysis, and introspectiveness. But apparently, there is already enough self-regard built into the organism; it does not have to be stimulated. It is a

master code, and it flares up at the slightest threat, with injurious consequences to reality functioning. Ego-involvement must be an intrinsic part of
the survival reflex: When self is threatened, the organism automatically forces
attention onto the self. Obviously, mild and brief reactions of ego-involvement
are adaptive; they alert us to the seriousness of a situation and speed up code-
controlled processing. But under intense and prolonged conditions, this
defensive process seems to over-correct the problem, leading to extremely subjective and impaired attentional processing. This might be comparable to the
stress diseases seen in the physiological realm; healing, when subject to continual activation by prolonged stress, can lead to tissue damage and
psychosomatic illness. In somewhat similar fashion, when self is continually
threatened, the organism instinctively keeps focusing attention on self, and
ends up allocating too much control to the internal determinants.

Ego-involvement seems to represent a flaw in the system; at higher levels
of functioning, internal processing loses its effectiveness. It lets us down when
we need it the most. If ego-involvement did not occur, people might come
closer to sailing through life's troubles — the greater the test, the more effective
the processing, the greater the likelihood of passing the test. Unfortunately,
this is not the case.

Chapter 14

Low-Processing Psychological States

Sleep that sometimes shuts up sorrow's eye,
Steal me awhile from mine own company.
— *William Shakespeare*

Like every other system, the human organism has two vital functions—
one pertaining to foreign relations, the other to domestic relations. The
psychological states are designed to take care of these functions. The high-
processing states are concerned with foreign relations, i.e., interactions with
the environment and the processing of tasks, tests, and threats. The low-
processing states—sleep and absorbed diversion—are concerned with
domestic relations such as rest, relaxation, and the renewal of aliveness.

Sleep and absorbed diversion may seem like passive conditions where
nothing happens, at least nothing important. It is undoubtedly for this reason
that these states have been generally neglected by the scientific establishment.
In the case of sleep, that neglect came to an end in the 1950s when the first
formal investigations were undertaken. Since then, our knowledge of the sleep
state has steadily increased and has often been enriched with unexpected insights. Obviously, one of the most important lessons learned is that sleep is
a highly complex state, anything but a passive, nihilistic condition.

Neither is absorption such a negatory state, defined only by the absence
of workaday qualities. As we have tried to show throughout this book, absorbed diversion is a unique psychological orientation, induced under certain
conditions, and containing its own qualities of experience.

As low-processing states, sleep and absorption can develop only through
mental relaxation; both require a suspension of evaluative business and a
withdrawal from everyday reality. There is indeed a kinship between these
two psychological states. In most cultural patterns, diversion occurs in the
evening, almost as a prelude to sleep; the mental lulling that characterizes absorbed diversion puts us on the path to sleep. Hypnotic trance, the epitome
of absorption, mimics sleep so closely that for a long time it was thought to
be a variation of sleep. Other types of absorption seem to be associated with
sleep. For example, inspirations often occur around sleep time. Meditation

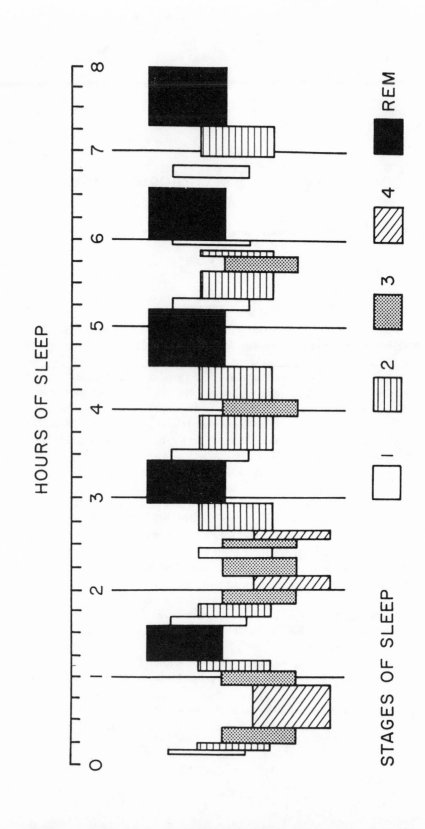

HOURS OF SLEEP

STAGES OF SLEEP

REM   4   3   2   1

is a near-sleep condition. And most amazing of all, sleep has its own kind of story entertainment in the form of dreams.

Sleep and Dreams

> The pleasure of the true dreamer does not lie in the substance of the dream, but in this: that there things happen without any interference from his side, and altogether outside his control. — *Isak Dinesen*

Clinical psychologists often use a procedure called "The Sentence Completion Test" in order to learn about the feelings and attitudes of their patients.[1] In administering this test, the psychologist starts a sentence with a particular phrase, but then lets the patient complete it in whatever way he likes. One of the sentences begins "I am best when. . . ." It is not unusual for highly distressed patients to complete this by saying: "I am best when I'm asleep."

What a revealing response — to be at one's best when unconscious! Such a response speaks volumes about the utter misery of mental distress, but also about the blessed relief that sleep can provide. Sleep is the most radical diversion, the end point of mental relaxation. Next to death, it is the most complete way of escaping the business of living. While other diversions suspend self-consciousness, sleep does away with consciousness itself. Master code processing is terminated, and therefore sense of self, reality, and thinking vanish in an absolute way. Sleep is our daily portion of diversion that is guaranteed by the organism. We cannot live without this diversion; physiological codes at first nudge us toward sleep, and eventually force us into it.

Although sleep is a negation of consciousness, it does not entail a complete shutdown of the psychological apparatus. Brain activity and general arousal do not stop but seem to go into a holding pattern consisting of sequential cycles, as show in Figure 2.[2] The first part of each cycle consists of a slowdown of the EEG and a lowering of arousal level. These drop steadily through different stages till the bottom of the cycle is reached, which is considered the deepest level of sleep. Following this, EEG and arousal steadily increase, reaching a peak that constitutes the top of the cycle. At this point, the sleeper's physiological status is close to that of the waking state, and it is here that dreaming occurs. After about fifteen or twenty minutes of dreaming, the cycle is repeated, with another descent to lower levels of sleep, and then an ascent to the dream stage. In the typical eight-hour sleep period, this cycle is repeated about five times.[3]

The discovery of these sleep cycles represented a historic breakthrough

Figure 2. The cycles of sleep formed by different stages of arousal. (Adapted from Clark et al., "The Mystery of Sleep," p. 50.)

in modern sleep research. The simplest explanation of this cycling process is that it seems to provide a fixed pattern of variability to brain activity and the arousal system. It makes possible a continuous change of pace, an exercising of different levels of functioning. It is a way of "idling" the brain to keep it going at a minimal level while the overall organism is resting. This programmed variability keeps the overall system functional but at a low level. Thus the variability of organismic functioning that is so characteristic of awake existence is retained in the otherwise nonvariable state of sleep.

Dreaming is but an aspect of this cycling process, and it can best be understood as a further mechanism for producing variable functioning. The variability so evident in the cycling of EEG and arousal is carried on into consciousness by means of the dream, which is the epitome of variability, according to Havelock Ellis.

> Perhaps the most elementary fact about dream vision is the perpetual and unceasing change which it is undergoing at every moment. . . . The commonest kind of dream is mainly a picture, but it is always a living and moving picture, however inanimate the objects which appear in vision before would be in real life. No man ever gazed at a dream picture which was at rest to his sleeping eyes. . . . Sleeping consciousness is a stream in which we never bathe twice, for it is renewed every second.[4]

Dreaming is a burst of aroused and variable conscious experience. It is in fact a diversion from the unconsciousness of sleep. In the past, dreams were thought to bubble up randomly from the void of unconsciousness, and so they were seen, not as an inherent part of sleep, but in terms of extraneous factors. Dreams were believed to be messages from the gods, communications from the unconscious mind, or unfinished business from everyday life. Such views, however, are invalidated by the findings of modern research, which show that everybody dreams, and does so regularly throughout the night. The finding that dreaming is correlated with observable rapid eye movements (REM) allowed investigators to plot dream frequency in an objective way.[5] It has been well established that dreaming occurs about every ninety mintues as an inherent part of the sleep cycle.[6] Therefore, dreaming is not an isolated occurrence that has mysterious significance. Rather, it seems to be a periodic "jolt" of consciousness, helping to keep the sleeping organism functional at a minimal level.

During sleep the organism achieves its periodic excursion into consciousness (dreaming) by stimulating itself with attention-getting images, high in arousal and fascination value. Variability, novelty, and suspense are some typical attention-getters, and they are very much in evidence in dream images.[7] Even though these images are at times derived from everyday life, they are strung together in a loose way that makes them interesting and even strange. Dream images are not connected in terms of logic or reality (master code processing) but in terms of other associational links that make the overall result seem unusual, implausible, imaginative, even witty and creative. Often, dreams are downright fantastic, as are some of the fairly common ones of flying; of being lost, pursued, or naked in public; or of interacting with people from childhood or those who are dead.

Such images are likely to be associated with relatively high arousal, which is at its peak during the dream phase of the cycle. As Luce and Segal reported in their book on sleep, dreaming is "a kind of built-in shock therapy," and the dreaming brain is "hot," i.e., aroused.[8]

Dream arousal usually equals or exceeds that of waking life.[9] Why then, does this dream jolt not wake us up?

The answer is that the dream is a kind of absorbed trance; it is, in fact, an extreme trance state. We are *awake* during the dream; we are conscious, experiencing, and paying attention.[10] But this consciousness exists in a psychological vacuum because it is absolutely cut off from everyday self and reality. Not only are the master codes and evaluative processing negated, but also sensory thresholds are raised by sleep, further sealing us off from environmental influences and distractions. Because sleep is physiologically determined, the shutdown of these systems is much more complete than in other kinds of absorbed experience. Thus, the dream always exists as an island of experience, completely cut off from everyday existence; it is no wonder that there is always a feeling of being in a different reality. Likewise, as in all absorbed experience where self and will are negated, one feels carried along by the dream events, with no sense of choice. The dream unfolds as a series of related images which are experienced as events happening to us. Havelock Ellis long ago noted that dream attention is involuntary, spontaneous, and automatic — in other words, very different from everyday consciousness.[11] If perchance we should awaken enough to try to exert our will (forebrain) to change the dream, then it stops.

When we attempt to recall a dream after sleep is over, usually our memory of it is weak and fragmentary. This is due to the fact that the dream is sealed off so completely; the cognitive vacuum in which it exists precludes labeling and evaluation. However, the dream is certainly not weakly experienced. Electrophysiological data indicate that the dream is an intense attentional state, and that the entire organism is wrapped up in it,[12] as in other absorbed trance states. The EEG waves in particular indicate aroused and focused attention and a censoring of distraction. Luce and Segal wrote that "the dreaming mind seems to be almost undistractible, exhibiting a force of concentration that most people could not sustain half so long when awake."[13] The tenacity of this attentional state is dramatized by the fact that sleepers are most resistant to waking up when they are dreaming. They can be more easily awakened in any other stage of the sleep cycle. Even though their arousal and EEG levels are close to the waking state, dreamers seem immune to distraction. Apparently this is so because attention is totally captured by the dream images and distraction is resisted. It has been hypothesized that the rapid eye movements, which can be quite vigorous, reflect the extent to which the dreamer is involved in the visual experience, or they may actually be a mechanism for maintaining focus and resisting distraction.[14]

There is yet another reason why dreaming is best conceptualized as absorbed trance. As is the case with absorption in general, dreaming consists of relaxed arousal — that paradoxical combination of high arousal and mental and physical relaxation. Studies show that the aroused dream condition is accompanied by a surprising degree of muscular relaxation. Usually arousal is associated with increased bodily tension, but according to Luce and Segal, a "silken" relaxation is one of the chief characteristics of the body of the dreamer. There is a general loss of body tone, spinal reflexes may be absent, and neck and head muscles are likely to be flaccid.[15] Likewise, the body seems more immobilized during dreaming than in any other stage of sleep. Sleep-walking, tossing, snoring, sleep-mumbling, and bed-wetting seldom occur during the dream stage when the sleeper is totally relaxed. This physical immobilization that characterizes dreaming has impressed various investigators as being similar to that of the spectator who is absorbed in entertainment.

> Dreaming often began just after a series of body movements ceased. The sleeper usually remained almost motionless, showing only the telltale rapid eye-movements, and stirred again when the eye-movements stopped.... the metaphor that captured the essence of this situation ... compared the dreamer to a spectator at a theater: fidgeting in his seat before the curtain goes up; then sitting quietly, often "spellbound" by the action, following the motions of the actors with his eyes; then stirring again when the curtain falls.[16]

As we have seen in earlier chapters, the most common source of absorbed experience is story entertainment. How interesting that the dream is essentially a story format. There is usually a cast of characters, and there are action sequences that develop according to an internal logic. Like a story, the dream edits and restructures reality; it is not just a representation of everyday life. It is generally accepted that a dream is a symbolic transformation of reality, seeming to fuse, condense, and displace various reality elements in a way that produces a novel product.[17] Not surprisingly, dreams have often inspired the creation of stories. A great many writers have admitted to getting their ideas from dreams.[18]

There are some differences between awake story entertainment and dreaming, but they do not seem significant. For example, the central character in the dream is usually oneself; this is not so in story entertainment. The dream self, however, tends to be a passive observer and is more or less controlled by the events. It is not self as executive function, exercising choice and making decisions. Dream reports obtained in a sleep lab from subjects who had been awakened at the end of the REM period showed that the most common mental orientation was one of "reflective contemplation," involving "silent observation and detached musing about dream events external to the self."[19]

Another difference between awake story entertainment and dreaming is that one is voluntary and the other is not. If a conventional story does not absorb us, we can walk away from it. Dreaming, on the other hand, is involuntary story experience. We are locked into it by the sleep codes of the organism. The dream images that are served up, although arousing, may not always be entertaining, but we are forced to stay involved in them.

Overall, however, there seem to be good reasons to conclude that dream experience is absorbed experience. All of the basic elements are there: fascinating stimuli (storylike dream images), resistance to distraction, and relaxed arousal. In scientific circles, dreaming is sometimes referred to as "paradoxical sleep." This term is used because on the one hand the dreamer seems to be deeply asleep (extremely relaxed and hard to awaken), but on the other hand he seems to be awake (high arousal and having conscious experience). But the paradox dissolves when sleep is viewed in the context of absorption and relaxed arousal.

Sleep not only offers diversion, it even has traces of workaday consciousness. In a reversed way, sleep functioning seems to mimic awake functioning. Most people are probably not aware of the fact that we continue to think during sleep; apparently some type of "mentation" continues to go on at a reduced level during the non–REM phases. The sleeper is not aware of this mentation, nor is it recalled after awakening. This phenomenon was discovered by researchers who simply woke up sleeping subjects and asked them what was going through their minds at that moment.[20] Generally the subjects reported they were thinking about something that had happened during the previous day. Thus sleep mentation seems to be fragmentary residual cognitive activity; it is very different from dreams, which are pictorial and experienced. Sleep mentation occurred only when REMs were absent, thus it has been referred to as "pre–REM" or "NREM" (non–REM) mentation.

As in everyday life, then, sleep gives evidence of the two kinds of attention — what we have called *everyday evaluative processing* and *absorption*. During awake existence, these two kinds of attention form the basis of work and play. During sleep they form the basis of pre–REM mentation and dreaming. Thus, from wakefulness to sleep there is a reversal of function. Evaluative thinking dominates awake existence, but in the state of sleep absorption (dreaming) stands out as the dominant experience.

People are usually intrigued by the phenomenon of dreaming, and have tried to understand it by analyzing its content. Because sleep was thought to be a psychological void, it followed that dreams must be related to everyday life, containing special messages, answers, or solutions to everyday problems.

Freud's system of dream interpretation was simply a continuation of this model, with a psychiatric slant. According to Freud, the dream is a neurotic manifestation. It is a disguised discharge of repressed wishes and pent-up tensions that occurs in order to protect sleep. Thus the occurrence of the dream is presumably dependent on certain personality dynamics which can be ascertained by interpreting the psychoanalytic symbols in the dream content.[21]

Without lab technology, of course, all that we can know about dreaming is its content, but this may be of only trivial significance. Although dream interpretation has been going on since prehistory, the enterprise has yet to yield reliable techniques or important knowledge. Modern sleep research tells us it is the *process* of dreaming that is important — not the content of the dream. After all, dreaming occurs regularly according to a fixed physiological cycle, and this process occurs in adults, children, infants, and animals. Thus dreaming cannot be a neurotic manifestation, nor is it likely to be dependent on the person's psychiatric status or personality functioning.

It is likely that the organism manufactures a dream from whatever is available at the beginning of the REM phase, so that content selection is probably more fortuitous than determined. Since the master codes are dormant, dream content takes shape from a variety of sources. "The elements of dream life," wrote Havelock Ellis, "are drawn from a wider field than is normally accessible to waking consciousness."[22] The day residues and memories carried into sleep by means of pre–REM mentation must be an important determinant of dream content. This explains why dream content is culture-bound; for example, today people dream of automobiles, not horses and buggies. In a similar manner, it seems that simple mental sets and subcodes can be maintained throughout sleep. For example, it is known that dream content and recall can be affected by post-hypnotic suggestion, going into psychoanalysis, or undertaking the study of dreams — all of which create expectations about dreams.[23] Another source of dream content would be unconscious associations and old memories which are more available in the absence of the master codes. Sensory input that intrudes into sleep is also a factor, e.g. noises, postural pressure, gastric upsets, etc.

Stimuli from all of these sources seem to have a role in dream formation. There is probably a free interplay among these associations, and they are combined on some nonrational basis — much like the bisociation process discussed in the chapter on inspiration. Although the input into dreams may contain bits and pieces that are relevant to everyday life, such content is secondary to the sleep cycle, which is impersonal and autonomous. As Luce and Segal noted, researchers are now moving toward the view that "dreams are manufactured by certain physiological cycles that are independent of the individual's history."[24]

According to the view presented here, therefore, dreaming is more biology than psychology, more process than content, and it can be best understood as an indigenous aspect of sleep activity rather than a reflection of waking life. At the allotted time in the sleep cycle, the organism is programmed to feed itself dream images, much as it would feed itself insulin after the ingestion of sugar. Physiologically, one dream is like another; its function is served by mobilizing arousal and consciousness. Psychologically, the dream content serves as a focus for consciousness and the intense attentional state that develops. In this manner, the sleep cycle provides periodic variability to brain processes that are nearly dormant during sleep. Dreams, therefore, probably have little to do in resolving the unfinished business of everyday life, but rather function to enhance experiencing — which is always the purpose of absorption in awake existence.

Sleep and dreams show that diversion and absorbed experience are vital functions of the organism. Because sleep and dreaming are instinctive to the organism and independent of culture, they can be considered prototypical diversions. Just on this basis, even if we knew nothing at all about awake existence, we might suspect that diversion and absorbed experience would have a role elsewhere in the functioning of the organism. And of course they do — in the domain of recreation. No other theory of play can relate recreational experience to the vital physiological functions of sleep and dreaming. It seems a theoretical advance to be able to connect these two major areas of human existence — dreaming and play — since both exist outside the bounds of workaday life.

To know why the organism dreams when sleeping is to know why the person plays when awake. Dreaming provides a jolt of consciousness to the sleeping brain. Much the same is true of play; it provides a jolt of experiencing to the routinized brain.

A Declaration of Independence for the State of Absorption

Like sleep, absorption occurs outside the bounds of selfhood. It is made possible by broader functions of the organism, such as the ability to suspend the master codes, to experience figure-ground reversal, and to be emotionally aroused and mentally relaxed at the same time. Unlike sleep, however, absorption allows us to be completely awake, even though self and reality are tuned out. And, ironically, we feel enlivened, even though we are relaxed and inactive.

In scientific circles, there is little recognition that such a unique and intriguing state is possible. But such recognition is necessary if we are to understand some of the paradoxes of play. In addition to that of relaxed arousal, the most obvious paradox is the fact that fictional and unrealistic stimuli can produce intensely real experience, as we have seen throughout this book. There is no way to explain this except with the concept of absorption, which stipulates that some kind of enlivening liberation takes place in the organism when the reality orientation and other master codes are suspended.

The current theories of play "explain away" our enjoyable diversions by attempting to show that their function is merely to satisfy self-related needs; play is a continuation of everyday business under more leisurely conditions. [25] Thus we hear that people read novels and watch movies primarily to release pent-up emotions or to learn about themselves. For example, Simon Lesser asserted that "narrative art deals with and attempts to resolve our emotional conflicts." [26] Jay Haley wrote that people go to the movies in order to learn how to behave; modern entertainment media "are an up-to-the-minute guide which people use to find their way in an increasingly complicated environment." [27] From this view it is a short step to the belief that stories are worthless unless they have a lesson. Everything must serve some goal of the self. Dreams must be messages about everyday problems; meditation is just a tension reduction technique; peak experiences must reflect a high degree of self-actualization; art and music must make a statement about everyday life; sexual fantasy is a perversion because it violates the taboos of everyday public life.

All of this represents a kind of egocentrism that often characterizes human understanding. Egocentrism is the belief that self is the center, and that all psychological roads must lead back to the self. Developmentally, the conceptions that humans have about things always start out as highly egocentric, and only gradually become more objective. The young child is initially aware only of himself, and sees himself as all-powerful, the center of the universe; it takes a long socialization process to divest him of this self-centeredness. Likewise, the first conceptions of the human race were highly distorted by self-reference. It has taken ages of scientific work to correct such egocentricities as the belief that the earth is the center of the universe, that there was a special creation in the Garden of Eden, and that people have free will and complete self-determination.

But there continue to be vestiges of this kind of egocentrism in the very notions of self currently held in psychology and the humanities. Self is viewed as a fixed, beneficent, and omnipresent trait in psychological functioning. It is seen as a constant and imperious function whose needs are served not only by workaday existence but even by play experiences. But the belief that play is a form of self-expression may be comparable to the belief that the earth is the center of the universe.

An example of egocentric thinking is found in the often-made claim that the primary purpose of our entertainments is to provide a catharsis for pent-up everyday emotions. However, one study that had angry subjects watch a movie seemed to discredit this theory. [28] The subjects were first made angry by being administered electric shocks, and then they watched fight scenes from a boxing film (*Champion*). Measures taken after the movie gave no indication that it had drained off the anger; there was no support for the hypothesis that the movie provided an outlet for hostile feelings. More significantly, what did happen relates to the importance of absorbed attention in entertainment. According to the ratings, the more angry the subjects were, the less they were able to get involved in the movie. As we have seen, intense emotions make us self-preoccupied — which makes it difficult to forget oneself, get absorbed, and experience *relaxed* arousal.

In his book *Homo Ludens,* Johan Huizinga made a general indictment of the various egocentric views that attempt to explain away the absorbed enjoyments of play by reducing them to merely the satisfaction of self-referent needs.

> The numerous attempts to define the ... functions of play show a striking variation. By some the origin and fundamentals of play have been described as a discharge of superabundant vital energy, by others as the satisfaction of some "imitative instinct." ... According to one theory play constitutes a training of the young creature for the serious work that life will demand later on. According to another it serves as an exercise in restraint needful to the individual. Some find the principle of play in an innate urge to exercise a certain faculty, or in the desire to dominate or compete. Yet others regard it as an "abreaction" — an outlet for harmful impulses, as the necessary restorer of energy wasted by one-sided activity, as "wish-fulfillment," as a fiction designed to keep up the feeling of personal value, etc.
>
> All of these hypotheses have one thing in common: they all start from the assumption that play must serve something which is *not* play, that it must have some kind of biological purpose. They all enquire into the why and the wherefore of play. The various answers they give tend rather to overlap than to exclude one another. It would be perfectly possible to accept nearly all the explanations without getting into any real confusion of thought — and without coming much nearer to a real understanding of the play-concept. They are all only partial solutions of the problem. If any of them were really decisive it ought either to exclude all the others or comprehend them in a higher unity. Most of them only deal incidentally with the question of what play is *in itself* and what it means for the player. They attack play direct with the quantitative methods of experimental science without first paying attention to its profoundly aesthetic quality. As a rule they leave the primary quality of play as such, virtually untouched. To each and every one of the above "explanations" it might well be objected: "So far so good, but what actually is the *fun* of playing? Why does the baby crow with pleasure? Why does the gambler lose himself in his passion? Why is a huge crowd roused to frenzy by a football match?" This intensity of, and absorption in, play finds no explanation in biological analysis. Yet in this intensity, this absorption, this power of maddening, lies the very essence, the primordial quality of play.[29]

According to the view presented in this book, play is a contrasting and emergent condition that enhances the organism's sense of aliveness, rather than just serving the self's need for expression and satisfaction. Although the content of play is usually derived from everyday life, this is of secondary importance. What is of primary importance is the sense of diversion and contrast that is achieved, and the enlivening effect this has on the organism. All in all, it must be recognized that self is not a fixed trait in awake existence: it is a variable function that is "down" when play experience occurs. Self has an optimal level in everyday living, but depending on the conditions it can vary from this level. It can be intensified to a malignant degree, as it is in mental distress. And it can also be suspended to a beneficial degree, making possible play and mental relaxation.

The conception of psychological states presented in the previous chapter (Figure 1) is a testament to organismic flexibility. The organism has the capability of switching into different modalities, each a fairly separate and discrete condition. In particular, there is a dissociation between the high-processing and low-processing states. Sleep is certainly separate from the everyday business of living, and so is absorption. Failure to understand this principle of separate states has confounded scholars and social critics, who are often fearful that transient absorbed experiences will corrupt everyday personality. This may be true to some extent in children; since they are not completely socialized, they might be affected, for example, by the violence on television. But with adults, psychological *states* do not lead to psychological *traits*.

There are many examples of the dissociation between absorption and everyday life; these are two different kinds of consciousness, and the one does not determine the other. For example, story experience and everyday life do not normally interact. To lose ourselves in the violence and horror of a movie does not make us violent and fearful in everyday life. Similarly, people can and do enjoy pornographic fantasy in the midst of their sexual relations, and still lead decent and competent lives.

Many kinds of absorbed diversions approach the sublime, but they do not make everyday personality sublime. Creative inspiration is a lofty kind of absorbed experience, but it has no influence on everyday conduct; it is well known that inspiration often occurs to creative people who are vain, selfish, and immature in their day-to-day lives. Maslow originally thought that peak experiences reflected superior psychological adjustment, but after extensive research he concluded that these peak states were not really related to adjustment.[30] In a similar vein, no amount of intoxicating highs or psychedelic flights can improve our workaday lives or cure our personal ills. Finally, if there were no dissociation between absorption and everyday life, how could one explain the disturbing observation that ruthless, even psychopathic personalities—such as the elite Nazis, for example—are apparently capable of tender and rapturous experiences while enjoying aesthetic diversions like art or classical music? We can only conclude that everyday personality is suspended when we lose ourselves in the purity and nobility of classical music, and so the music itself does not make us pure and noble in everyday life.

The business of living and absorbed diversion are two separate domains, and we cannot expect them to agree or be consistent with each other. The one cannot be judged or evaluated by the criteria of the other. Except for addiction, which is a special case and relatively infrequent, absorption is but a fragile spell which cannot overrun everyday personality. Once society can accept this, it is likely to be more tolerant of nonself experience, rather than attempting to tone it down, subvert it, demean it, or replace it with more cognitive activity. Absorption presents no threat to everyday personality; the dissolution of self that occurs in absorption is brief, and the reversals are reversible in turn.

Absorption is the weakest psychological state; it has the briefest duration and is easily disrupted. Nevertheless, the conditions favorable for its development have come together in modern society: free time, affluence, technologies to create and distribute fascination objects, and the need to enliven existence that is increasingly regulated and monotonous. In fact, as we come to understand the full potential of hypnotic absorption, this psychological state may have broad historic implications, much as the inventions of writing and the printing press did for civilizations. What these verbal capabilities did for workaday life, the absorbed capability may do for play in the age of leisure.

Today, scholars claim that Western civilization is being transformed by a new "wave" or "mutation," characterized by affluence among the masses and the upsetting of the traditional work-and-play relationship.[31] Affluence favors play, leisure, and diversion — as it has for the wealthy and the privileged throughout history. Affluence allows people to move beyond work and business, and develop the impractical but enjoyable aspect of the organism — experiencing for its own sake. This, of course, is the specialty of absorption.

Chapter Notes

Introduction: Psychological Diversion as Adult Play

1. Mihaly Csikszentmihalyi and Eugene Rochberg-Halton, *The Meaning of Things* (Cambridge: Cambridge University Press, 1981), pp. 147–8.

Chapter 1. Absorbed Attention

1. William James, *The Principles of Psychology,* Vol. 1 (New York: Holt, 1890), p. 402.

2. Erik H. Erikson, *Childhood and Society,* 2nd ed. (New York: Norton, 1963), p. 222.

3. Ernest R. Hilgard, *The Experience of Hypnosis* (New York: Harcourt, Brace & World, 1968), pp. 10–14 and 24–6.

4. Gardner Murphy, *Personality* (New York: Harper, 1947), pp. 919–20 and 921–2.

5. John F. Hall, "Motivation and Affectivity," in *Contemporary Approaches to Psychology,* ed. Harry Helson and William Bevan (Princeton, N.J.: Van Nostrand, 1967), p. 240; Bernard Berelson and Gary A. Steiner, *Human Behavior: An Inventory of Scientific Findings* (New York: Harcourt, Brace & World, 1964), p. 89.

6. Charles S. Myers, "Individual Differences in Listening to Music," in *The Effects of Music,* ed. Max Schoen (New York: Harcourt, Brace, 1927), pp. 36–7.

7. David Riesman, *Individualism Reconsidered, and Other Essays* (Glencoe, Ill.: Free Press, 1954), p. 206; Roger Caillois, *Man, Play, and Games* (New York: Free Press, 1961), p. 167.

8. John P. Robinson, "Daily Participation in Sport Across Twelve Countries," in *The Cross-Cultural Analysis of Sport and Games,* ed. Gunther Luschen (Champaign, Ill.: Stipes, 1970), pp. 156–73.

9. U.S. Bureau of Outdoor Recreation, *Outdoor Recreation, A Legacy for America* (Washington, D.C.: U.S. Government Printing Office, 1973), p. 23.

10. Robert Heilbroner, "Automation in the Perspective of Long-Term Technological Change," in *Seminar on Manpower Policy and Program* (Washington, D.C.: U.S. Dept. of Labor, 1966), pp. 4–15.

11. Richard D. Altick, *The English Common Reader: A Social History of the Mass Reading Public 1800–1900* (Chicago: University of Chicago Press, 1975), pp. 86–7.

12. Sebastian De Grazia, *Of Time, Work, and Leisure* (New York: Twentieth Century Fund, 1962), p. 441.

13. C. Wright Mills, *White Collar: The American Middle Classes* (New York: Oxford University Press, 1953), p. 236.

14. J.D. Hodgson, "Leisure and the American Worker," in *Leisure Today: Selected Readings*, ed. Larry L. Neal (Washington, D.C.: American Alliance for Health, Physical Education and Recreation Publications, 1975), pp. 12–3.

15. Alvin Toffler, *Future Shock* (New York: Random House/Bantam, 1970), Chap. 10.

16. Thomas M. Kando, *Leisure and Popular Culture in Transition* (St. Louis: Mosby, 1975), p. 216.

17. Michael Ellis, *Why People Play* (Englewood Cliffs, N.J.: Prentice-Hall, 1973), Chaps. 3, 4, and 5.

Chapter 2. Breaking Out of Everyday Consciousness

1. Gene Bammel and Lei Lane Burrus-Bammel, *Leisure and Human Behavior* (Dubuque, Iowa: Brown, 1982), p. 13.

2. William Stephenson, *The Play Theory of Mass Communication* (Chicago: University of Chicago Press, 1967), p. 150.

3. Johan Huizinga, *Homo Ludens* (Boston: Beacon, 1964), p. 13.

4. Jay S. Shivers, *Principles and Practices of Recreational Service* (New York: Macmillan, 1967), p. 86.

5. *The American Heritage Dictionary of the English Language,* 1981, s.v. "fascinate."

6. Loyd W. Rowland, "The Somatic Effects of Stimuli Graded in Respect to their Exciting Character," *Journal of Experimental Psychology* **19** (1936): 547–60.

7. Ronald E. Shor, "The Three-Factor Theory of Hypnosis as Applied to the Book-Reading Fantasy and to the Concept of Suggestion," *International Journal of Clinical and Experimental Hypnosis* **18** (1970): 97.

8. George Matheson and John F. Grehan, "A Rapid Induction Technique," *Journal of Clinical Hypnosis* **21** (1979): 298.

9. Ronald E. Shor, Martin T. Orne, and Donald N. O'Connell, "Validation and Cross-Validation of a Scale of Self-Reported Personal Experiences Which Predicts Hypnotizability," *Journal of Psychology* **53** (1962): 58.

10. Arvid As, John W. O'Hara, and Michael Munger, "The Measurement of Subjective Experiences Presumably Related to Hypnotic Susceptibility," *Scandanavian Journal of Psychology* **3** (1962): 63–4.

11. Evelyn Lee-Teng, "Trance-Susceptibility, Induction-Susceptibility, and Acquiescence as Factors in Hypnotic Performance," *Journal of Abnormal Psychology* **70** (1965): 384.

12. Nicholas P. Spanos and John D. McPeake, "Involvement in Everyday Imaginative Activities, Attitudes Toward Hypnosis, and Hypnotic Suggestibility," *Journal of Personality and Social Psychology* **31** (1975): 594.

13. Theodore X. Barber, Nicholas P. Spanos, and John F. Chaves, *Hypnosis, Imagination, and Human Potentialities* (New York: Pergamon, 1974), p. 11.

14. *Ibid.,* p. 43.

15. Lynn S. Johnson, "Self-Hypnosis: Behavioral and Phenomenological Comparisons with Heterohypnosis," *International Journal of Clinical and Experimental Hypnosis* **27** (1979): 240–64.

16. David Van Nuys, "Meditation, Attention, and Hypnotic Susceptibility: A Correlational Study," *International Journal of Clinical and Experimental Hypnosis* **21** (1973): 59–69; Susanne M. Barmark and Samuel C. Gaunitz, "Transcendental Meditation and Heterohypnosis as Altered States of Consciousness," *International Journal of Clinical and Experimental Hypnosis* **27** (1979): 227–39.

17. Nicholas P. Spanos, Stephen M. Rivers, and Jack Gottlieb, "Hypnotic Responsivity, Meditation, and Laterality of Eye Movements," *Journal of Abnormal Psychology* **87** (1978): 566–9.

18. Auke Tellegen and Gilbert Atkinson, "Openness to Absorbing and Self-Altering Experiences ('Absorption'), A Trait Related to Hypnotic Susceptibility," *Journal of Abnormal Psychology* **83** (1974): 268.

19. Theodore X. Barber, *LSD, Marijuana, Yoga, and Hypnosis* (Chicago: Aldine, 1970).

20. Spencer E. Sherman, "Very Deep Hypnosis: An Experiential and Electroencephalographic Investigation" (Ph.D. diss., Stanford University, 1971).

21. James H. Leuba, *The Psychology of Religious Mysticism* (1925; reprint, London: Routledge & Kegan Paul, 1972), p. 170.

22. José Ortega y Gasset, *On Love* (New York: New American Library, 1957).

23. Sigmund Freud, "Psychology and the Analysis of the Ego," in *The Complete Psychological Works of Sigmund Freud,* Vol. 18, ed. James Strachey (1921; reprint, London: Hogarth, 1955), p. 114.

24. Josephine R. Hilgard, *Personality and Hypnosis* (Chicago: University of Chicago Press, 1970), pp. 4–5.

25. Joseph Kamiya, "Operant Control of the EEG Alpha Rhythm and Some of Its Reported Effects on Consciousness," in *Altered States of Consciousness: A Book of Readings,* ed. Charles T. Tart (New York: Wiley, 1969), p. 514.

26. Rowland, "Somatic Effects of Stimuli," p. 548.

27. William James, *The Principles of Psychology,* Vol. 2 (1890; reprint, Cambridge, Mass.: Harvard University Press, 1981), p. 1132.

28. George A. Miller, Eugene Galanter, and Karl Pribram, *Plans and the Structure of Behavior* (New York: Holt, 1960), pp. 105–6.

29. Hannes Lindemann, *Relieve Tension the Autogenic Way* (New York: Peter H. Wyden, 1973); Edmund Jacobson, *Progressive Relaxation* (University of Chicago Press, 1929).

30. Donald B. Lindsley, "Physiological Psychology," *Annual Review of Psychology* **7** (1956): 323–48; Harry Helson, "Perception," in *Contemporary Approaches to Psychology,* ed. Harry Helson and William Bevan (Princeton, N.J.: Van Nostrand, 1967), pp. 311–43.

31. J.Z. Young, *Programs of the Brain* (Oxford: Oxford University Press, 1978), pp. 7–8.

32. Arthur Koestler, *The Act of Creation* (New York: Macmillan, 1964), Pt. 1.

33. Young, *Programs of the Brain,* p. 44.

34. Muriel D. Lezak, *Neuropsychological Assessment* (New York: Oxford University Press, 1983), p. 38.

35. Charles Darwin, *The Expression of the Emotions in Man and Animals* (1872; reprint, Chicago: University of Chicago Press/Phoenix books, 1965), pp. 226–7.

Chapter 3. The Enjoyments of Being Absorbed

1. Bernard Berelson and Gary A. Steiner, *Human Behavior: An Inventory of Scientific Findings* (New York: Harcourt, Brace & World, 1964), pp. 104–5.

2. Gardner Murphy, *Personality: A Biosocial Approach to Origins and Structure* (New York: Harper, 1947), pp. 498–502.

3. Karl Zener and Mercedes Gaffron, "Perceptual Experience: An Analysis of Its Relations to the External World Through Internal Processings," in *Psychology: A Study of a Science,* Vol. 4, ed. Sigmund Koch (New York: McGraw-Hill, 1962), p. 523.

4. Jerome S. Bruner and Cecile C. Goodman, "Value and Need as Organizing Factors in Perception," *Journal of Abnormal and Social Psychology* **42** (1947): 33–44; Jerome S. Bruner, "Personality Dynamics and the Process of Perceiving," in *Perception — An Approach to Personality,* ed. Robert R. Blake and Glenn V. Ramsey (New York: Ronald, 1951), pp. 121–47; Ernest R. Hilgard, "Human Motives and the Concept of the Self," *American Psychologist* **4** (1949): 374–82.

5. Abraham H. Maslow, *Motivation and Personality* (New York: Harper, 1954), Chap. 14.

6. Abraham H. Maslow, *Toward a Psychology of Being* (New York: Van Nostrand/Insight, 1962), p. 74.

7. William Stephenson, *The Play Theory of Mass Communication* (Chicago: University of Chicago Press, 1967), pp. 158 and 51–2.

8. William James, *The Varieties of Religious Experience* (1902; reprint, New American Library/Mentor, 1958), p. 321.

9. Walter N. Pahnke, "LSD and Religious Experience," in *LSD, Man & Society,* ed. Richard C. Debold and Russell C. Leaf (Middletown, Conn.: Wesleyan University Press, 1967), p. 63.

10. Ludwig Eidelberg, ed., *Encyclopedia of Psychoanalysis* (New York: Collier-Macmillan/Free Press, 1968), pp. 280–1.

11. Donald O. Hebb, *A Textbook of Psychology* (Philadelphia: Saunders, 1966), pp. 39 and 252.

12. Theodor Lipps, "Empathy, Inner Imitation, and Sense-Feeling" (1903), in *A Modern Book of Esthetics: An Anthology,* ed. Melvin Rader (New York: Holt, Rinehart and Winston, 1979), pp. 374–5.

13. Maureen Kovich, "Sport as an Art Form," *Journal of Health, Physical Education and Recreation* **42** (October 1971): 42.

14. Bruce Buchenholz, "The Motivating Action of Pleasure," *Journal of Nervous and Mental Disease* **124** (1956): 574.

15. Auke Tellegen and Gilbert Atkinson, "Openness to Absorbing and Self-Altering Experiences ('Absorption'), A Trait Related to Hypnotic Susceptibility," *Journal of Abnormal Psychology* **83** (1974): 275.

16. Maslow, *Toward a Psychology of Being,* p. 74.

17. Jean Piaget, *The Child's Conception of the World* (1929; London: Routledge & Kegan Paul, 1971), Chap. 4.

18. Munro S. Edmonson, *Lore: An Introduction to the Science of Folklore and Literature* (New York: Holt, Rinehart and Winston, 1971), p. 54.

19. Aldous Huxley, *The Devils of Loudun* (New York: Harper, 1952), p. 67.

20. Maslow, *Toward a Psychology of Being,* p. 76.

21. Jean Piaget, *The Construction of Reality in the Child* (New York: Basic, 1954).

22. Ronald E. Shor, "Hypnosis and the Concept of the Generalized Reality-Orientation," *American Journal of Psychotherapy* **13** (1959): 585.

23. Robert Ornstein, *The Psychology of Consciousness* (San Francisco: W.H. Freeman, 1972), Chap. 2.

24. Ernest R. Hilgard, *The Experience of Hypnosis* (New York: Harcourt, Brace & World, 1965), p. 9.

25. Shor, "Hypnosis and the Concept of the Generalized Reality-Orientation," p. 591.

26. Robert W. White, "A Preface to the Theory of Hypnotism," *Journal of Abnormal and Social Psychology* **36** (1941): 501–2.

27. William James, *The Principles of Psychology,* Vol. 2 (1890; reprint, Cambridge, Mass.: Harvard University Press, 1981), p. 918.

28. William Hamilton (1859), quoted by Dominic W. Massaro, *Experimental Psychology and Information Processing* (Chicago: Rand McNally, 1975), p. 241.

29. Nicholas P. Spanos and John D. McPeake, "Involvement in Suggestion-Related Imaginings, Experienced Involuntariness, and Credibility Assigned to Imaginings in Hypnotic Subjects," *Journal of Abnormal Psychology* **83** (1974): 687–90.

30. Maslow, *Toward a Psychology of Being*, p. 67.

31. Thomas M. Kando, *Leisure and Popular Culture in Transition* (St. Louis: Mosby, 1975), p. 95; Max Kaplan, *Leisure in America: A Social Inquiry* (New York: Wiley, 1960), p. 211.

32. Robert W. McIntosh, *Tourism Principles, Practices and Philosophies* (Columbus, Ohio: Grid, 1972), p. 7; Arlin F. Epperson, *Private and Commercial Recreation* (New York: Wiley, 1977), p. 11; Donald E. Lundberg, *The Tourist Business* (Chicago: Institutions/Volume Feeding Management Magazine, 1972), p. 12.

33. Lundberg, *The Tourist Business*, p. 114.

34. Sigmund Freud, *A General Introduction to Psychoanalysis* (Garden City, New York: Doubleday/Permabooks, 1938), p. 325; Irwin Edman, *Arts and the Man* (New York: Norton, 1939), p. 16.

35. John Dewey, "Having An Experience" (1934), in *A Modern Book of Esthetics: An Anthology*, ed. Melvin Rader (New York: Holt, Rinehart and Winston, 1979), pp. 137, 140, and 143.

36. D.E. Berlyne, *Conflict, Arousal, and Curiosity* (New York: McGraw-Hill, 1960), Chap. 9.

37. Bernard DeVoto, *The World of Fiction* (Boston: The Writer, 1950), p. 145.

38. Edman, *Arts and the Man*, p. 17.

39. Dewey, "Having an Experience," pp. 137–8.

40. James, *Varieties of Religious Experience*, pp. 301–2.

41. Frances V. Clark, "Exploring Intuition: Prospects and Possibilities," *Journal of Transpersonal Psychology* **5** (1973): 156–70.

42. Arthur J. Deikman, "Experimental Meditation," *Journal of Nervous and Mental Disease* **136** (1963): 333–4.

43. Pauline Kael, *Reeling* (Boston: Little, Brown, 1972), p. xii.

Chapter 4. Story Enjoyment

1. Q.D. Leavis, *Fiction and the Reading Public* (1932; New York: Russell and Russell, 1965), p. 56.

2. Jay Haley, "The Appeal of the Moving Picture," *Quarterly of Film, Radio and Television* **6** (1952): 373.

3. Guido Majno, *The Healing Hand: Man and Wound in the Ancient World* (Cambridge, Mass.: Harvard University Press, 1975), p. 142.

4. James O'Donnell Bennett, *Much Loved Books: Best Sellers of the Ages* (New York: Liveright, 1927), p. 78.

5. *Encyclopaedia Britannica*, 15th ed., s.v. "Comedy."

6. Tyrone Guthrie, "Is Lady Macbeth Really Walking in Her Sleep?" *New York Times*, 28 August 1966, Sect. 2, p. 1.

7. Norman Holland, *The Dynamics of Literary Response* (New York: Oxford University Press, 1968), p. 66.

8. Josephine R. Hilgard, *Personality and Hypnosis* (Chicago: University of Chicago Press, 1970), pp. 23, 24 and 35.

9. Joseph Conrad, *A Conrad Argosy* (Garden City, New York: Doubleday, Doran, 1942), p. 82.

10. A.L. Schafer, *Hypno-fiction: Hypnosis and the Writing of Fiction* (Arvada, Colorado: Capstone, 1968), p. 103.

11. Holland, *Dynamics of Literary Response,* p. 63.

12. Bernard DeVoto, *The World of Fiction* (Boston: The Writer, 1950), p. 210.

13. Holland, *Dynamics of Literary Response,* p. 69.

14. Wallace A Bacon and Robert S. Breen, *Literature as Experience* (New York: McGraw-Hill, 1959), p. 48.

15. *Collier's Encyclopedia,* s.v. "Fiction."

16. Wayne Shumaker, "The Cognitive Value of Literature," in *Aesthetics and the Arts,* ed. Lee Jacobus (New York: McGraw-Hill, 1968), p. 118.

17. Holland, *Dynamics of Literary Response,* pp. 69–70.

18. DeVoto, *World of Fiction,* pp. 205–6.

19. Samuel McKechnie, *Popular Entertainments Through the Ages* (London: Sampson Low, Marston, 1931), Chap. 4.

20. *The Diary of Samuel Pepys,* Vol. 8 (1896; reprint, London: Bell, 1929), p. 110.

21. *The Random House Dictionary of the English Language,* college ed., s.v. "vicarious."

22. Richard S. Lazarus, Edward M. Opton, Markellos S. Nomikos, and Neil O. Rankin, "The Principle of Short-Circuiting of Threat: Further Evidence," *Journal of Personality* **33** (1965): 622–35.

23. Hans Kreitler and Shulamith Kreitler, *Psychology of the Arts* (Durham, N.C.: Duke University Press, 1972), p. 260.

24. James Mann, "What Is TV Doing to America?" *U.S. News & World Report* **93**, No. 5 (2 August 1982): 27–30.

25. DeVoto, *World of Fiction,* p. 50.

26. John Harvey, "The Content Characteristics of Best-Selling Novels," *Public Opinion Quarterly* **17** (1953): 91–114.

27. Harvey Wallerstein, "An Electromyographic Study of Attentive Listening," *Canadian Journal of Psychology* **8** (1954): 228–38.

28. Nathan Kleitman, "The Effect of Motion Pictures on Body Temperature," *Science* **101** (1945): 507.

29. Arthur Koestler, *The Act of Creation* (New York: Macmillan, 1964), p. 159.

30. Allardyce Nicoll, "Film and Theatre," in *Film: A Montage of Theories,* ed. Richard D. MacCann (New York: Dutton, 1966), p. 122.

31. Bernard Bosanquet, "Easy and Difficult Beauty," in *A Modern Book of Esthetics,* ed. Melvin Rader (New York: Holt, Rinehart, and Winston, 1979), p. 418.

32. Michael Dirda, "Perils of Fiction," *Washington Post Book World,* 31 August 1980, p. 3.

33. Isak Dinesen, *Last Tales* (New York: Random House, 1957), pp. 23–4.

34. Irving Singer, *The Nature of Love: Plato to Luther* (New York: Random House, 1966), p. 17.

35. William James, *The Principles of Psychology,* Vol. 2 (1890; reprint, Cambridge, Mass.: Harvard University Press, 1981), p. 918.

36. Simon O. Lesser, *Fiction and the Unconscious* (Boston: Beacon, 1957), pp. 201–3.

Chapter 5. Ever More Absorbing Stories

1. Richard Kraus, *Recreation and Leisure in Modern Society* (Pacific Palisades, Calif.: Goodyear, 1971), Chap. 6.

2. Daniel J. Crowley, "I Could Talk Old-Story Good: Creativity in Bahamian Folklore," *Folklore Studies: 17* (Berkeley and Los Angeles: University of California Press, 1966), p. 1.

3. David Riesman, *The Lonely Crowd* (New York: Doubleday/Anchor, 1956), pp. 24-8.

4. *Encyclopaedia Britannica*, 15th ed., s.v. "Folk Literature."

5. Q.D. Leavis, *Fiction and the Reading Public* (1932; New York: Russell and Russell, 1965), pp. 106 and 130.

6. Patricia M. Spacks, *Imagining a Self: Autobiography and Novel in Eighteenth-Century England* (Cambridge, Mass.: Harvard University Press, 1976), p. 10.

7. Ingmar Bergman, "Film Has Nothing To Do With Literature," in *Film: A Montage of Theories*, ed. Richard D. MacCann (New York: Dutton, 1966), p. 144.

8. Michael Roemer, "The Surfaces of Reality," in *Film: A Montage of Theories*, ed. Richard D. MacCann (New York: Dutton, 1966), p. 257.

9. Shirley Weitz, *Nonverbal Communication* (New York: Oxford University Press, 1979).

10. Bela Balazs, "The Faces of Men," in *Film: A Montage of Theories*, ed. Richard D. MacCann (New York: Dutton, 1966), pp. 150-1.

11. Dudley Nichols, "The Writer and the Film," in *Film: a Montage of Theories*, ed. Richard D. MacCann (New York: Dutton, 1966), p. 79.

12. Pauline Kael, *Reeling* (Boston: Little, Brown, 1972), p. xi.

13. Elizabeth Bowen, "Why I Go to the Cinema," in *Film: A Montage of Theories*, ed. Richard D. MacCann (New York: Dutton, 1966), pp. 241-2.

14. Gustav Janouch, *Conversations with Kafka*, trans. Goronwy Rees (London: Derek Verschoyle, 1953), p. 89.

15. Ernest R. Hilgard, Richard C. Atkinson, and Rita L. Atkinson, *Introduction to Psychology*, 6th ed. (New York: Harcourt Brace Jovanovich, 1975), p. 150.

16. Clifford T. Morgan and Richard A. King, *Introduction to Psychology* (New York: McGraw-Hill, 1966), p. 343.

17. David Riesman, *The Oral Tradition, the Written Word, and the Screen Image* (Yellow Springs, Ohio: Antioch, 1956), p. 31.

18. Lewis Jacobs, "Movement: Real and Cinematic," in *The Movies as Medium*, ed. Lewis Jacobs (New York: Farrar, Straus & Giroux, 1970), pp. 77-8.

19. Raymond Durgnat, *Films and Feelings* (Cambridge, Mass.: M.I.T. Press, 1967), p. 28.

20. Herbert Lightman, "The Subjective Camera," in *The Movies as Medium*, ed. Lewis Jacobs (New York: Farrar, Straus, & Giroux, 1970), pp. 62-3.

21. Richard S. Lazarus and Edward M. Opton, "The Study of Psychological Stress: A Summary of Theoretical Formulations and Experimental Findings," in *Anxiety and Behavior*, ed. Charles D. Spielberger (New York: Academic, 1966), pp. 225-62; Walter A. Brown, Donald P. Corrineau, and Peter M. Monti, "Anger Arousal by a Motion Picture: A Methodological Note," *American Journal of Psychiatry* **134** (1977): 930-1.

22. Walter A. Brown and George Heninger, "Cortisol, Growth Hormone, Free Fatty Acids, and Experimentally Evoked Affective Arousal," *American Journal of Psychiatry* **132** (1975): 1175.

23. Kael, *Reeling*, pp. xii and xi.

24. Thomas M. Kando, *Leisure and Popular Culture in Transition* (St. Louis: Mosby, 1975), p. 95.

25. Jerry Mander, *Four Arguments for the Elimination of Television* (New York: Morrow, 1978), Chap. 8.

26. Marshall McLuhan, *Understanding Media: The Extensions of Man* (New York: McGraw-Hill Paperbacks, 1964), Chap. 1.

27. Leo Bogart, *Age of Television* (New York: Ungar, 1972), p. 50.

28. Irving J. Weiss, "Sensual Reality in the Mass Media," in *McLuhan: Pro & Con,* ed. Raymond Rosenthal (New York: Funk & Wagnalls, 1968), p. 55.

29. Craig Norback, ed., *The Complete Book of American Surveys* (New York: New American Library, 1980), p. 80.

30. William A. Mindak and Gerald D. Hursh, "Television's Functions on the Assassination Weekend," in *The Kennedy Assassination and the American Public,* ed. Bradley S. Greenberg and Edwin B. Parker (Stanford, Calif.: Stanford University Press, 1965), pp. 134–5.

31. Tom Pettit, "The Television Story in Dallas," in *The Kennedy Assassination and the American Public,* ed. Bradley S. Greenberg and Edwin B. Parker (Stanford, Calif.: Stanford University Press, 1965), pp. 63–6.

32. Stephen Rosen, *Future Facts: A Forecast of the World as We Will Know It Before the End of the Century* (New York: Simon and Schuster, 1976), pp. 431–8.

33. Alvin Toffler, *Future Shock* (New York: Random House/Bantam, 1970), pp. 234 and 231–32.

34. Jeff Greenfield, "TV," *Washington Post,* 7 May 1978, p. C4.

35. Mander, *Arguments for Elimination of Television.*

36. Bogart, *Age of Television,* p. xxix.

37. Martin Mayer, *About Television* (New York: Harper, 1972), p. 389.

Chapter 6. Recreational Drugs

1. Andrew I. Malcolm, *The Pursuit of Intoxication* (New York: Washington Square, 1971), p. 4.

2. Lawrence A. Young, Linda G. Young, Marjorie M. Klein, Donald M. Klein, and Dorianne Beyer, *Recreational Drugs* (New York: Macmillan/Collier, 1977), p. 3.

3. *Encyclopaedia Britannica,* 15th ed., s.v. "Alcohol Consumption."

4. Jack S. Margolis, *Complete Book of Recreational Drugs* (Los Angeles: Cliff House, 1978), p. 157.

5. John Rublowsky, *The Stoned Age* (New York: Putnam/Capricorn, 1974).

6. *Ibid.,* p. 197.

7. Aldous Huxley, *The Devils of Loudun* (New York: Harper, 1952), pp. 314–5.

8. Paul Nash, "Education 2000 A.D.," *Journal of Education* 155 (1973): 20.

9. Jerome L. Singer, "Ongoing Thought: The Normative Baseline for Alternate States of Consciousness," in *Alternate States of Consciousness,* ed. Norman E. Zinberg (New York: Free Press, 1977), p. 111.

10. Margolis, *Recreational Drugs,* p. 185; M.M. Glatt, *Drugs, Society and Man: A Guide to Addiction and its Treatment* (New York: Wiley, 1974), p. 35.

11. Glatt, *Drugs, Society and Man,* Chap. 2.

12. John T. Partington, "Dr. Jekyll and Mr. High: Multidimensional Scaling of Alcoholics' Self-Evaluations," *Journal of Abnormal Psychology* 75 (1970): 131–8.

13. Thomas Storm and Reginald G. Smart, "Dissociation: A Possible Explana-

tion of Some Features of Alcoholism, and Implication for Its Treatment," *Quarterly Journal of Studies on Alcohol* **26** (1965): 112; Henry Murphree, "Some Possible Origins of Alcoholism" in *Alcohol and Alcohol Problems,* ed. William Filstead *et al.* (Cambridge, Mass.: Ballinger, 1976, p. 152.

14. John S. Tamerin *et al.,* "The Alcoholic's Perception of Self: A Retrospective Comparison of Mood and Behavior during States of Sobriety and Intoxication," *Annals of the New York Academy of Sciences* **233** (1974): 48–60.

15. Sheldon Weiner *et al.,* "Familial Patterns in Chronic Alcoholism: A Study of a Father and Son During Experimental Intoxication," *American Journal of Psychiatry* **127** (1971): 1646–51.

16. John S. Tamerin and Jack H. Mendelson, "The Psychodynamics of Chronic Inebriation: Observations of Alcoholics During the Process of Drinking in an Experimental Group Setting." *American Journal of Psychiatry* **125** (1969): 886–99.

17. Tamerin *et al.,* "Alcoholic's Perception of Self," p. 49.

18. William James, *The Varieties of Religious Experience* (1902; New American Library/Mentor, 1958), p. 297.

19. Herbert Barry, "Alcohol," in *Drug Abuse: Clinical and Basic Aspects,* ed. Sachindra Pradhan and Samarendra Dutta (St. Louis: Mosby, 1977), pp. 82–3.

20. Gillian Leigh, J.E. Tong, and J.A. Campbell, "Effects of Ethanol and Tobacco on Divided Attention," *Journal of Studies on Alcohol* **38** (1977): 1233.

21. Herbert Moskowitz and Dennis DePry, "Effect of Alcohol on Auditory Vigilance and Divided-Attention Tasks," *Quarterly Journal of Studies on Alcohol* **29** (1968): 54–63.

22. Barry, "Alcohol," p. 91.

23. *Ibid.*

24. *Ibid.*

25. Young *et al., Recreational Drugs,* p. 3.

26. Barry, "Alcohol," p. 85.

27. *Ibid.,* pp. 84–5.

28. *Ibid.*

29. David C. McClelland, William N. Davis, Rudolf Kalin, and Eric Wanner, *The Drinking Man* (New York: Free Press, 1972).

30. Craig MacAndrew and Robert B. Edgerton, *Drunken Comportment: A Social Explanation* (Chicago: Aldine, 1969), p. 168.

31. "The Colombian Connection," *Time* **29** January 1979, p. 22.

32. *Ibid.*

33. U.S. Congress, Senate Committee on the Judiciary, Subcommittee to Investigate Administration of the Internal Security Act, "Marihuana-Hashish Epidemic and Its Impact on U.S. Security: The Continuing Escalation," *Hearings, 94th Congress, 1st Session* (Washington, D.C.: U.S. Government Printing Office, 1975).

34. Robert C. Petersen, "Marihuana Research Findings," *National Institute of Drug Abuse Research Monograph,* no. 14 (Washington, D.C.: U.S. Government Printing Office, 1976), p. 10.

35. Erich Goode, *The Marijuana Smokers* (New York: Basic, 1970), p. 159.

36. Glatt, *Drugs, Society and Man,* p. 167.

37. William G. Drew and Loren L. Miller, "Cannabis: Neural Mechanisms and Behavior—A Theoretical Review," *Pharmacology* **11** (1974); 13–32; Robert G. Heath, "Marihuana Effects on Deep and Surface Electroencephalograms of Man," *Archives of General Psychiatry* **26** (1972): 577–84.

38. Walle Nauta, "The Problem of the Frontal Lobe: A Reinterpretation," *Journal of Psychiatric Research* **8** (1971): 182.

39. Morton D. Low, Harry Klonoff, and Anthony Marcus, "The Neurophysiological Basis of the Marijuana Experience," *Canadian Medical Association Journal* **108** (1973): 164.

40. Charles T. Tart, "Work with Marijuana: II. Sensations," *Psychology Today* **4** (May 1971): 43.

41. Bert S. Kopell, J.R. Tinklenberg, and L.E. Hollister, "Contingent Negative Variation Amplitudes: Marihuana and Alcohol," *Archives of General Psychiatry* **27** (1972): 809–11.

42. Irwin Rinder, "Effects of Marijuana: A Social Psychological Interpretation," *Psychiatry* **41** (1978): 203.

43. Reese Jones, "Human Effects," in *Drug Abuse: Clinical and Basic Aspects,* ed. Sachindra Pradhan and Samarendra Dutta (St. Louis: Mosby, 1977), pp. 128–78.

44. Joel S. Hochman, *Marijuana and Social Evolution* (Englewood Cliffs, N.J.: Prentice-Hall, 1972), p. 68.

45. Andrew T. Weil, Norman E. Zinberg, and Judith M. Nelson, "Clinical and Psychological Effects of Marihuana in Man," *Science* **162** (1968): 1240.

46. Jack H. Mendelson *et al.,* "Behavioral and Biologic Aspects of Marijuana Use," *Annals of the New York Academy of Sciences* **282** (1976): 198.

47. Low *et al.,* "Neurophysiological Basis of Marijuana;" Abram Hoffer and Humphry Osmond, *The Hallucinogens* (New York: Academic, 1967), p. 92.

48. Howard D. Cappell and Patricia Pliner, "Volitional Control of Marijuana Intoxication: A Study of the Ability to Come Down on Command," *Journal of Abnormal Psychology* **82** (1973): 428–34.

49. Sidney Cohen, *The Beyond Within: The LSD Story* (New York: Atheneum, 1967), pp. 168–9.

50. *Ibid.,* p. 36.

51. Margolis, *Recreational Drugs,* p. 149.

52. *Ibid.,* pp. 330–32.

53. Gordon Claridge, *Drugs and Human Behavior* (New York: Praeger, 1970), p. 120.

54. R.A. Durr, *Poetic Vision and the Psychedelic Experience* (Syracuse, N.Y.: Syracuse University Press, 1970), p. 3.

55. William Marshall and Gilbert W. Taylor, *The Art of Ecstasy: An Investigation of the Psychedelic Revolution* (Burns & MacEachern Limited, 1967), p. 75.

56. Sachindra Pradhan and Leo E. Hollister, "Abuse of LSD and Other Hallucinogenic Drugs," in *Drug Abuse: Clinical and Basic Aspects,* ed. Sachindra Pradhan and Samarendra Dutta (St. Louis: Mosby, 1977), p. 276.

57. Harriet L. Barr *et al., LSD: Personality and Experience* (New York: Wiley-Interscience, 1972), pp. 150 and 162.

58. Margolis, *Recreational Drugs,* p. 328.

59. Paul D. MacLean, "The Triune Brain, Emotion, and Scientific Bias," in *The Neurosciences,* ed. Francis O. Schmitt (New York: Rockefeller University Press, 1970), 336–49.

60. Walter N. Pahnke, "LSD and Religious Experience," in *LSD, Man & Society,* ed. Richard C. Debold and Russell C. Leaf (Middletown, Conn.: Wesleyan University Press, 1967), pp. 60–84.

61. Allan Watts, "A Psychedelic Experience: Fact or Fantasy?" in *LSD: The Consciousness-Expanding Drug,* ed. David Solomon (New York: Putnam, 1964), p. 125.

62. Aldous Huxley, *The Doors of Perception, and Heaven and Hell* (New York: Harper, 1956), p. 33.

63. *Encyclopaedia Britannica,* 15th ed., *s.v.* "Drug Problems."

Chapter 7. The Recreational Value of People

1. George C. Homans, "Social Behavior as Exchange," *American Journal of Sociology* **63** (1958): 597–606; John Thibaut and Harold Kelley, *The Social Psychology of Groups* (New York: Wiley, 1959).

2. Gary Van Gorp, John Stempfle, and David Olson, "Dating Attitudes, Expectations, and Physical Attractiveness," unpublished paper (University of Michigan, 1969).

3. William Glasser, *Reality Therapy* (New York: Harper, 1965); O. Hobart Mowrer, *The New Group Therapy* (Princeton, N.J.: Van Nostrand, 1964).

4. Timothy Leary, *Interpersonal Diagnosis of Personality* (New York: Ronald, 1957); Robert C. Carson, *Interaction Concepts of Personality* (Chicago: Aldine, 1969), Chaps. 4, 5, and 6.

5. Eric Berne, *Games People Play* (New York: Grove, 1964).

6. Neil S. Jacobson and Gayla Margolin, *Marital Therapy* (New York: Brunner/Mazel, 1979).

7. Zick Rubin, *Liking and Loving* (New York: Holt, Rinehart and Winston, 1973), p. 157.

8. Alvin Toffler, *Future Shock* (New York: Random House/Bantam, 1970), Pt. 2.

9. Christopher Lasch, *The Culture of Narcissism* (New York: Warner, 1979), pp. 127–8, 126, and 69.

10. Carl R. Rogers, *Client-Centered Therapy* (New York: Houghton Mifflin, 1951).

11. Toffler, *Future Shock*, p. 97.

12. Roger Caillois, *Man, Play, and Games* (New York: Free Press, 1961), Chap. 3.

13. Max Kaplan, *Leisure in America: A Social Inquiry* (New York: Wiley, 1960), p. 201.

14. Jeanne Watson, "A Formal Analysis of Sociable Interaction," in *Current Perspectives in Social Psychology,* ed. E.P. Hollander and Raymond G. Hunt (New York: Oxford University Press, 1963), p. 289.

15. Bernard Berelson and Gary A. Steiner, *Human Behavior: An Inventory of Scientific Findings* (New York: Harcourt, Brace & World, 1964), p. 328.

16. Rubin, *Liking and Loving*, p. 137.

17. Watson, "Analysis of Sociable Interaction," p. 284.

18. Michael and Eleanor Brock, ed., *H.H. Asquith: Letters to Venetia Stanley* (Oxford: Oxford University Press, 1982), p. 2.

19. Ralph Waldo Emerson, "Love," in *The Complete Essays and Other Writings of Ralph Waldo Emerson,* ed. Brooks Atkinson (New York: Modern Library, 1940), p. 213.

20. Rubin, *Liking and Loving*, p. 224.

21. John Money, *Love and Love Sickness: The Science of Sex, Gender Difference, and Pair-Bonding* (Baltimore: Johns Hopkins University Press, 1980), p. 151.

22. Sigmund Freud, "Civilization and Its Discontents," in *The Standard Edition of the Complete Psychological Works of Sigmund Freud,* Vol. 21, ed. James Strachey (1930; reprint, London: Hogarth Press, 1961), pp. 65–6.

23. Ignace Lepp, *The Psychology of Loving* (Baltimore: Helicon, 1963), p. 30.

24. Sigmund Freud, "Psychology and the Analysis of the Ego," in *The Complete Psychological Works of Sigmund Freud,* Vol. 18, ed. James Strachey (1921; reprint, London: Hogarth Press, 1955), p. 114.

25. Lepp, *Psychology of Loving*, p. 30.

26. Emerson, "Love," pp. 214–5.

27. Stendhal, *On Love* (1822; reprint, New York: Liveright, 1947), p. 35.

Chapter 8. Sexual Experience

1. Roger W. Libby, "Today's Changing Sexual Mores," in *Handbook of Sexology,* ed. John Money and Herman Musaph (Amsterdam: Excerpta Medica, 1977), pp. 564–76.

2. Robert A. Wilson, "Modern Attitudes Toward Sex," in *The Encyclopedia of Sexual Behavior,* Vol. 1, ed. Albert Ellis and Albert Abarbanel (New York: Hawthorn, 1961), p. 186.

3. William Masters and Virginia Johnson, "Why 'Working' at Sex Won't Work," in *Masters & Johnson Explained,* ed. Nat Lehrman (New York: Playboy Paperbacks, 1970).

4. William Masters and Virginia Johnson, "Ten Sex Myths Exploded," in *Masters & Johnson Explained,* ed. Nat Lehrman (New York: Playboy Paperbacks, 1970), p. 235.

5. Alfred C. Kinsey, Wardell B. Pomeroy, and Clyde E. Martin, *Sexual Behavior in the Human Male* (Philadelphia: Saunders, 1948), p. 568.

6. Shere Hite, *The Hite Report on Male Sexuality* (New York: Knopf, 1981), pp. 148 and 142.

7. Shere Hite, *The Hite Report: A Nationwide Study on Female Sexuality* (New York: Macmillan, 1976), p. 134.

8. Alex Comfort, *More Joy of Sex* (New York: Simon and Schuster, 1974), p. 12.

9. Albert Ellis, *Sex without Guilt* (New York: Stuart, 1966), Chap. 1; Hite, *Hite Report on Female Sexuality,* p. 118.

10. John Money, *Love and Love Sickness: The Science of Sex, Gender Difference, and Pair-Bonding* (Baltimore: Johns Hopkins University Press, 1980), p. 145.

11. Hite, *Hite Report on Female Sexuality,* pp. 303–4.

12. Comfort, *More Joy of Sex,* p. 70.

13. Bernard I. Murstein, *Love, Sex, and Marriage through the Ages* (New York: Springer, 1974), pp. 561 and 563.

14. Albert Ellis, "Frigidity," in *The Encyclopedia of Sexual Behavior,* Vol. 1, ed. Albert Ellis and Albert Abarbanel (New York: Hawthorn, 1961), p. 453.

15. Hite, *Hite Report on Female Sexuality,* pp. 194–5.

16. Herman Nunberg, *Principles of Psychoanalysis* (New York: International Universities Press, 1955), p. 100.

17. Robert Wood, "Sex Life in Ancient Civilizations," in *The Encyclopedia of Sexual Behavior,* Vol. 1, ed. Albert Ellis and Albert Abarbanel (New York: Hawthorn, 1961), p. 120.

18. Murstein, *Love, Sex, and Marriage through the Ages,* p. 560.

19. Vance Packard, *The Sexual Wilderness* (New York: McKay, 1968).

20. Abraham H. Maslow, *The Farther Reaches of Human Nature* (New York: Penguin, 1971), p. 169; Marghanita Laski, *Ecstasy* (Bloomington, Ind.: Indiana University Press, 1961), Chap. 14.

21. Colin Wilson, *Origins of the Sexual Impulse* (New York: Putnam, 1963), pp. 28–9.

22. Hite, *Hite Report on Female Sexuality,* pp. 66–8 and 111.

23. Money, *Love and Love Sickness,* p. 119.

24. Hite, *Hite Report on Female Sexuality,* p. 194.

25. William Masters and Virginia Johnson, *Human Sexual Response* (Boston: Little, Brown, 1966), p. 183.

26. Edward Dengrove, "Sex Differences," in *The Encyclopedia of Sexual Behavior,* Vol. 2, ed. Albert Ellis and Albert Abarbanel (New York: Hawthorn, 1961), p. 936.

27. Masters and Johnson, *Human Sexual Response,* p. 266.

28. Ellis, "Frigidity," p. 452.

29. Nat Lehrman, "A Report on Human Sexual Inadequacy," in *Masters & Johnson Explained,* ed. Nat Lehrman (New York: Playboy Paperbacks, 1970), p. 25.

30. Herant A. Katchadourian and Donald T. Lunde, *Fundamentals of Human Sexuality* (New York: Holt, Rinehart, and Winston, 1972), p. 252.

31. Masters and Johnson, *Human Sexual Response,* pp. 118 and 133.

32. Alan W. Watts, *Nature, Man, and Woman* (New York: Random House/Vintage, 1970), p. 163.

33. Wilson, *Origins of Sexual Impulse,* p. 155.

34. Denis de Rougemont, *Love Declared* (New York: Pantheon, 1963), p. 42.

35. Bengt Danielsson, "Sex Life in Polynesia," in *The Encyclopedia of Sexual Behavior,* Vol. 2, ed. Albert Ellis and Albert Abarbanel (New York: Hawthorn, 1961), p. 833.

36. Wilson, *Origins of Sexual Impulse,* p. 148.

37. *Ibid.,* p. 39.

38. *Ibid.,* p. 228.

39. Harry Benjamin, "Prostitution," in *The Encyclopedia of Sexual Behavior,* Vol. 2, ed. Albert Ellis and Albert Abarbanel (New York: Hawthorn, 1961), p. 877.

40. Robert V. Sherwin, "Laws on Sex Crimes," in *The Encyclopedia of Sexual Behavior,* Vol. 2, ed. Albert Ellis and Albert Abarbanel (New York: Hawthorn, 1961), p. 624.

41. Charles Winick and Paul M. Kinsie, *The Lively Commerce: Prostitution in the United States* (Chicago: Quadrangle, 1971), p. 193.

42. Martha L. Stein, "Prostitution," in *Handbook of Sexology,* ed. John Money and Herman Musaph (Amsterdam: Excerpta Medica, 1977), p. 1077.

43. Peter Dally, *The Fantasy Game* (New York: Stein and Day, 1975), p. 75.

44. Katchadourian and Lunde, *Fundamentals of Human Sexuality,* p. 211.

45. Barbara E. Hariton and Jerome L. Singer, "Women's Fantasies During Sexual Intercourse," *Journal of Consulting and Clinical Psychology* **42** (1974): 313–22.

46. Dally, *Fantasy Game,* p. 3.

47. Wilson, *Origins of Sexual Impulse,* p. 21.

48. Joseph P. Slade, "Pornographic Theaters off Times Square," in *The Pornography Controversy,* ed. Ray C. Rist (New Brunswick, N.J.: Transaction, 1975), p. 137.

49. Hariton and Singer, "Women's Fantasies During Intercourse," pp. 320–21.

50. Nancy Friday, *Men in Love* (New York: Dell, 1980).

51. Eberhard Kronhausen and Phyllis Kronhausen, "The Psychology of Pornography," in *The Encyclopedia of Sexual Behavior,* Vol. 2, ed. Albert Ellis and Albert Abarbanel (New York: Hawthorn, 1961), pp. 849.

52. Don Byrne, "The Imagery of Sex," in *Handbook of Sexology,* ed. John Money and Herman Musaph (Amsterdam: Excerpta Medica, 1977), p. 336.

53. Friday, *Men in Love,* p. 24.

54. Hariton and Singer, "Women's Fantasies During Intercourse."

55. Dally, *Fantasy Game,* p. 16.

56. Friday, *Men in Love,* pp. 463–4.

57. Erich Fromm, *The Art of Loving* (New York: Harper, 1956), p. 16.

58. Stein, "Prostitution," p. 1079.

59. George F. Will, "Birthplace of the Sex Business," *Washington Post,* 1 October 1978, p. C7.

Chapter 9. Motion and Emotion in Music

1. Vernon Lee, "The Riddle of Music," *Quarterly Review* **204** (1906): 211.

2. Eduard Hanslick, "The Effects of Music" (1891), in *Aesthetics and the Arts,* ed. Lee A. Jacobus (New York: McGraw-Hill, 1968), p. 174.

3. Richard Wagner, quoted by Susanne Langer, *Philosophy in a New Key* (Cambridge, Mass.: Harvard University Press, 1967), pp. 221–2.

4. Carroll C. Pratt, *Music as the Language of Emotion* (Washington, D.C.: Library of Congress, 1950), pp. 7 and 21.

5. *Ibid.,* p. 26; Carroll C. Pratt, *The Meaning of Music* (New York: McGraw-Hill, 1931), p. 198.

6. John Colbert, "On the Musical Effect," *Psychiatric Quarterly* **37** (1963): 434.

7. William C. Robinson, "The Musical Preferences of Mental Patients Based on Cattell's Interpretations of Factors Associated with Certain Aspects of Personality" (Ph.D. diss., University of Miami, 1976).

8. George du Maurier, "Trilby," *Harper's Monthly* **88** (January 1894): 180.

9. Carl E. Seashore, *Psychology of Music* (New York: McGraw-Hill, 1938), pp. 142–3.

10. Dominick A. Barbara, *Questions and Answers on Stuttering* (Springfield, Ill.: Thomas, 1965), pp. 8–9.

11. William Butler Yeats, *Essays and Introductions* (New York: Macmillan, 1961), p. 159.

12. William Sargant, *Battle for the Mind* (New York: Harper/Perennial Library, 1971), Chap. 5.

13. Aldous Huxley, *The Devils of Loudun* (New York: Harper, 1952), p. 322.

14. Ian Oswald, "Experimental Studies of Rhythm, Anxiety and Cerebral Vigilance," *Journal of Mental Science* **105** (1959): 269–94.

15. George Santayana, *Reason in Art* (1906; reprint, New York: Collier, 1962), p. 39.

16. John Rublowsky, *Popular Music* (New York: Basic, 1967), Chap. 3.

17. *Ibid.,* p. 97.

18. Jeremy Larner, "What Do They Get from Rock 'n' Roll?" *Atlantic Monthly* **214** (August 1964): 45–6.

19. Richard Bobbitt, *Harmonic Technique in the Rock Idiom* (Belmont, Calif.: Wadsworth, 1976), p. 176.

20. John P. Robinson and Paul Hirsch, "It's the Sound That Does It," *Psychology Today* **3** (October 1969): 42–5.

21. Bobbitt, *Harmonic Technique in Rock,* pp. i and ii.

22. Rublowsky, *Popular Music,* p. 108.

23. *Ibid.,* p. 104.

24. Mihaly Csikszentmihalyi, *Beyond Boredom and Anxiety* (San Francisco: Jossey-Bass, 1975), p. 105.

25. *Ibid.*

26. Mike Sager, "Discomania," *Washington Post,* 1 July 1979, p. B1.

27. *Ibid.*

28. Max Schoen, "The Aesthetic Attitude in Music," *Psychological Monographs* **39** (1928): 174.

29. John M. Roberts and Cecilia Ridgeway, "Musical Involvement and Talking," *Anthropological Linguistics* **11** (1969): 223–46.

30. Bennett Reimer and Edward G. Evans, *The Experience of Music* (Englewood Cliffs, N.J.: Prentice-Hall, 1972), p. 50.

31. *Ibid.,* p. 55.

32. Josephine R. Hilgard, *Personality and Hypnosis* (Chicago: University of Chicago Press, 1970), p. 83.

33. Robert E. Ornstein, *The Psychology of Consciousness* (San Francisco: Freeman, 1972), Chap. 3.

34. Elda Franklin, "An Investigation of Auditory Laterality Effects for Verbal and Melodic Stimuli Among Musicians and Nonmusicians" (Ph.D. diss., University of North Carolina at Greensboro, 1977).

35. Robert Panzarella, "The Phenomenology of Peak Experience in Response to Music and Visual Art and Some Personality Correlates" (Ph.D. diss., City University of New York, 1977), p. 5.

36. *Ibid.,* pp. 233, 231, 214–15, and 215.

37. Santayana, *Reason in Art,* p. 37.

38. Charles S. Myers, "Individual Differences in Listening to Music," in *The Effects of Music,* ed. Max Schoen (New York: Harcourt, Brace, 1927), p. 37.

39. Paul Elmer More, *Selected Shelburne Essays* (New York: Oxford University Press, 1935), p. 39.

40. Abraham Maslow, *The Farther Reaches of Human Nature* (New York: Penguin, 1971), p. 170.

10. Cultivated Diversions: Art

1. Melvin Rader, ed., *A Modern Book of Esthetics: An Anthology* (New York: Holt, Rinehart and Winston, 1973), p. 14.

2. Clive Bell, *Art* (New York: Stokes, 1914), pp. 225 and 25.

3. William James, *The Principles of Psychology,* Vol. 1 (1890; Cambridge, Mass.: Harvard University Press, 1981), p. 420.

4. Bell, *Art,* p. 3.

5. Kate Hevner, "The Aesthetic Experience: A Psychological Description," *Psychological Review* 44 (1937): 252.

6. Elsie Murray, "Some Uses and Misuses of the Term 'Aesthetic,'" *American Journal of Psychology* 42 (1930): 641.

7. Bernard Berenson, *Sunset and Twilight: From the Diaries of 1947–1958* (New York: Harcourt, Brace & World, 1963), pp. 47 and 130; Bernard Berenson, quoted by Hanna Kiel, *Looking at Pictures with Bernard Berenson* (Jerusalem: Massada, 1974), pp. 17–8.

8. Paul Klee, quoted by Paul Weiss, *Nine Basic Arts* (Carbondale, Ill.: Southern Illinois University Press, 1961), p. 45; Marshall McLuhan, "Foreword," in *The Interior Landscape,* ed. Eugene McNamara (New York: McGraw-Hill, 1969), p. xiv.

9. Rudolf Arnheim, *Art and Visual Perception* (Berkeley and Los Angeles: University of California Press, 1965), p. 2.

10. George Santayana, "The Elements and Function of Poetry," in *Aesthetics and the Arts,* ed. Lee A. Jacobus (New York: McGraw-Hill, 1968), p. 100.

11. Walter Pater, *The Renaissance* (1873; reprint, London: Macmillan, 1925), pp. 137–8 and 238; Bernard Berenson, *Aesthetics and History* (Garden City, N.Y.: Doubleday, 1954), p. 150.

12, Thomas M. Kando, *Leisure and Popular Culture in Transition* (St. Louis: Mosby, 1975), p. 122.

13. Harold Wilensky, "Mass Society and Mass Culture: Interdependence or Independence?" *American Sociological Review* 29 (1964): 194.

14. Edward Bullough, "'Psychical Distance' as a Factor in Art and an Aesthetic Principle," *British Journal of Psychology* 5 (1912): 89.

15. *Ibid.*, pp. 99 and 108.

16. *Ibid.*, p. 94.

17. Clement Greenberg, "The Case for Abstract Art," in *TLE Six: Options for the 1970s*, ed. Louis G. Locke *et al.* (New York: Holt, Rinehart and Winston, 1972), pp. 314 and 316.

18. Theodor Lipps, "Empathy, Inner Imitation, and Sense-Feeling" (1903), in *A Modern Book of Esthetics: An Anthology,* ed. Melvin Rader (New York: Holt, Rinehart and Winston, 1979), p. 372.

19. Rader, *Modern Book of Esthetics,* p. 335.

20. Eliseo Vivas, "A Definition of the Esthetic Experience," in *The Problems of Esthetics,* ed. Eliseo Vivas and Murray Krieger (New York: Rinehart, 1953), pp. 408–410.

21. Henry James (1883), quoted by James E. Miller, *Theory of Fiction: Henry James* (Lincoln, Neb.: University of Nebraska Press, 1972), p. 93.

22. T.S. Eliot, *The Sacred Wood* (1920; reprint, London: Methuen, 1950), pp. 58 and viii.

23. George Steiner, "On Literature, Language, and Culture," *Bill Moyers' Journal Transcript,* 22 May 1981, p. 1.

24. Abraham H. Maslow, "Lessons from the Peak-Experiences," *Journal of Humanistic Psychology* 2 (1962): 9.

25. Berenson, *Aesthetics and History,* pp. 79 and 93.

26. Abraham H. Maslow, *Toward a Psychology of Being* (Princeton, N.J.: Van Nostrand Insight, 1962), Chap. 6.

27. L. Eugene Thomas and Pamela E. Cooper, "Incidence and Psychological Correlates of Intense Spiritual Experiences," *Journal of Transpersonal Psychology* 12 (1980): 78.

28. Basil Douglas-Smith, "An Empirical Study of Religious Mysticism," *British Journal of Psychiatry* 118 (1971): 549–54.

29. Marghanita Laski, *Ecstasy: A Study of Some Secular and Religious Experiences* (Bloomington, Ind.: Indiana University Press, 1961), pp. 17–8.

Chapter 11. Cultivated Diversions of Body and Mind

1. Henry Doering, ed., *Book of Buffs, Masters, Mavens and Uncommon Experts* (New York: World Almanac, 1980).

2. George Plimpton, *Paper Lion* (New York: Harper, 1966).

3. Mihaly Csikszentmihalyi, *Beyond Boredom and Anxiety* (San Francisco: Jossey-Bass, 1975), p. 36.

4. *Ibid.*, pp. 43, 86, and 87.

5. *Ibid.*, pp. 76 and 77.

6. Robert W. Creamer, *Stengel: His Life and Times* (New York: Simon and Schuster, 1983), p. 16.

7. Kenneth Ravizza, "Peak Experiences in Sport," *Journal of Humanistic Psychology* 17 (1977): 38–9.

8. George Sheehan, *Running and Being* (New York: Warner, 1978), p. 172.

9. *Ibid.*, pp. 230–1.

10. Eugen Herrigel, *Zen in the Art of Archery* (1953; New York: Random House/Vintage, 1971), pp. 54 and 69–70.

11. Robert M. Nideffer, *The Inner Athlete* (New York: Crowell, 1976), pp. 179–80.

12. Timothy W. Gallwey, *The Inner Game of Tennis* (New York: Random House, 1974), p. 33.

13. Roger Caillois, *Man, Play, and Games* (New York: Free Press, 1961), pp. 137–8.

14. William James and Petr Ilich Tchaikovsky, quoted by Rosamond Harding, *An Anatomy of Inspiration* (Cambridge, England: Heffer, 1940), p. 8; Logan Pearsall Smith, quoted by Robert Gathorne-Hardy, *Recollections of Logan Pearsall Smith* (New York: Macmillan, 1950), p. 249; Henri Poincaré, quoted by Melvin Rader, ed., *A Modern Book of Esthetics* (New York: Holt, Rinehart and Winston, 1979), p. 14; and Bernard Berenson, *Sunset and Twilight* (New York: Harcourt, Brace & World, 1963), p. 136.

15. Sigmund Koch, "Behavior as 'Intrinsically' Regulated: Work Notes towards a Pre-Theory of Phenomena Called 'Motivational,'" in *Nebraska Symposium on Motivation, 1956,* ed. Marshall R. Jones (Lincoln: University of Nebraska Press, 1956), pp. 67–8.

16. C.M. Bowra, *Inspiration and Poetry* (Freeport, N.Y.: Books for Libraries, 1970), p. 9.

17. *Ibid.,* p. 19.

18. Patricia Bowers, "Hypnotizability, Creativity and the Role of Effortless Experiencing," *International Journal of Clinical and Experimental Hypnosis* 26 (1978): 184–202.

19. Rollo May, "The Nature of Creativity," in *Creativity and Its Cultivation,* ed. Harold H. Anderson (New York: Harper, 1959), pp. 62–3.

20. Harding, *Anatomy of Inspiration,* p. 16.

21. Gardner Murphy, *Personality* (New York: Basic, 1966), p. 460.

22. John W. Haefele, *Creativity and Innovation* (New York: Reinhold, 1962), Chap. 7; Eliot Dole Hutchinson, "The Nature of Insight," *Psychiatry* 4 (1941): 31–43.

23. Rudolf Flesch, *The Art of Clear Thinking* (New York: Harper, 1951), p. 146.

24. Hermann von Helmholtz (1896), quoted by Robert S. Woodworth and Harold Schlosberg, *Experimental Psychology* (New York: Holt, 1954), p. 838.

25. Henri Poincaré, quoted by Arthur Koestler, *The Act of Creation* (New York: Macmillan, 1964), p. 115.

26. Alden Whitman, "Arnold Toynbee, Who Charted Civilizations' Rise and Fall, Dies," *New York Times,* 23 October 1975, pp. 1 and 42.

27. Woodworth and Schlosberg, *Experimental Psychology,* p. 837; Wilbert S. Ray, *The Experimental Psychology of Original Thinking* (New York: Macmillan, 1967), Chap. 5.

28. Frank Barron and David M. Harrington, "Creativity, Intelligence, and Personality," in *Annual Review of Psychology,* ed. Mark R. Rosenzweig and Lyman W. Porter (Palo Alto, Calif.: Annual Reviews, 1981), pp. 439–76.

29. Colin Martindale, "What Makes Creative People Different?" *Psychology Today* 9 (July 1975): 44–50.

30. Koestler, *Act of Creation,* Chap. 6.

31. May, "Nature of Creativity," pp. 62–3.

32. Abraham H. Maslow, "Creativity in Self-Actualizing People," in *Creativity and Its Cultivation,* ed. Harold H. Anderson (New York: Harper, 1959), p. 92.

33. Koestler, *Act of Creation,* pp. 208 and 146.

34. William V. Shannon, "An Irish Renaissance Man," *Washington Post Book World,* 8 May 1983, p. 12.

35. Jerome S. Bruner, *On Knowing: Essays for the Left Hand* (Cambridge: Harvard University Press, 1962), p. 17.

36. T.S. Eliot, *The Sacred Wood* (1920; reprint, London: Methuen, 1950), pp. 52–3.

37. Joyce Carol Oates, quoted by Edward F. Murphy, *The Crown Treasury of Relevant Quotations* (New York: Crown, 1978), p. 404.

38. Neil Simon, quoted by Stanley Rosner and Lawrence E. Abt, eds., *The Creative Experience* (New York: Grossman, 1970), p. 359.

39. Russell R. Monroe, "The Episodic Psychoses of Vincent Van Gogh," *Journal of Nervous and Mental Disease* **166** (1978): 480-8.

40. Ralph Waldo Emerson, "The Poet," in *The Complete Essays and Other Writings of Ralph Waldo Emerson,* ed. Brooks Atkinson (1844; reprint, New York: Modern Library, 1940), p. 332.

41. Elia Kazan, quoted by David Richards, "Elia Kazan: The Director and His Gifts," *Washington Post,* 4 December 1983, p. F8.

42. Bernard Berelson and Gary A. Steiner, *Human Behavior: An Inventory of Scientific Findings* (New York: Harcourt, Brace & World, 1964), p. 234.

43. Frank Barron, *Creative Person and Creative Process* (New York: Holt, Rinehart and Winston, 1969), p. 180.

44. Robert B. Martin, *Tennyson: The Unquiet Heart* (New York: Oxford University Press, 1980.

45. Winifred Gerin, "Eminent Victorians," *Washington Post Book World,* 21 December 1980, pp. 6 and 8.

Chapter 12. Meditation: The Cleansing of Awareness

1. Richard J. Davidson, Daniel J. Goleman, and Gary E. Schwartz, "Attentional and Affective Concomitants of Meditation: A Cross-Sectional Study," *Journal of Abnormal Psychology* **85** (1976): 235-8; Nicholas P. Spanos *et al.,* "Meditation, Expectation and Performance on Indices of Nonanalytic Attending," *International Journal of Clinical and Experimental Hypnosis* **28** (1980): 244-51; David Van Nuys, "A Novel Technique for Studying Attention During Meditation," *Journal of Transpersonal Psychology* **3** (1971): 125-33.

2. "The TM Craze: Forty Minutes to Bliss," *Time,* 13 October 1975, pp. 71-4.

3. *Encyclopaedia Britannica,* 15th ed., *s.v.* "Buddhism."

4. Arthur Koestler, *The Lotus and the Robot* (New York: Macmillan, 1961), Chap. 2.

5. B.K. Anand, G.S. Chhina, and Baldev Singh, "Some Aspects of Electroencephalographic Studies in Yogis," *Electroencephalography and Clinical Neurophysiology* **13** (1961): 452-6.

6. John Welwood, "Meditation and the Unconscious: A New Perspective," *Journal of Transpersonal Psychology* **9** (1977): 8.

7. Nyanaponika Mahathera, "The Power of Mindfulness," in *Pathways of Buddhist Thought,* ed. Nyanaponika Mahathera (New York: Barnes and Noble, 1971), p. 103.

8. Claudio Naranjo and Robert E. Ornstein, *On the Psychology of Meditation* (New York: Viking, 1971), pp 194-5.

9. Alan Watts, *Meditation* (New York: Pyramid, 1974), pp. 27, 29, and 37.

10. Walpola Rahula, *What the Buddha Taught* (New York: Grove, 1962), pp. 72-3.

11. Akira Kasamatsu and Tomio Hirai, "An Electroencephalographic Study on the Zen Meditation (Zazen)," in *Altered States of Consciousness,* ed. Charles T. Tart (New York: Wiley, 1969), pp. 489-501.

12. Koestler, *The Lotus and the Robot,* p. 257.

13. Naranjo and Ornstein, *Psychology of Meditation,* Pt. 2.

14. Erich Fromm, "Psychoanalysis and Zen Buddhism," *Psychologia* **2** (1959): 79-99.

15. Robert Ornstein, *The Psychology of Consciousness* (San Francisco: W.H. Freeman, 1972), pp. 122–3.

16. "TM Craze," *Time,* p. 73.

17. Joel Younger *et al.,* "Sleep during Transcendental Meditation," *Perceptual Motor Skills* **40** (1975): 953–4.

18. Robert Pagano *et al.,* "Sleep during Transcendental Meditation," *Science* **23** January 1976, pp. 308–9.

19. Kasamatsu and Hirai, "Electroencephalographic Study of Zen Meditation."

20. R. Hebert and D. Hehmann, "Theta Bursts: An EEG Pattern in Normal Subjects Practicing the Transcendental Meditation Technique," *Electroencephalography and Clinical Neurophysiology* **42** (1977): 397–405.

21. Barry D. Elson, Peter Hauri, and David Cunis, "Physiological Changes in Yoga Meditation," *Psychophysiology* **14** (1977): 52–7.

22. Edward Maupin, "Individual Differences in Response to a Zen Meditation Exercise," *Journal of Consulting Psychology* **29** (1965): 139–45.

23. R. Keith Wallace, "Physiological Effects of Transcendental Meditation," *Science* **167** (1970): 1751–4; Roger N. Walsh, "Meditation Research: An Introduction and Review," *Journal of Transpersonal Psychology* **11** (1979): 161–74; Herbert Benson, *The Relaxation Response* (New York: Avon, 1975).

24. Naranjo and Ornstein, *Psychology of Meditation,* p. 8.

25. John P. Zubek, "Sensory and Perceptual-Motor Processes," in *Sensory Deprivation: Fifteen Years of Research,* ed. John P. Zubek (New York: Appleton-Century-Crofts, 1969), pp. 207–53; John P. Zubek *et al.,* "Perceptual Changes After Prolonged Sensory Isolation (Darkness and Silence)," *Canadian Journal of Psychology* **15** (1961): 83–100.

26. John Welwood, "Befriending Emotion: Self-Knowledge and Transformation," *Journal of Transpersonal Psychology* **11** (1979): 158.

27. Arthur J. Deikman, "Implications of Experimentally Induced Contemplative Meditation," *Journal of Nervous and Mental Disease* **142** (1966): 103.

28. Arthur J. Deikman, "Experimental Meditation," *Journal of Nervous and Mental Disease* **136** (1963): 332.

29. Arthur J. Deikman, "De-Automatization and the Mystic Experience," *Psychiatry* **29** (1966): 331.

30. Deikman, "Experimental Meditation," p. 339.

31. James Leuba, *The Psychology of Religious Mysticism* (1925: reprint, London: Routledge & Kegan Paul, 1972), p. 179.

32. Herbert Moller, "Affective Mysticism in Western Civilization," *Psychoanalytic Review* **52** (1965).

33. *Ibid.,* p. 116.

34. Leuba, *Psychology of Mysticism,* p. 170.

35. José Ortega y Gasset, *On Love* (New York: New American Library, 1957), pp. 60 and 62–3.

36. Woodburn Heron, "The Pathology of Boredom," *Scientific American* **196** (1957): 54; Donald O. Hebb, "The Mammal and His Environment," *American Journal of Psychiatry* **111** (1955): 826–31.

37. Heron, "Pathology of Boredom," pp. 53–4.

38. Walter N. Pahnke, "LSD and Religious Experience," in *LSD, Man & Society,* ed. Richard C. DeBold and Russell C. Leaf (Middletown, Conn.: Wesleyan University Press, 1967), pp. 60–84.

39. José Ortega y Gassett, *On Love,* p. 62.

40. Leuba, *Psychology of Mysticism,* p. 299.

Chapter 13. High-Processing Psychological States

1. Bernard Berelson and Gary A. Steiner, *Human Behavior: An Inventory of Scientific Findings* (New York: Harcourt, Brace & World, 1964), pp. 99–100.

2. C.P. Snow, *The Two Cultures: and a Second Look* (Cambridge: Cambridge University Press, 1969), p. 6.

3. Thomas S. Szasz, "The Myth of Mental Illness," *American Psychologist* **15** (1960): 118.

4. Marvin A. Iverson and Mary E. Reuder, "Ego Involvement as an Experimental Variable," *Psychological Reports* **2** (1956): 147–81.

5. George Mandler and Seymour B. Sarason, "A Study of Anxiety and Learning," *Journal of Abnormal and Social Psychology* **47** (1952): 166–73.

6. Irwin G. Sarason, "Empirical Findings and Theoretical Problems in the Use of Anxiety Scales," *Psychological Bulletin* **57** (1960): 411.

7. Jeri Wine, "Test Anxiety and Direction of Attention," *Psychological Bulletin* **76** (1971): 92.

8. J.A. Easterbrook, "The Effect of the Cue Utilization and the Organization of Behavior," *Psychological Review* **66** (1959): 183–201.

9. Wilbert S. Ray, *The Experimental Psychology of Original Thinking* (New York: Macmillan, 1967), p. 56.

10. Enoch Callaway and George Stone, "Re-Evaluating Focus of Attention," in *Drugs and Behavior,* ed. Leonard Uhr and James G. Miller (New York: Wiley, 1960), p. 395.

11. Otto F. Ehrentheil, "Thought Content of Mute Chronic Schizophrenic Patients: Interviews after Injection of Amobarbital Sodium (Sodium Amytal) and Methamphetamine Hydrochloride (Methedrine)," *Journal of Nervous and Mental Disease* **137** (1963): 187–97.

12. Steven Starker, "Fantasy in Psychiatric Patients: Exploring a Myth," *Hospital and Community Psychiatry* **30** (1979): 25–30.

13. Lucile Dooley, "The Concept of Time in Defense of Ego Integrity," *Psychiatry* **4** (1941): 17.

14. Walter J. Coville, Timothy W. Costello, and Fabian L. Rouke, *Abnormal Psychology* (New York: Barnes and Noble, 1960), p. 105.

15. Harold I. Kaplan and Benjamin J. Sadock, *Modern Synopsis of Comprehensive Textbook of Psychiatry/III* (Baltimore: Williams and Wilkins, 1981), p. 310.

16. James Chapman, "The Early Symptoms of Schizophrenia," *British Journal of Psychiatry* **112** (1966): 225–51.

17. Andrew McGhie and James Chapman, "Disorders of Attention and Perception in Early Schizophrenia," *British Journal of Medical Psychology* **34** (1961): 103–15.

18. Sid J. Schneider, "Selective Attention in Schizophrenia," *Journal of Abnormal Psychology* **85** (1976): 167–73.

19. P.J. Korboot and N. Damiani, "Auditory Processing Speed and Signal Detection in Schizophrenia," *Journal of Abnormal Psychology* **85** (1976): 287–95.

20. Bob Trotter, "Fifth Kittay Symposium: Focus on Cognition," *APA Monitor,* May 1977, p. 4.

21. Coville, Costello, and Rouke, *Abnormal Psychology,* p. 106.

22. Quoted in William James, *The Varieties of Religious Experience* (1902; reprint, New York: New American Library/Mentor, 1958), pp. 134–5.

23. Anton T. Boisen, "The Form and Content of Schizophrenic Thinking," *Psychiatry* **5** (1942): 24–5.

24. Daniel P. Schreber, *Memoirs of My Nervous Illness,* ed. and trans. Ida Macalpine and Richard A. Hunter (London: W. Dawson, 1955), p. 197.

25. Thelma G. Alper, "An Electric Shock Patient Tells His Story," *Journal of Abnormal and Social Psychology* 43 (1948): 201–10.

26. Coville, Costello, and Rouke, *Abnormal Psychology,* p. 163.

27. Ronald D. Laing, *The Divided Self* (Chicago: Quadrangle, 1960), Chap. 7.

28. Seymour Krim, "The Insanity Bit," in *The Inner World of Mental Illness,* ed. Bert Kaplan (New York: Harper, 1964), p. 64.

29. Walter Freeman and James Watts, "Frontal Lobes and Consciousness of Self," *Psychomatic Medicine 3* (1941): pp. 117 and 114–5.

30. Maude Harrison, *Spinners Lake* (London: Lane, 1941), p. 39.

Chapter 14. Low-Processing Psychological States

1. Julian Rotter, "Word Association and Sentence Completion Methods," in *An Introduction to Projective Techniques,* ed. Harold Anderson and Gladys Anderson (Englewood Cliffs, N.J.: Prentice-Hall, 1951), pp. 279–311.

2. Matt Clark *et al.,* "The Mystery of Sleep," *Newsweek,* 13 July 1981, p. 50.

3. Nathaniel Kleitman, *Sleep and Wakefulness* (Chicago: University of Chicago Press, 1963), Pt. 2.

4. Havelock Ellis, *The World of Dreams* (London: Constable, 1931), pp. 20–1.

5. Eugene Aserinsky and Nathaniel Kleitman, "Regularly Occurring Periods of Eye Motility and Concomitant Phenomena During Sleep," *Science* 118 (1953): 273–4.

6. Kleitman, *Sleep and Wakefulness,* Chap. 11.

7. David G. Schwartz, Lissa N. Weinstein, and Arthur M. Arkin, "Qualitative Aspects of Sleep Mentation," in *The Mind in Sleep: Psychology and Psychophysiology,* ed. Arthur M. Arkin, John S. Antrobus, and Steven J. Ellman (Hillsdale, N.J.: Lawrence Erlbaum Associates, 1978), pp. 143–241.

8. Gay G. Luce and Julius Segal, *Sleep* (New York: Lancer, 1966), p. 231.

9. *Ibid.,* pp. 206–7.

10. William Dement, "An Essay on Dreams: The Role of Physiology in Understanding their Nature," in *New Directions in Psychology II* (New York: Holt, Rinehart, and Winston, 1965), p. 210.

11. Ellis, *World of Dreams,* p. 26.

12. Luce and Segal, *Sleep,* Chap. 9.

13. *Ibid.,* p. 208.

14. Kleitman, *Sleep and Wakefulness,* p. 95; Luce and Segal, *Sleep,* p. 205.

15. Luce and Segal, *Sleep,* Chap. 9.

16. Nathaniel Kleitman, "Patterns of Dreaming," in *Altered States of Awareness: Readings from Scientific American* (San Francisco: Freeman, 1972), pp. 48–9.

17. Sigmund Freud, "The Interpretation of Dreams," in *The Standard Edition of the Complete Psychological Works of Sigmund Freud,* Vol. 4, ed. James Strachey (1900; reprint, London: Hogarth Press, 1953), Chaps. 4 and 6.

18. Charles Rycroft, *The Innocence of Dreams* (New York: Pantheon, 1979), Chaps. 3 and 9.

19. Schwartz, Weinstein, and Arkin, "Qualitative Aspects of Sleep Mentation," p. 149.

20. David Foulkes, "Theories of Dream Formation and Recent Studies of Sleep Consciousness," *Psychological Bulletin* 62 (1964): 241.

21. Freud, "The Interpretation of Dreams," Chap. 6.

22. Ellis, *World of Dreams,* p. 44.

23. C. Scott Moss, *The Hypnotic Investigation of Dreams* (New York: Wiley, 1967), p. 12.

24. Luce and Segal, *Sleep,* p. 215.

25. Michael Ellis, *Why People Play* (Englewood Cliffs, N.J.: Prentice-Hall, 1973), Chaps. 3, 4, and 5.

26. Simon O. Lesser, *Fiction and the Unconscious* (Boston: Beacon, 1957), p. 94.

27. Jay Haley, "The Appeal of the Moving Picture," *Quarterly of Film, Radio and Television* **6** (1952): 368.

28. A.L. Carlisle and Robert J. Howell, "Comparison of Filmed Violence and Anger as Measured by Changes in Affective States," *Psychological Reports* **34** (1974): 1259–66.

29. Johan Huizinga, *Homo Ludens* (Boston: Beacon, 1964), pp. 2–3.

30. Abraham H. Maslow, "Lessons from the Peak-Experiences," *Journal of Humanistic Psychology* **2** (1962): 10.

31. Alvin Toffler, *The Third Wave* (New York: Morrow, 1980), John Brookes, *The Great Leap: The Past Twenty-Five Years in America* (New York: Harper, 1966).

Index